Praise for Aspire

Matt Rogers' *Aspire* is a theologically-sound and missionally-savvy workbook for pastors to use when raising up young leaders in their churches. He helps pastors build a leadership pipeline in three semesters which center on the three concepts of gospel, ministry, and mission. Rogers is the perfect person to write the book—he has nearly 20 years of experience as a church planter and pastor and is a Ph.D. candidate at Southeastern Baptist Theological Seminary. Highly recommended.

—Dr. Bruce Ashford
Provost and Associate Professor of Theology & Culture
Southeastern Baptist Theological Seminary

Aspire is just what the church has needed to equip it in theologically grounded, yet practical, ways to make disciples! Matt Rogers is notcoming at this subject as a theorist, but he is a practitioner who has labored tirelessly in the context of the local church to live out the principles found on these pages. You will enjoy reading and then implementing what you discover in this book.

—Aaron Coe
Vice President for Mobilization and Marketing
North American Mission Board

Matt Rogers has provided a thorough and comprehensive tool for making solid disciples. It is a resource that demands time and commitment. As Matt says, "It is better to train disciples well than to train them quickly." We live in a day when we can no longer have disciples who only go an inch deep. The world needs to see men and women who know God's Word, have a grasp on biblical doctrine, and who know how to live the Christian life successfully. With this resource, churches will be producing disciples who truly impact the world for Christ.

—Dr. Greg Faulls
Senior Pastor, Bellevue Baptist Church, Owensboro, Kentucky
Adjunct Professor, Liberty Baptist Theological Seminary

In *Aspire*, Matt Rogers has given the church a gift. Not merely a book that addresses the concept in theory, but a practical book that walks with us as we walk with others into a deeper relationship with Christ. If you care about making disciples through the local church, this book should be a welcome addition to your library.

—Micah Fries,
Vice President, Lifeway Research

If we are going to fulfill Christ's Great Commission, it will happen on the backs of Spirit-filled disciple makers. I am thrilled that Matt Rogers has put together such high quality content in a format that is not only easy to use but which also facilitates reproduction and multiplication. May God use *Aspire* to catalyze a fresh and multiplying disciple-making culture in all our churches!

—Dr. Mark Liederbach,
Professor of Theology, Ethics, and Culture,
Vice President, Dean of Students Research Fellow
for the L. Russ Bush Center for Faith and Culture,
Southeastern Baptist Theological Seminary

The great need for local churches is to empower their members and mobilize them to fulfill the Great Commission. Before we can send out qualified church planters and missionaries, they need to be equipped through a mentor-driven discipleship plan. This is why I appreciate what Matt Rogers has given us with *Aspire*. Now we have a resource to help people reach their God-given potential for ministry and mission as they grow in the grace and knowledge of our Lord and Savior Jesus Christ. *Aspire* teaches us that God can transform people's lives through growth in: (1) what they know, (2) who they are, (3) what they do, and (4) how they love. I am excited to implement this well-rounded approach to discipleship in my church and in our church-planting training. I am also excited for local church leaders to have this valuable resource at their disposal.

—Dr. Dwayne Milioni
Senior Pastor, Open Door Baptist Church, Raleigh, NC;
Board Chairman, The North American Church Planting Foundation;
Assistant Professor of Preaching, Southeastern Baptist Theological Seminary

Matt Rogers has done a great service for the cause of Christ! Discipleship is the need of the day, and he gives us a guide that is practical, workable, and effective. You will benefit from this manual in meaningful, eternal ways as you apply the principles and live out the methodology. *Aspire* will make a difference in your life and in your church. Use it!

—Dr. Doug Munton
Senior Pastor, FBC O'Fallon, IL

After teaching almost 25 years—20 at Southeastern Seminary—I sometimes need to be reminded of why I teach. Students like Matt Rogers take their education and apply it well to their real ministries. Matt has done just that with this book. We are called not merely to win converts but to make disciples, and Matt has given us a great plan to develop disciple-making disciples of Jesus. I for one am inspired by *Aspire*!

—Dr. Alvin Reid
Professor of Evangelism and Student Ministry
and the Bailey Smith Chair of Evangelism,
Southeastern Baptist Theological Seminary

In *Aspire*, Matt offers a framework for discipleship that comes from his personal journey as a "disciple-making practitioner." Churches and pastors worldwide are starving for a method of discipleship that is both reproducing *and* reproducible. Matt offers a clear and concise path that anyone could use to make disciples. Every church should have *Aspire* in their toolbox for making disciples!

—Dr. Steve Wright
Pastor of Discipleship and Church Planting,
First Baptist Church, West Palm Beach, FL

Aspire

Developing and Deploying Disciples in the Church for the Church

Matt Rogers

Seed Publishing Group, LLC
Timmonsville, South Carolina

Aspire: Developing and Deploying Disciples in the Church for the Church

Copyright © 2014 by Matt Rogers

Published by:
Seed Publishing Group, LLC
2570 Double C Farm Ln
Timmonsville, SC 29161

Library of Congress Cataloging-in-Publication Data
Rogers, Matt, 1977-
Aspire : developing and deploying disciples in the church for the church / Matt Rogers.
pages cm
ISBN 978-1-890586-44-7
1. Discipling (Christianity) I. Title.
BV4520.R645 2014
253—dc23
2014025324

Produced by TIPS Technical Publishing, Inc.
www.technicalpublishing.com

Printed in the United States of America

2   3   4   5   20   19   18   17   16   15

Some books you write and some books you live. Establishing a process for intentionally developing disciples and leaders was at the top of my priority list shortly after planting a church in Greenville, South Carolina in the summer of 2009. God had used such a process to drastically alter my life, and I was committed to doing everything I could to replicate this experience in the church that I now pastor. The writings that follow are my attempt to aid other churches in creating their own method for developing disciples and leaders.

Thankfully, God gave me a group of men who let me experiment with their lives using the ideas in this book. To them I owe a great debt of gratitude. Their faithful and humble service to Christ's church fueled the fire of this dream and brought the process of *Aspire* to life. Any investment I have made in their lives is vastly outweighed by the extent to which they have shaped mine.

I am specifically thankful to the men and women who read early drafts of this manuscript, such as James Nugent, Jeff Doyle, and Trevor Hoffman. Seed Publishing Group was gracious to publish my work, and for that I am grateful. Pastors Dwayne Milioni and Bill Curtis provided valuable insight throughout the various stages of this work.

Finally, my family is the real hero of this story. The publication of one's first book is a daunting undertaking, especially while planting and pastoring a local church. The only way this has happened is through the sacrificial love and support of a godly wife, Sarah, and precious children, Corrie, Avery, and Hudson. Sarah has served as a constant encouragement and support—making me feel far wiser than I actually am. Not only that, but she exemplifies the life of disciple-making outlined in this book.

My prayer is that God will use *Aspire* to equip churches to make disciples and train leaders until He returns.

—Matt Rogers
Pastor, The Church at Cherrydale

Contents

Foreword...ix
Preface: A Word to the Church..xi

Trimester 1: Gospel...1
    Week 1: Creation 5
    Week 2: Rebellion 17
    Week 3: Covenant 29
    Week 4: People 39
    Week 5: Kingdom 51
    Week 6: Judgment 61
    Week 7: Incarnation 73
    Week 8: Life 83
    Week 9: Cross 93
    Week 10: Resurrection 109
    Week 11: Church 117
    Week 12: Consummation 125
    Suggested Reading List 133

Trimester 2: Ministry 135
    Week 1: Worship 137
    Week 2: Transformation 147
    Week 3: Idolatry 155
    Week 4: Character 165
    Week 5: The Spirit 177
    Week 6: Discipleship 187
    Week 7: Gifting...197
    Week 8: Calling...213
    Week 9: Marriage 223
    Week 10: Parenting 231
    Week 11: Time 239
    Week 12: Rest 253
    Suggested Reading List 261

Contents

Trimester 3: Mission **263**

    Week 1: Mission of God...265

    Week 2: The Mission of the Church 273

    Week 3: The Mission of the Disciple 283

    Week 4: The Nations 293

    Week 5: Your Culture 303

    Week 6: Your City 311

    Week 7: Pray 319

    Week 8: Invest 327

    Week 9: Declare 339

    Week 10: Demonstrate...353

    Week 11: Connect..361

    Week 12: Disciple 375

    Suggested Reading List 384

Appendix 1: Overview..387

Appendix 2: How does *Aspire* address the four critical areas of growth? 391

Appendix 3: Frequently Asked Questions 395

Foreword

Last words are meant to be lasting words. They are meant to make an impact and leave an impression. As the Lord Jesus prepared to ascend back to heaven, He called His disciples to Himself and said these words: "All authority has been given to Me in heaven and on earth. Go, therefore, and make disciples of all nations, baptizing them in the name of the Father and of the Son and of the Holy Spirit, teaching them to observe everything that I have commanded you. And remember, I am with you always, to the end of the age" (Matt 28:18–20, HCSB). These well known words of our King are often referred to as the Great Commission. Their greatness is found both in their content and in the one who spoke them. These words are nothing less than a strategic mandate for the Church of the Lord Jesus to passionately obey until He returns again to consummate all things.

So, we are told to make disciples. You would think this would be an easy assignment, but my 35 plus years in ministry have convinced me that this is an area where the Church has stumbled about in confusion. Too often we have settled for cheap substitutes that have produced anemic followers of the crucified Galilean. How few there are in our churches who truly deny themselves, take up their cross, and follow Jesus (Mark 8:34). In many cases the problem is the *will* to follow; in other cases it is *how* to follow.

In this superb treatment on discipleship, Matt Rogers provides a model for how to make devoted followers of King Jesus—people who will learn His ways, reflect His character, and then reproduce themselves in others. Now, at this point I need to make something crystal clear: this book is not a quick fix. Why? The process of discipleship is not a quick fix. Jesus took three years to disciple the 12. Do we think we can make disciples better and quicker than our Savior? No! Forming disciples is a time intensive process, and *Aspire: Developing and Deploying Disciples in the Church for the Church* will guide you well in accomplishing this divine goal within the Body of Christ.

I was struck as I read the book not only by how comprehensive it is but also by how practical it is. This is a rare balance you seldom find in most books of this nature. As a result, it is with great delight that I commend this book to all who would take seriously the final marching orders of our Commander-in-Chief. It is my sincere prayer that it will be widely distributed and used for the building up of the Lord's Church and for the sending of an army of disciples among every tribe, tongue, people, and nation. I know this: it will be the first book I turn to and recommend when asked, "How can my church truly become a discipleship catalyst for the glory of God and the good of the nations?" I now have a tool I can confidently put in the hands of others.

—Dr. Daniel L. Akin

Preface: A Word to the Church

"We proclaim Him, warning and teaching everyone with all wisdom,
so that we may present everyone mature in Christ. I labor for this,
striving with His strength that works powerfully in me."[1]

—*Colossians 1:28–29*

You know John.

God did a great work in John's life after graduation from high school. He had been a typically rebellious teenager who had heard the gospel but was not truly converted. But God, in His kindness, reclaimed John's prodigal life and brought him to a point of repentance and faith in his college years.

He immediately connected with a group of Christians from the local church adjacent to his home and poured himself into its ministry. His life was marked by an insatiable hunger for the Word, a longing for relationships with other Christians, a humble desire to serve, and a genuine pursuit of a life that honored God.

Before long, John found himself overseeing a group of middle-school boys and assuming increasing levels of leadership within the church. While John was honored to be asked to lead, he knew that there was a problem.

He had never been discipled.

Sure, he attended the church service each week, went to the classes offered by the church, and occasionally listened to his favorite preacher via podcast. However, no one assumed spiritual responsibility for him or walked with him through a process of understanding and applying the gospel to his life. Even worse, he was now being asked to make disciples without having been discipled himself.

John felt trapped. He knew that he was ill-equipped for the task. It was exposing all sorts of sin in his heart and he knew that he lacked the maturity and training necessary to lead well. Not only that, but the stress of leadership in the church was having a negative impact on his family. On most days, he masked this insecurity behind sheer,

---

1. All Scripture quotations are taken from the Holman Christian Standard Bible (HCSB) unless otherwise noted, Holman Christian Publishers, 2003.

white-knuckled will power. He worked hard and pretended that he knew what he was doing. But he didn't. And he, his family, and the church were suffering as a result.

The church felt trapped, too. The pastor was busy, and the never-ending needs of the church always seemed to crowd out meaningful time to train John. And what's worse, he really didn't have a good plan for discipling guys like John anyway. He had never been discipled either. So, on a good week he might share a meal with John and ask how he was doing or give him a book that had proved valuable in his own ministry. What else could he do? The only other option was to send him off to seminary and run the risk of never seeing him again. Young leaders were too rare and too valuable to the church to make this choice.

Our churches are filled with people like John. They love Jesus and the church, and they are looking to the church for discipleship. They are not all college-aged men. Some are teenage girls, some business professionals, some elderly church members. They need the church to create an intentional plan to disciple new converts toward maturity and leadership in the church. This task is not optional for the church. Paul reminded Timothy that his primary task was this: "The things you have heard me say in the presence of many witnesses entrust to reliable men who will also be qualified to teach others (2 Tim 2:2)." Churches have a responsibility to create a culture of disciple-making and multiplication.

Healthy disciples are vital for the church's effectiveness in seeing the lost saved, leaders produced, and new churches started. And, the best leaders are often new Christians. They are people who know the grace of God and have connections with those who are far from God.

If the task of discipleship is neglected, the results are predictable. Developing disciples will have to do the following things on their own:

- Understand the gospel message and how it shapes their own spiritual formation;

- Apply the gospel to their lives and the lives of others through intentional disciple-making;

- Develop the fruit of the Spirit and the character of a leader in the church;

Preface: A Word to the Church

- Learn how to practice key spiritual disciplines and grow in the grace and knowledge of God;

- Make key life decisions, such as choosing a spouse or a career;

- Join a healthy church and become a meaningful member;

- Discern their own gifting and calling;

- Find a leadership role that fits that gifting and calling;

- Learn how to care for fallen and broken people.

This is a weighty task that cannot be accomplished by simply shuffling people off to a new Bible study class in the hopes that they will grow. More often than not potential disciples will end up frustrated, burned-out, and stagnant in their own spiritual formation, because they are being asked to do in isolation what is meant to be done in the community of the church.

Churches who lack a strategy for disciple-making and leadership development will experience the following problems:

- See a host of their members fall away due to the sin or neglect that results from a lack of maturity;

- Lament the lack of trained and skilled leaders for the ministries that God has entrusted to the church—small group leaders, Sunday School teachers, or future staff members;

- Depend on classes and programs to do the arduous work of disciple-making;

- See new believers come to faith in Christ and yet lack any strategy for nurturing them to maturity;

- Fail to equip the church to do their most important task—make disciples;

- Place people in leadership roles that may exceed their maturity;

- Determine a good fit for staff positions in the church based on a resume alone;

- Depend on seminaries or parachurch agencies to train its leaders in the hopes that this feeder system will consistently produce enough leaders for the church's needs;

- Remove leaders whose calling, character, or competence do not match the leadership needs to which they are called.

The result is wasted potential, immature church attendees, poorly led churches, and thousands of unreached men, women, and children. The surpassing riches of God's grace in the gospel and the vast lostness of the world compel the church to reproduce theologically robust, missionally active, and Spirit-led disciples (Eph 2:6–10). The development and deployment of future disciples **in** the church and **for** the church is vital for the church to thrive in the coming generation.

This is a stewardship responsibility that we must not neglect.

Thankfully, God is actively calling people to Himself and to His church. Young Christians will, by nature of their salvation, aspire to grow in the grace and knowledge of the Lord Jesus Christ (2 Pet 3:18). Young leaders will, by nature of their calling, aspire to lead, teach, and shepherd God's people faithfully (1 Tim 3:1). The task of discipling and training these men and women is the responsibility of the local church, regardless of whether they are everyday missionaries, summer interns, small group leaders, women's ministry leadership, pastors, church planters, or missionaries to an unreached people group.

Churches can train leaders—but most need tools to aid them in this task. *Aspire* is written in an effort to not only motivate churches to engage in this vital work but also to provide them with the basic framework for developing disciples and leaders in their specific context. There is no such thing as a plug-and-play model. What works for us in Greenville, SC may not work exactly the same way in an urban context on the West coast. *Aspire* can, however, provide the church with a vital resource for creating a pathway for discipleship.

This requires intentionality from the following people:

- **Pastors:** Pastors must embrace the multiplication of disciples as a vital aspect of their responsibility, whether they disciple a part-time youth leader in their church or a young man that has just come to Christ under their preaching. Pastors must personally be about the mission of disciple-making. They must also lead their church to understand that the creation of an intentional, disciple-making strategy is crucially important to the mission of the church. Pastors must lead the church's disciple-making mission by actively making disciples themselves (Heb 13:17).

- **Disciple-Makers:** All Christians are commanded to make disciples, yet many do not know how. Thus, any Christian can benefit from *Aspire* as they seek to make disciples in their daily lives (Mt 28:18–20). For example, a stay-at-home mom could utilize *Aspire* to disciple a younger wife and mom in her small group during a weekly play date with the kids. Or, a business professional could meet with a college student over lunch to utilize the plan outlined in this book.

- **Young Christians:** Young Christians are spiritually hungry and will often have an insatiable appetite for spiritual nourishment. Churches that have a plan for their growth will see far more fruit than those that passively assume growth will happen through another sermon or Bible-study class (1 Jn 2). These young believers should seek out mature leaders in the church and ask them to mentor them through *Aspire*.

- **Young Leaders:** Young leaders will seek out churches that have an intentional on-ramp for gospel ministry and mission. Such churches will quickly become magnetic to those seeking to be effectively positioned for a fruitful ministry (1 Tim 4:12). *Aspire* will provide a valuable tool for training such leaders, whether they are recent college or seminary graduates or seeking to be a new small-group leader in the local church.

The exact contours of a leadership development strategy will need to be catered to the needs of the local church and its leaders. But the basic values that are essential for the development of a disciple-making culture remain the same.

- **Gospel Transformation:** Disciples will only be produced by the power of the gospel, which means that any development plan must submerge them in the water of the gospel and allow them to soak in its life-giving truth (Gal 3:1–5).

- **Character Formation:** Disciples cannot be mass-produced through content-laden curriculum. They are produced through the intense process of walking with a person in the context of a loving relationship as they grow in gospel understanding and application (Rom 5:3–5).

- **Ongoing Mentorship:** Disciples cannot train themselves (or at least they should not have to). Rather, what they need is for a mature leader to mentor them through an intentional process of development. This process will build into them the tools that they are sure to need to multiply and make more disciples (2 Tim 3:14; 2 Tim 2:2).

- **Biblical Community:** Disciples are not made in isolation. The local church provides the context for them to form relationships with other aspiring leaders with whom they can grow and internalize what it means to follow Jesus and serve the church (Heb 13:17).

- **Gift Utilization:** There is no omni-competent disciple and leader. They come in all shapes and sizes, and developing disciples need a process by which they can try on various roles in the church and discover their best fit for fruitful ministry (1 Cor 12:14–26).

- **Leadership Experience:** Disciple-multiplication happens in the context of real-life relationships with messy people, not simply in a classroom. The skills necessary to connect theological training with practical wisdom are only forged in the local church (1 Tim 3:6–7).

- **Theological Education:** Disciple-making has a vital truth component. Churches should be intentional about theological training in the context of the local church and in partnership with mission-minded seminaries, which can serve as a catalyst for the church's mission (1 Tim 3:6–7).

- **Ongoing Assessment:** Developing disciples need someone who loves them enough to have hard conversations. The local church context provides the relational network necessary for such personalized assessment and direction in their service to God and His church (Titus 1:5–16; 1 Tim 3).

How do you make a disciple?

This answer is multifaceted. Clearly, God is the chief catalyst of a disciple. He calls disciples to Himself and places them in the church. However, the church is not passive in this process. Peter's exhortation to the church highlights the active role people play in disciple-making:

> By these He has given us very great and precious promises, so that through them you may share in the divine nature, escaping the corruption that is in the world because of evil desires. For this very reason, make every effort to supplement your faith with goodness, goodness with knowledge, knowledge with self-control, self-control with endurance, endurance with godliness, godliness with brotherly affection, and brotherly affection with love (2 Pet 1:4–7).

The very great and precious promises of God are meant to grow a disciple in knowledge, character, obedience, and love. Thankfully, these areas of focus are the same whether you are training a young disciple or a future pastor, thus they provide the foundation for the *Aspire* model.

Know

Disciples must know and embrace the message of the good news of Jesus Christ. The gospel cannot be an abstract concept, but must infuse every facet of the disciple's life. In turn, the gospel will begin to seep out of their lives as they both declare and display the glory of God (Ps 131:1–3; 139:17; Eccl 5:1–20; Is 26:3; Jer 33:3; Jn 3:1–36; Rom 12:2;

1 Cor 2:11–16; 2 Cor 4:4,10:3–6; Eph 4:22–24; Philemon 2:5; 4:4–9; Col 3:1–2; 2 Tim 1:6–8; 2:2; James 1:8; 3:1; 2 Pet 1:3).

Be

The gospel then transforms the hearts of the disciples so that they exemplify the fruit of the Spirit. Character formation, driven by a rich gospel understanding, is at the heart of the disciple-making journey and is essential for leadership among the people of God (Pr 4:23; Pr 27:19; Mt 5:1–48; 6:21; 12:31–34; 15:18; 22:37; Mk 7:21–22; Lk 6:45; Jn 7:38; 15:1–17; Rom 5:5; Gal 5:16–26; Eph 3:16–18; 1 Tim 3:1–7; Titus 1:5–9).

Do

Obedience to Christ is the proper response to a right understanding of the gospel. Disciples should increasingly live lives worthy of the gospel, not in order to earn God's favor, but because they have already been graciously given God's favor in Christ. This understanding should also transform a person to live a life of mission through humble service to others and bold proclamation of the gospel (Is 42:1–4; 52:13–53:3; Mt 20:25–28; 28:18–20; Mk 10:42–45; Lk 4:18–21; 9:1–62, 22:26; Jn 1:14; 13:3–17, 34–35; Acts 6:1–15; 20:28–35; Rom 12:1–21; Eph 4:11–12; Philemon 1:1; 2:5–11; 1 Tim 3:1–7; 2 Tim 4:5; Heb 13:7; 1 Pet 5:1–14).

Love

Finally, disciples live a life of love knowing that they have been richly loved in Christ Jesus. The relationships (such as family, spouse, children) of the developing disciple serve as a vital training ground by which the fruit of a person's life can mature and be assessed (Mal 2:16; Mk 12:31; Lk 6:31–35; Eph 5:22–33; Eph 6:1–3; 1 Cor 13:4–8; 1 Tim 3:2–5; Titus 1:6; 1 Pet 3:3–6, 4:8; 1 Jn 4:7, 18–19).

God transforms a person's life through growth in what they know, who they are, what they do, and how they love.

TRIMESTER 1
Gospel

Trimester 1: Gospel

I remember the first time someone said that they wanted to disciple me. Honestly, it felt weird. While I was raised in the church, I did not understand discipleship. I did not know if I had done something wrong to attract the notice of this older Christian or whether my clear inadequacy as a follower of Jesus had prompted them to seek me out.

For whatever reason I agreed. In the years that followed, my process of growth as a disciple of Jesus, and my ability to make other disciples has been far from seamless. There were times when godly men intentionally discipled me and taught me what it meant to love God with all of my heart, soul, mind, and strength and to love my neighbor as myself. Two seasons in my life deserve mention. First, I spent two years at North Wake Church in Wake Forest, NC under the mentorship of Jeff Doyle and pastoral leadership of their staff. I went to Wake Forest to get an education at Southeastern Baptist Theological Seminary and, by God's grace, fell in love with the local church. Along with a host of other young, passionate men (many of whom far better leaders and pastors than I will ever be), I set about the task of being trained to walk with God and pastor a local church. I look back on those days with fond memories and know that, around the world, God's Kingdom is blessed by the work of churches like North Wake.

From there, I spent two years serving alongside the pastoral staff at Crosspoint Church in Clemson, SC. Ken Lewis, Jeremy Chasteen, and Jason Finley modeled what it means to create a culture of discipleship in the local church. They were gracious to allow me to glean wisdom through these years and humbly sent me to pastor a church in Greenville, SC in the summer of 2009. To this day, I continue to partner with these brothers to develop and send leaders through the North American Church Planting Foundation (www.nacpf.org) and GenerationLink (www.generation-link.org).

I see no greater task before the church than the making of disciples and leaders for God's church. As the pastor of The Church at Cherrydale (www.tccherrydale.com), I have given my life to multiplying disciples both in a local church setting and throughout the world. This book may as well be my journal. It is the result of a decade of notes scribbled anywhere I could find space—from the back of a dinner napkin to the pages of numerous notebooks. In many ways it is the tool that I wish someone had used with me as a new believer and leader in the local church. Now, I seek to apply these truths to the lives of the young men I disciple, even as I continue to allow them to transform my own heart.

My prayer is that God would use this process to bring fruit from your life as well, whether you are a new Christian, a maturing disciple, a seminary student, or a vocational servant in God's church. For this to happen you are going to need the following:

- **A Humble Posture:** Let me guess—you feel inadequate and ill-equipped to be a disciple of Jesus and to make other disciples. Be encouraged. Allow your inadequacy and fears to drive you to a humble dependence on the grace of God and the leading of the Holy Spirit (1 Pet 5:6).

- **An Authoritative Bible:** The Scriptures are the basis for knowing God and understanding what it means to follow Him. The Scriptures will serve as our guide throughout *Aspire*. This will allow you to see the amazing depth and beauty of the promises and plans of God revealed in the person of His Son (2 Tim 3:16–17).

- **A Healthy Church:** Discipleship is meant to happen through the local church. A missionary disciple will not be able to consistently apply the truths of God's word in isolation. If you have not already found a Bible-centered, healthy church in which to plant your life, do so immediately. If you are in a healthy church, praise God—you are going to grow to love and rely on that community in the days ahead (Acts 2:41–47).

- **A Godly Mentor:** The local church in which you serve should provide a host of exemplary disciples who can guide you through the implementation of the tools you develop each week. Find someone who is marked by a discernable love for God and others, and ask if they will walk with you through *Aspire*. The questions provided in this guide should give you ample fodder for discussion (1 Cor 4:15–16).

- **An *Aspire* Book:** This book is written to not merely be read, but to be used. In the pages that follow, I will often ask questions and provide space for you to interact with the ideas being discussed. Do not neglect this process. Thoughtful reflection on these questions will be essential for the discipleship process in your life. In addition, your mentor may provide additional reading at his/her discretion. Finally, at the end of each trimester, you will find a lengthy list of suggested reading for further study. These books have been selected for their biblical foundations and proven benefits to the church (Eccl 12:11–12).

- **A Prayer Journal:** Journaling is helpful to record the thoughts, motives, and prayers of your heart, and to collect tangible evidence of God's grace in your life for years to come. Purchase a simple journal, or locate an online tool, that will allow you to collect your thoughts as you walk through the discipleship process (Lk 2:19).

Thankfully God has provided all that you need in order to grow as a disciple of Jesus and a leader in His church. Peter states, "His divine power has given us everything required for life and godliness through the knowledge of Him who called us by His own glory and goodness (2 Pet 1:3)." May *Aspire* fan the flames of godliness in your life, and may you then use it to make disciples of others until the great and glorious day when Jesus returns "the earth will be filled with the knowledge of the Lord's glory as the waters covers the sea (Hab 2:14)."

—Matt Rogers

Week 1: Creation

"Our Lord and God, You are worthy to receive glory and honor and power, because You have created all things, and because of Your will they exist and were created."

—Revelation 4:11

"The pursuit of pleasure is bound up with God himself. We were made initially by God and for God, and the best and highest pleasure is a God-centeredness that secular hedonists cannot possibly imagine. Their pleasure is too fleeting, too small, too narrow."[1]

—D.A. Carson

Gospel clarity is essential for a disciple of Jesus.

What is the gospel? Sadly, Christians and church leaders alike often neglect the answer to this question. We often assume that someone understands the gospel if they come to church gatherings, express faith in Jesus, live a morally upright life, and serve in the church's various ministries.[2]

This lack of clarity on the gospel is true at all stages in the life of the church. Many picture their initial expression of faith in Christ (be it praying a prayer, walking an isle, or being baptized) as the finish line of faith when in fact it is only the starting line. This may result in decades of church attendance, religious performance, and even church leadership without any real growth in spiritual maturity.

Discipleship Defined: The process of growing in your understanding of God, love for God, and obedience to God through intentional relationships.

---

1. D.A. Carson, *The God Who Is There: Finding Your Place in God's Story* (Grand Rapids: Baker, 2010), 26.
2. The author has intentionally limited the number of citations throughout *Aspire*. Following each trimester, however, a detailed list of suggested reading will be provided that addresses the subject matter of each trimester in far greater detail. Consult this resource list for a compilation of the sources that were most instrumental in developing the *Aspire* material.

Trimester 1: Gospel

What about you? What form has discipleship taken in your spiritual journey up to this point?

_____

_____

What are the consequences of a lack of discipleship in your life or in the life of a new Christian?

_____

_____

A lack of discipleship is not only rampant among church members, but also it is rampant in the leaders of the church as well. Many Christians lack a gospel foundation substantial enough to sustain the weight of walking with Jesus and serving in His church. Young Christians often place their faith in Christ and are thrust into leadership roles and responsibilities that far exceed their understanding or maturity. They may *feel* ready to move on to the meat of gospel ministry—how to lead a small group, preach a rousing sermon, or even launch the next church campus. They are spiritually impoverished, however. If these young disciples are given a mantel of leadership in the local church the results may be catastrophic. The church is littered with the shrapnel of church members and leaders who serve week in and week out without a clear understanding of the gospel and its application for their lives and ministries—devastating their lives, their families, and their churches.

Any journey towards maturity and leadership in the church must be driven by the gospel of Jesus Christ. The rich truth of the gospel is the foundation on which one's Christian life and ministry in the church must be built. Thus, a robust understanding of the gospel is the place to start our journey through *Aspire*.

Consider what is neglected in each of the following definitions of the gospel:

• The gospel is the way a person lives in order to please God.

_____

_____

- The gospel is the first four books of the New Testament.

  _____

  _____

- The gospel is the fact that Jesus died for my sins.

  _____

  _____

- The gospel is what a person believes in order to go to heaven when they die.

  _____

  _____

Your Christian life is impossible without gospel clarity. You cannot live a faithful and fruitful life that makes much of the glory of God without a deep and robust understanding and application of the gospel.

Think through your definitions of the gospel at different stages of your life. How did you define the gospel when:

- You were five:

  _____

  _____

- You were twelve:

  _____

  _____

- You were a senior in high school:

  _____

  _____

- You graduated from college:

  _____

  _____

How about now? What is the good news of Jesus Christ? How would you summarize the gospel in three sentences?

_____

_____

The goal of the first trimester of *Aspire* will be to build in you a clear and compelling understanding of the gospel. You will return to these truths again and again. You will grow in your understanding and ability to articulate the gospel throughout your life. And your breathtaking awe of the gospel will only deepen from here. In order to do this we will approach the Bible in sequential stages, as you might a story, looking at the plan of God from creation in the garden to recreation in the new heavens and the new earth.

Such a macro-level framework is essential because the gospel is far more than Jesus' death on the cross. While the substitutionary atonement of Jesus Christ is an essential part of the gospel, the gospel does not start on a cross but in a garden. Or more exactly, the gospel begins prior to the garden—in the eternal purpose and plan of God before the creation of the world (Eph 1:3–14). Our first glimpses into this story are found in the opening pages of our Bibles, where God begins to map out His plan for humanity. Read Genesis 1–2 and note what you observe about:

- God: _____

  _____

- Mankind:_____

  _____

- The World: _____

  _____

Paul recounts the story of God's creation in his letter to the church in Colossae. There he writes:

> *He is the image of the invisible God, the firstborn over all creation. For everything was created by Him, in heaven and on earth, the visible and the invisible, whether thrones or dominions or rulers or authorities—all things have been created through Him and for Him. He is before all things, and by Him all things hold together. He is also the head of the body, the church; He is the beginning, the firstborn from the dead, so that He might come to have first place in everything (Col 1:15–18).*

Here we see two vital foundations for a proper understanding of the gospel.

Foundation 1: Creation is BY GOD

The Triune God (Father, Son, and Spirit) is the author of creation. The Spirit hovers over the water and the Word of God (Jesus) brings all things into existence at the bidding of the Father (Gen 1; Jn 1:1–4). God creates *ex nihilo*—"out of nothing" by the power of His spoken Word (Heb 11:3). Romans 4:17 refers to God as the one who "calls things into existence that do not exist." The power of the Word of God is on display from the outset of creation.

God the Creator is also God the Sustainer, who continues to execute Lordship over his good creation through his providential care. He upholds it by "His powerful word (Heb 1:3)." Similarly, the Colossians passage above notes that "in [Christ] all things hold together (Col 1:15–18)." In the words of Albert Wolters, "From day to day every detail of our creaturely existence continues to be constituted by the 'Let there Be's of the sovereign will of the Creator."[1] God created all that is and continues to rule the world by His powerful word.

Why is it important to understand the role of God's spoken word in creation? How should the Word of God continue to lead His people?

_____

_____

---

1. Albert Wolters, *Creation Regained: Biblical Basics for a Reformational Worldview, 2nd ed.* (Grand Rapids: Eerdmans, 2005), 14.

What role does the Word of God currently play in your life?

_____

_____

God creates the world and all that is in it (Acts 17:24), including the pinnacle of creation—human beings (Gen 1:26–28). People are uniquely constructed from the dust of the ground and given life by the very breath of God. They are created as embodied souls, intricately formed by God and bearing the unique imprint of His image. As such, they are infused with worth and dignity and are uniquely capable of relationship with God.

What does it mean to be made in the image of God based on Genesis chapters 1–2?

_____

_____

How does this truth serve as an encouragement to you?

_____

_____

But God does not stop with the creation of an isolated individual. Rather, He blesses Adam with a helpmate in the person of Eve. God provides relationship for man at the outset of creation, demonstrating that His design is not simply the creation of isolated individuals but rather a community of image-bearers modeled after the Trinitarian God Himself.

What evidence do you see that people were made for relationships?

_____

_____

Why are relationships vital for the Christian life?

_____

_____

Foundation 2: Creation is FOR GOD

Creation was not necessary for an all-sufficient God, nor was it an accident. Instead, God created out of His own pleasure and for His own joy (Is 43:7; 48:11). But why?

If God is sovereign and knew that mankind would rebel from Him (which He is and He did) why would He create?

_____

_____

It is often assumed that the creation of the world was primarily for those who inhabit it. Yet, the biblical authors go out of their way to make the point that the end (*teleos)* of creation is not humanity but God. The Colossians passage you read earlier echoes Paul's words in the letter to the church at Rome. There he writes, "For *from him* and through him and *to him* are all things. To him be the glory forever. Amen (Rom 11:36)."

Creation is for God. He is the rightful ruler of that which He has made. Paul says that everything, including people, exist in order to declare the preeminence, or worth, of God (Col 1:18).

Define preeminent. How would you know if a person considers God to be preeminent?

_____

_____

How do you know whether or not God is preeminent in your life right now?

_____

_____

God's preeminence is a response to an essential attribute of God—His glory. The word "glory" means to be weighty or heavy. This word still creeps into our language regularly. Imagine that you receive a phone call from a good friend who confesses to you that his marriage is in trouble, and he is considering divorce. Perhaps you would not say it out loud but your thought is "Man, that is heavy!" Big, significant, weighty news is heavy.

The same would be true for objects of our affection. They simply have more weight. What my wife says to me matters far more than what some stranger says on Twitter. She has more significance in my life.

God is the most gloriously weighty person who exists. The Psalmist recounts that the "heavens declare the glory of God (Ps19:1–4)," and the prophet Isaiah comments, "His glory fills the whole earth (Is 6:3)." Mankind is meant to declare that glory as well. This is the point of Jonathan Edwards' masterful work *The End for Which God Created the World.* Here, Edwards argues that God created the world for His own glory—so that He might be seen worshiped in all the earth.[1] All of creation, including humans, is meant to be a megaphone for God's praise.

Read the following texts. What role does God's glory play?

Isaiah 43:6–7 _____
_____

Isaiah 49:3 _____
_____

Psalm 106:7–8 _____
_____

2 Samuel 7:23 _____
_____

Ezekiel 36:22–32 _____
_____

John 7:18 _____
_____

---

1. For a full treatment of the centrality of God's glory in all that God does see John Piper, *God's Passion for His Glory: Living the Vision of Jonathan Edwards* (Wheaton: Crossway, 1998). Here Piper provides a full copy of Edwards' text *The End for Which God Created The World.*

John 14:13 _____

_____

John 12:27–28 _____

_____

Romans 1:22–23 _____

_____

Isaiah 43:25 _____

_____

John 16:14 _____

_____

God is jealous for His glory and seeks it from all those He created. And rightly so. As the author of life and the fount of goodness, He *is* glorious. He has graciously blessed his creatures with abundant provision, declaring himself to be the source of all that is good, pure, and beautiful (Js 1:17). Worship is the proper response to glory. Who would not want to worship a God this glorious? This is the task of humanity (Ps 19:1–6; 1 Pet 2:9).

God creates all things in order to fill the earth with His glory.

How would you explain the purpose of creation to each of the following people:

A ten-year old boy:

_____

_____

A 40-year old, widow who attends church regularly:

_____

_____

A 70-year old saint:

_____

_____

An atheist, urban 30-year old hipster:

_____

_____

In order to accomplish the task of filling the earth with the glory of God, He commands Adam and Eve to be fruitful and multiply, thus filling the world with image-bearing worshippers. The title of "image-bearer" provides a much-needed identity, but it also carries certain responsibilities. Image-bearers have a mission and a capacity for demonstrating the glory of God in ways that other created things cannot.

They are also given a cultural task. In Genesis 1:28, Adam is told to "subdue the earth" and "have dominion" over that which God has made. God gives his image-bearers a degree of dominion in a world where they serve as sub-regents of the King. They are to develop the world He has created. Mankind must steward the earth in a way that both honors God and gives glory back to Him.

Based on the creation narrative, what is the importance of each of the following facets of life:

Beauty _____

_____

Work _____

_____

Marriage_____

_____

Child-bearing_____

_____

Mission _____

_____

Stewardship _____

_____

Write a mission statement for mankind based on Genesis 1 and 2. How does the cultural mandate serve to inform all of your life?

_____

_____

God completes His creation work by resting from His labors and basking in the glow of His goodness. In doing so He establishes a pattern for all of mankind to follow. They are to work and rest for God's glory.

If humans had been faithful to their task, the world would be filled with worship, peace, beauty, and joy. In a word—*shalom*. Cornelius Plantinga defines *shalom* as a "universal flourishing, wholeness, and delight—a rich state of affairs in which natural needs are satisfied and natural gifts fruitfully employed, all under the arch of God's love."[1] *Shalom* is the way the world was intended to function. As *The Jesus Storybook Bible* so eloquently says:

> *God looked at everything he had made, "Perfect!" he said. And it was. But all the stars and the mountains and oceans and galaxies and everything were nothing compared to how much God loved his children. He would move heaven and earth to be near them. Always. Whatever happened. Whatever it cost him, he would always love them. And so it was that the wonderful love story began...*

Imagine a world of pure *shalom*. What would such a world look like?

_____

_____

What do you learn about the gospel from creation?

_____

_____

---

1. Cornelious Plantinga Jr, *Engaging God's World: A Christian Vision of Faith, Learning, and Living* (Grand Rapids: Eerdmans, 2002), 15.

Trimester 1: Gospel

How is a right understanding of creation necessary for the Christian life?

_____

_____

The act of creation sets the stage for all subsequent redemptive history. This understanding will pave the way for you to rightly understand what went wrong, and what God is doing to make all things right again, in Christ Jesus.

Week 2: Rebellion

"They exchanged the truth of God for a lie, and worshiped and served something created instead of the Creator, who is blessed forever. Amen."

—Romans 1:25

"Most people think of sin as failing to keep God's rules of conduct but, while not less than that, Jesus' definition of sin goes beyond it."[1]

—Tim Keller

The depth of sin reveals the beauty of the gospel.

God created all things in order to declare and demonstrate His glory in all the world. This is the view from Genesis chapter 2. But it does not last long. In one hideous episode, Adam and Eve plunge themselves, the world, and all subsequent humanity into the depths of sin. Our world attests to this reality as death, suffering, injustice, fears, illness, pain, sorrow, grief, boredom, annoyances, and nuisances reveal that something is terribly wrong with the world. What is wrong? The scriptural answer to this question is SIN.

The Fall

Read Genesis 3:1–7. What observations would you make about this text?

_____

_____

_____

_____

In most Bibles, this section of Genesis chapter 3 is known as "The Fall," yet the word itself does little to attest to the catastrophic nature of what transpires in these few verses. On the surface, it is hard to imagine how this could happen at all. Adam and Eve have

---

1. Timothy Keller, *The Prodigal God: Recovering the Heart of the Christian Faith* (New York: Riverhead, 2008), 37–38.

everything—perfect communion with God, intimacy and fellowship with one another, meaningful work to do, and bountiful provision in a pristine world.

However, it is there that the serpent meets them. Satan himself tempts them to disobey God and eat from the forbidden tree. Hoping to be "like God, knowing good and evil," they willingly and culpably break relationship with God by living outside of His rule and reign. Simply put, they sin.

How would you define sin based on Genesis 3?

_____

_____

Perhaps you remember the first time you were aware of sin in your own life. I recall a time when my parents bought me a pair of brand-new, white, Reebok pumps. You know—the kind where you pressed an inflatable basketball on the tongue of the shoe and it supposedly pumped air into the shoe cushion, making it possible for all kids to dunk a basketball. These shoes were expensive, and I knew that I had to take good care of them. So, what did I do? The first day I had them I put them on and went exploring through the woods around my house, covering my new shoes with red clay and mud. When my parents saw them, I did what any kid would do—I blamed my best friend!

I knew I was guilty in my heart. I had disobeyed my parents, taken advantage of their generosity, and placed blame where it did not belong. I was a sinner and I knew it.

Can you remember the first time you recall knowing that you were a sinner? What happened and how did you feel?

_____

_____

Based on Genesis 3 and your own experience with sin, how would you explain sin to:

- Your 7-year-old son: _____

  _____

  _____

- A 75-year-old deacon in a Baptist church: _____

  _____

  _____

- A Catholic university student: _____

  _____

  _____

Sin reveals itself in a thousand ways making it difficult to define properly. Scripture is clear what sin is not; sin is not a mere error in judgment; sin is not a sickness; sin is not some form of psychological maladjustment.

Scripture, in particular the story of Genesis 3, provides the reader with a number of images that help us understand sin's heinous nature. Much like a kaleidoscope which, when turned, reveals different dimensions and shapes, the concept of sin can be analyzed from different angles to help one see the scope and significance of human depravity.

Sin is Rebellion

The scene in the garden is a clear case of rebellion, similar to what you might see from a teenage girl who has been told that she cannot date a certain, wayward guy. God told the first couple that one tree was off limits, yet they willingly rebelled and pursued what God had told them to avoid.

R.C. Sproul writes that sin is "cosmic treason." He notes that the sin in the garden, and all subsequent sin, was a willing act of rebellion against the sovereign rule of God.[1] The mutiny of the first couple is evidenced by their unwillingness to worship God and make His glory known in the world. Elsewhere, the Bible defines sin as missing the mark, wandering from the path, and straying from the fold, which all point to the rebellious nature of sin (Rom 3:23; Eph 2:1–3; 1 Jn 3:4). Sin is as an affront to the King of the Universe.

---

1. R.C. Sproul, *The Holiness of God* (Carol Stream, IL: Tyndale House, 1985), 116.

This understanding of sin is seen in the propensity of humans to pursue that which is off-limits (i.e. the forbidden boyfriend) simply because they draw pleasure from the mere act of rebellion.

How are you most tempted to rebel against God?

_____

_____

How might you help others see their sin as rebellion against God?

_____

_____

Sin is Idolatry

Another turn of the kaleidoscope reveals that sin is idolatry. In Eden, the first couple worship and serve God's creation (the fruit of the tree) rather than God Himself. They make a terrible exchange. In Romans, Paul recounts that this is in fact a fundamental way in which sin happens as people "exchange the glory of the immortal God for images resembling mortal man (Rom 1:23)."

This image is pervasive in the Old Testament as well. The nation of Israel was consistently guilty of idolatry—worshiping something other than God as god. This notion of exchange is at the heart of idolatry. The glory that is rightly due to God alone is exchanged for another object. Objects that lack glory, weight, and significance are given glory through the affections, sacrifices, and actions of humanity. In this way, things that are not God become functional gods, which are pursued in lieu of their intended purpose of promoting the worship of God.

This can happen with any object. In fact, sin results when good objects (work, money, family, sex, food) are turned into ultimate things and worshiped in place of God. Calvin writes that the heart of a human is "a perpetual factory of idols," constantly producing a steady stream of god-substitutes.[1]

---

1. John Calvin, *Institutes of the Christian Religion, vol. 1* (John T. McNeill, ed.: Philidelphia; Westminister, 1960), I.XI.8., 108.

In what areas are you most tempted to idolatry?

_____

_____

Imagine you are talking to a young Christian girl who is struggling in a relationship with a non-Christian boyfriend. She claims to love him but knows that the relationship is causing her to falter in her walk with God.

How could you use the idea of idolatry to help her see and understand her sin?

_____

_____

Sin is Adultery

Sin is a worship disorder (idolatry) because sin is a love disorder (adultery). In the garden, the tree was a delight to the eyes and desirable to make one wise. Adam and Eve found it lovely—more lovely in fact than God Himself. Throughout the Bible, the people of God are consistently reproved for their forays into adulterous loves (see the book of Hosea). Rather than remaining faithful to their covenant with God they chose to dabble with mistresses. God's people, like the church today, often settled for the temporary, fleeting pleasure of sin rather than the loving security of their relationship with God.

Respond to the following statement: "People sin because they love sin more than God." Do you agree or disagree?

_____

_____

Sin is Selfishness

The sin in the garden is a plea for autonomy. This is astounding considering God's love and provision yet the first couple wants to be free from the constraints of His authority as they attempt to be like God themselves; the sole arbitrators of right and wrong. Paul succinctly states that apart from God, people "live for themselves (2 Cor 5:15)." This has led many theologians to conclude that pride is at the root of all sin, as people live pursuing their own desires, pleasures, hopes, and dreams. Interestingly, this self-aware-ness is seen immediately after the sin in the garden, not by the joyous freedom of a life without God, but by a desperate attempt to cover their sin and shame.

How do Adam and Eve respond to their sin in the garden? How is this similar to the way in which people respond to sin in our culture?

_____

_____

How could the three prototypical responses to sin (shame, hiding, and blame) serve as useful tools for helping other people respond to sin in their lives?

_____

_____

Sin is Corrupt Fruit

Interestingly, the sin in the garden is related to fruit, and that is just the image the later biblical authors will use to define sin. They point out that sinful behavior is merely fruit that evidences the root of sin in a person's life.

Because of the fall, **all people are sinners who sin**. They are sinners at the core of their being, and they demonstrate sinful actions by what they do. Jesus makes this point in Matthew 12:33–35 when He says, "Either make the tree good and its fruit good, or make the tree bad and its fruit bad; for a tree is known by its fruit… A good man produces good things from his storeroom of good, and an evil man produces evil things from his storeroom of evil."

The fruit reveals the root, and the root of human sin is a depraved human heart that is bent towards rebellion, idolatry, and adultery. Sin is more than what people do; it is who they are. They sin by nature and by choice. Consider Romans 1. Paul goes to great length to establish the reality that all people are dead in their sins and morally guilty before a holy God. Following this, he lists a host of sinful actions that result from a sinful heart. The acts of sin are not the problem, but rather something much more dastardly.

What are the most common "fruit" manifestations of sin in your life?

What root issues might these reveal?

_____

_____

Sin is Unbelief

Satan tempts the couple in the Garden to doubt both the provision of God and the truthfulness of His word. In other words, unbelief is at the heart of the temptation. They are led to doubt God's word ("did God really say?") and the provision of God ("it seemed good to the eyes, etc."). Sinful people fail to trust the infinite God to be true to his word and provide for their needs, and they seek comfort, provision, and security elsewhere. This leads people to put their hope in objects that are ill equipped to carry the weight they put on them; it causes them to live anxious and restless lives anticipating that objects of their devotion may collapse.

How is all sin linked to a lack of belief in God?

_____

_____

Sin is Pollution

Sin pollutes the world of shalom, breaking the rich state of flourishing that God intended in His created design. Rather than remaining pure and holy (set apart), sin contaminates that which God created. Sin drags God's good creation through the mud and soils that which he has made beautiful. As a result the world is a broken and tattered reflection of God's created design.

How does sin mess up the world? How can the brokenness of our world serve as an inroad for talking to people about the gospel?

_____

_____

Sin is Folly

Sin is foolish. It is both *wrong* AND *dumb*. It is in mortal opposition to the biblical notion of wisdom. Cornelius Plantinga Jr. writes, "In the Biblical view, we not only sin because we are ignorant but we are also ignorant because we sin, because we find it convenient to misconstrue our place in the universe and to reassign divinity in it."[1] This ignorance and selfishness leads us to falsely believe that sin can fulfill its promises. The deceitfulness of sin results from futility in thinking and the darkening of the mind (Rom 1:21). Certainly, sin is fulfilling—for a while and in small measure. But it lacks the ability to fully and lastingly supply the longings of the human heart.

How can you help yourself and those you serve to see their sin as folly PRIOR to their sin rather than AFTER they sin?

_____

_____

Sin is Slavery

Sin results in slavery. Years later the people of God will find this to be all too true, as they will find themselves enslaved in Egypt. There they will be captive to a foreign master and unable to escape without outside help. They are hopeless and helpless. It begins in the garden as the first couple introduces the slavery of sin into the world. The closest modern language we might have to denote this reality would be that of "addiction." Sin causes a people to be held captive to the addictive desires of their heart.

How would the language of addiction aid you in discussing sinful behaviors that are not typically thought of as addictive (discontentment, worry, fear, anger, lust, etc.)?

_____

_____

Each of the turns of the kaleidoscope of sin demonstrate the way in which sin distorts and alters man's ability to worship God. They cannot worship God rightly—and neither can you.

---

1. Cornelius Plantinga, Jr, *Not the Way It's Supposed to Be: A Breviary of Sin* (Grand Rapids: Eerdmans, 1995), 18.

Which of these images of sin most connects with your current experience with sin?

_____

_____

What images of sin will be most helpful in talking about sin with others?

_____

_____

The Curse

It is no wonder that a holy God must deal swiftly and decisively with sin. There is simply no way God could, should, or would wink at sin and undermine its severity. He must act. As Plantinga writes, "Sin grieves God, offends God, betrays God, and not because God is touchy. God hates sin against himself, against neighbors, against a good creation, because sin breaks the peace—in the first place between the sinner and God."[1] His judgment consists of cursing the serpent to a life of bondage, the woman to pain in childbirth and discord in marriage, the man to pain and suffering in work and frustration in leadership, creation to futility, and humankind to death (Rom 8:18–24). They are banished from the garden, separating them both from God's presence.

His action is a just response to the sinful choices of His image-bearers. In a real way, God simply gives people over to the just implications of their foolishness. Paul tells the Roman church that God "gave them over" to the implications of their sin. The Psalmist makes the same point when his writes, "But my people did not listen to me…so I gave them over to their stubborn hearts to follow their own plans (Ps. 81:11–12)." The consequences for human sin are evident in the announcement of curse in the garden.

Read Genesis 3:14–19. What consequences for sin do you observe?

_____

_____

---

1. Plantinga, _Engaging_, 51.

Alienation from God

God removes humanity from the sphere of his gracious provision and blessing by driving them out of the garden and placing an angel at the entrance of the garden to prohibit their reentry. God is gracious in His dealings with man and gives him death rather than allowing him to eat of the Tree of Life and live forever apart from God. If not for the gracious intervention of God, this alienation would lead to an eternal separation from God for all people, since all "have sinned and fallen short of the glory of God (Rom 3:23)." The just wages of those sinful actions is death (Rom 6:23). The result of Adam's sin spreads to all humanity; "Just as sin entered the world through one man, and death through sin, in this way death spread to all men, because all sinned" (Rom 5:12). Therefore all people are born in a state of sin and misery resulting in their death (Eph 2:1–10) and are without excuse before a holy God (Rom 1:20). Eternal separation is the proper punishment for sinful humanity, and "the infinite horrors of hell are intended by God to be a vivid demonstration of the infinite value of the glory of God."[1]

Why does sin separate mankind from God?

_____

_____

Separation from Community

The implications of the curse are also relational. Graeme Goldsworthy says, "The rebellion of mankind caused all relationships of the Kingdom of God to be dislocated. God, mankind, and the rest of creation no longer relate in the perfect way that God intended."[2] The first couple, created to partner together to spread the glory of God, settle for blame-shifting and hiding in the garden. God indicates that their lives will be marked by relational friction as the woman will long to rule and the man will forcefully rule over her. Even that which is meant to be a means of spreading the glory of God, the act of fruitful reproduction, will be marked by pain.

---

1. John Piper, *Let the Nations be Glad!* (Grand Rapids: Baker, 1993), 22.
2. Graeme Goldsworthy, *According to Plan: the Unfolding Revelation of God in the Bible* (Downers Grove: IVP, 1991), 111.

How does this understanding of the consequences of sin help you understand issues like marital discord, jealously in friendships, or disunity among family members?

_____

_____

Brokenness of the World

Humankind is affected by the curse and all creation is likewise broken. Nothing escapes the curse of sin. Creation itself is subject to corruption and bondage, and it groans for redemption (Rom 8:19–22). The shalom state of the garden has been permanently altered by sin. As Albert Wolters says, "Every area of the created world cries out for redemption and the coming of the Kingdom of God."[1] Work will now be hard, and all of life will be marked by vanity, as people chase after the wind (Ecc 1:17).

How do these consequences inform how you interpret the daily news stories you watch on TV or read online? How does it help you interpret the seemingly chaotic events of this world?

_____

_____

Systems of Evil

James say that "after desire is conceived, it gives birth to sin, and when sin is fully grown, it gives birth to death (Js 1:15)." Sin grows, spreads, and kills everything it touches. And yet sin does not stop there. Sin is primarily personal, but it is also societal. Personal sin leads to societal and systemic sin in which all of the created order—its systems, structures, and institutions—are broken and distorted. In spite of the Enlightenment optimism about human progress, the reality is that people cannot stop being idolaters. In the end, gains in science, technology, and innovation may lead to great advances, but they often lead to greater and more pervasive forms of idolatry. Systems of evil such as sex trafficking, economic oppression, and political corruption are a consequence of the spread of sin.

---

1. Wolters, _Regained_, 68.

This is a far cry from the shalom found in the garden. People were created to fill the earth with the glory of God, but instead people fill the earth with sin. Needless to say, the bad news of sin is quite bad indeed. This is what makes the gospel such good news!

Why is a proper understanding of sin essential for a right understanding of the gospel?

_____

_____

How should an understanding of sin cause you to respond to temptation and sin in your own life?

_____

_____

Sin sets the stage for the next phase in the mission of God. How will He respond to the mess that his image-bearers have made with His created design? This is the story of the rest of the Bible.

Week 3: Covenant

"Blessed be the God and Father of our Lord Jesus Christ, who has blessed us with every spiritual blessing in the heavens, in Christ; for He chose us in Him, before the foundation of the world, to be holy and blameless in His sight. In love He predestined us to be adopted through Jesus Christ for Himself, according to His favor and will, to the praise of His glorious grace that He favored us with in the Beloved."

—Ephesians 1:3–6

"Only God's revelation can build a story where the end is anticipated from the beginning, and where the guiding principle is not chance or fate, but promise."[1]

—Edmund Clowney

God is on mission to reclaim worshippers to live in His Kingdom.

Over two-thirds of the Bible lies between Genesis 3 and the beginning of the New Testament. A vast amount of the revelation God chose to preserve for the church is found in the Old Testament. Sadly, this portion of the Scriptures is neglected.

What makes the Old Testament intimidating for you?

_____

_____

The reasons for the neglect of the Old Testament are many:

- The OT seems culturally distant;

- The OT is difficult to understand;

- The OT is filled with seemingly minor and obscure details;

---

1. Edmund P. Clowney, *The Unfolding Mystery: Discovering Christ in the Old Testament* (Phillipsburg: P&R, 1988), 11.

- The OT is written for the nation of Israel and has no relevance for the modern church;

- The OT is thought to be unrelated to the work of Jesus.

Because of this, the teaching from these Scriptures often amounts to little more than cute stories reserved for a children's Sunday school class or poorly extracted rules that seemingly lack coherence with the person and work of Christ. We must do a better job of connecting the dots on how Genesis 1–3 informs the Old Testament story and how the Old Testament story provides essential categories for understanding the person and work of Jesus.

Take a minute to try your hand at recounting the big story of the Old Testament. If you were asked by someone who was new to the Bible to explain what happened between the Fall and the incarnation of Jesus, what essential concepts would you want to communicate?

_____

_____

In a sense, all of the rest of the Scriptures are an outworking of Genesis 1–3. Thus far, we have established two dominant truths:

- God created all things so that His glory would fill the earth.

- Sin makes it impossible for humanity to give God glory.

Would God simply give up on his failed image-bearers? How would He respond to sin? Would His image-bearers ever again be able to rightly reflect His glory? How would a world broken and marred by sin be made right again?

Through the lens of Genesis 1–3 we are able to catch a glimpse of the means by which God would answer these questions. It is clear that the fall of mankind was not surprising to God, nor was his response to their sin some type of cosmic Plan B. He was not sitting helplessly on His throne, bewildered by the choices of Adam and Eve. Rather, from eternity past, God ordained a plan by which he would restore fallen humanity. God would put His glory on full display through this plan.

The Character of God

God's nature and character is the main focus of the Bible. He is the hero of the story, and His plan to rescue His creation helps us see Him clearly.

If all you had was Genesis 1–3, how would you describe the attributes of God?

_____

_____

Two attributes of God seem to rise above the rest, specifically in the way in which God deals with the sin of his image-bearers. First, we see the judgment of God. God is swift to enact a punishment for the sin of mankind, and his judgment is cosmic in scope. All that He has made is now distorted and broken by sin. Sin has fundamentally altered God's created order, even though the image of God in humanity remains intact. Paul demonstrates in Romans 1 that sin does not erase mankind's knowledge of God: We still know that He exists, but simply suppress that truth in unrighteousness (Rom 1:18–23).

Why must God respond to human sin with judgment? How is God's judgment connected to His holiness?

_____

_____

How do we see the judgment of God demonstrated in our world today?

_____

_____

Secondly, we see the mercy of God. God does not destroy His creation or kill his image-bearers immediately. While they are now faced with inevitable death and the potential doom of eternal separation from God, they are not given what their sin deserves—immediate, physical death. Instead, God allows them to continue to live. However, He also promises (as an act of grace) that they will die one day and not have to live in their sin-drenched state forever. God gives them hope that both their physical bodies and the world can be remade (Ps 103:8–11).

Define the word mercy. How do we see God's mercy continue to play out in the pages of the Old Testament?

_____

_____

How do we see the mercy of God demonstrated in our world today?

_____

_____

The Provision of God

God's nature is put on display alongside His gracious provision. Notice what God does in Genesis 3:21.

How does this verse compare with what Adam and Eve do in Genesis 3:7?

_____

_____

God does something for Adam and Eve that they have already tried to do for themselves —provide a covering for their sin. They have tried to cover their sin by sewing fig leaves together, and this has proven futile. Instead, God must provide a covering for their sins through a sacrifice. The covering of sin by the blood sacrifice of a substitute is an essential concept that provides clarity for a right understanding of the Old Testament.

How is this theme of blood sacrifice seen throughout the Old Testament?

_____

_____

The Promise of God

Finally, we see the amazing promise of God. As Bartholomew and Goheen write, "God did not turn his back on a world bent on destruction; he turned his face toward it in love. He set out on the long road of redemption to restore the lost as his people and the world as his kingdom."[1] God does not abandon his creation to destruction; rather, He promises to restore the broken world. He has a plan.

Read Genesis 3:15. What does this verse tell us about the plan of God?

_____

_____

God is on a relentless mission to reclaim worshippers. Specifically, we are introduced in Genesis 3:15 to the fact that ultimately God will emerge victorious. His plan involves the means by which the head of the serpent will be crushed, though this victory will come at a cost to God—Satan will strike the heel of the promised one. The crushing of the head of the serpent will happen through "the seed of the woman."

The seed of the woman maintains an enigmatic presence throughout the Old Testament. The purpose of the seed is clear—He will be the one who defeats sin and makes it possible for God to reclaim a people to worship Him rightly. The seed will fulfill the plan of God—He will be the one who will crush the head of the serpent. Yet, His identity remains in the shadows. How will God keep His promise to provide the seed? This is the story of the Bible.

I remember the first time I committed to reading through the Bible in a year. I did not make it out of Genesis. The stories seemed so archaic and repetitious. Why all this talk of babies, barrenness, and circumcision? So I turned to Matthew and started reading the part of the Bible that seemed to make a little bit of sense. Perhaps you've been in that position yourself. When the main themes of the Bible appear, however, your reading of the Scripture will grow more rich, more deep, and more clear.

What examples of God's mission to reclaim worshippers through the sending of a seed do you find in the book of Genesis and Exodus?

_____

_____

---

1. Craig G. Bartholomew and Michael W. Goheen, The *Drama of Scripture: Finding Our Place in the Biblical Story* (Grand Rapids: Baker, 2004), 12.

Covenant

In subsequent generations, God seals His character, promise, and provision in the form of a covenant. The idea of a covenant may sound strange to most modern ears. Perhaps you may hear the word used at a wedding, but that is about it.

What images or thoughts come to mind when you think of a covenant?

_____

_____

In the ancient Near-East, covenants would have been a standard practice for establishing the relationship between a King and his people. Covenants would serve to establish the terms of the relationship and the responsibilities that would be expected by both parties —the ruler and those ruled.

> *Covenant Defined*: An explanation of the nature of the relationship between God and His people.

The need for such a plan is all too clear. Sin is beginning to spread, and by Babel (Gen 6), human folly reaches an all-time high. The people gather in foolish pride and false worship, and God acts to protect them from the severe consequences of their sin. In a scene eerily reminiscent of the garden, God scatters His image-bearers over the face of the earth, not as worshippers—but as judged sinners. The handwriting is on the wall. Creation is careening to certain destruction. God, in His grace, still acts.

Noahic Covenant

God declares his purpose and plan to Noah in the form of a covenant. God is grieved by mankind and laments their very existence. However, instead of destroying them forever (which He would have full right to do), he preserves the life of a remnant worshipper and his family through the waters of judgment.

God begins the work of gathering a people through Noah, and to these people God pledges His everlasting fidelity and protection (Gen 6–9). Stunningly, He repeats His creation command to "be fruitful and multiply and fill the earth (Gen 9:1)." God's covenant with Noah is the first step in His plan to gather and reclaim a people to declare His glory in all the world.

What role did the grace of God play in His covenant with Noah? What role did Noah's obedience play?

_____

_____

How are both of these vital to an understanding of God's work in the world?

_____

_____

Abrahamic Covenant

God's covenant is further clarified in His promises to Abraham, a faithful man living in a pagan city in the East. God calls the aging Abram to leave all that he knows and pursue a new land of God's choosing. Abram believes and God counts this as righteousness.

Read Romans 4 and Galatians 3:1–9. What does Paul say Abram did? Why does that matter?

_____

_____

Abram and his family trust God, follow His call, and in so doing receive some of the most beautiful promises of God recorded in the Scriptures. Read Genesis 12:1–3:

> *The Lord said to Abram: "Go out from your land, your relatives, and your father's house to the land that I will show you. I will make you into a great nation, I will bless you, I will make your name great, and you will be a blessing. I will bless those who bless you, I will curse those who treat you with contempt, and all the peoples on earth will be blessed through you.*

God makes a wonderful promise to Abram. Through no merit of his own, Abram was given the promise of God—that He will (1) gather a people, (2) bless a people, and (3) make that people a blessing to the nations. How? Through his seed! This covenant serves as a fulfillment of the promises of God in the garden (Gen 3) and a precursor to the commission of Jesus following His resurrection (Mt 28:18–20).

The importance of this covenantal promise cannot be overstated. It reveals:

- **The Grace of God:** God calls a people to Himself, and graciously acts on their behalf in order that they may have the opportunity to have a relationship with Him. The covenant ceremony enacted with Abram in Genesis 17 is unilateral in nature; God's faithfulness trumps man's sinfulness. Here we see the rhythm of the Old Testament. God acts in mercy and grace to allow mankind to do that which they were created to do.

Consider what we have established thus far.

God is glorious;

GLORY

His glory is meant to lead to worship;

GLORY ➡ WORSHIP

Sin blocks the pathway from glory to worship;

GLORY ➡ SIN ➡ WORSHIP

God's grace overcomes human sin, making it possible for mankind to do what they were created to do—worship.

GLORY ➡ GRACE ➡ WORSHIP

Define grace. Why is God's grace vital for worship?

_____

_____

How is God's grace evident in your spiritual journey?

_____

_____

- **The Seed of God:** The plan of God will be impossible without the promised seed. His full identity will not be revealed in the Old Testament; however, we know that worshipful obedience will be possible only through Him. God confirms His covenant promises by circumcising the men in Abraham's family.

What do we know about the seed from the first twelve chapters of Genesis?

_____

_____

- **The Presence of God:** These reclaimed worshippers would not just be any people—they would be God's people. God's mission in humanity culminates in Him getting what He is after all along—the rightful worship of His people. His mantra in the Old Testament when referring to His people is this: "I will be their God and they will be my people." He is jealous for the worship of His people.

- **The Blessing of God:** God promises rich blessings to those who respond to His offer of grace. Not only do they get God Himself, but also they get the pledge of His kindness and protection.

The beauty of these covenant promises is that they are made by God. And God does not break promises. There is a biblical word for the faithfulness of God to keep His covenant promises—*hesed*. Our English versions have trouble translating this word because of the richness it possesses in the Hebrew language. It is used to refer to God's faithfulness and loving-kindness. God is always faithful to the promise He made with mankind. As a result we are to "give thanks to the Lord, for He is good, His love (*hesed*) is eternal (Ps 136:1–3)."

As you complete this session, look up the following passages which speak of the *hesed* of God. How do they prompt your heart to worship?

Exodus 34:6–7 _____

_____

Trimester 1: Gospel

Deuteronomy 7:9 _____

_____

Isaiah 54:8–10 _____

_____

Lamentations 3:22–23 _____

_____

Psalm 85:8–11 _____

_____

Unlike you and me, God always keeps His word. His faithfulness to His promises is at the core of the Bible. His *hesed* is seen in His next, great act—the gathering of His people.

Week 4: People

"He is the Lord our God; His judgments [govern] the whole earth. He forever remembers His covenant, the promise He ordained for a thousand generations- [the covenant] He made with Abraham, swore to Isaac, and confirmed to Jacob as a decree and to Israel as an everlasting covenant."

—Psalm 105:7–10

"We must recover the Old Testament as a book about Jesus."[1]

—Peter Leithart

God's covenant-keeping love relentlessly pursues His people.

God promises to reclaim a people. The following scenes of God's redemptive plan tell the story of the gathering of that people. As Graeme Goldsworthy notes, "God is refusing to allow human rebellion to divert him from his purpose to create a people to be his people in a perfect universe."[2] The people follow in the line that travels from Abraham to Isaac to Jacob, who is given the name that would define God's people—Israel.

The Israelites serve as the gracious recipients of God's covenant promises. Though the story has been fraught with tragedy and sin, it has resulted in great growth for the people of God (Gen 50:20). He has been faithful to preserve His seed through lines of barrenness, and He is clearly distinguishing between His people (those saved by grace) and those who are not His people (those judged in their sin).

However, as the book of Genesis comes to a close, God's people find themselves enslaved in Egypt. Not exactly what you would expect for God's chosen people. Rather than filling the earth with the worship of God, they are servants to a foreign king.

God does what God always does; He keeps His promises and redeems His people. This time, He does it by breaking the shackles of their captivity. Through His chosen servant Moses, God executes His judgment on the nations by showing Himself to be

1. Peter J. Leithart, *A House For My Name: A Survey of the Old Testament* (Moscow, ID: Canonpress, 2000), 26.
2. Goldsworthy, *According*, 115.

more powerful than any of their false gods, and He redeems a people to Himself so that they can worship Him (Ex 3:19–20; 7:3–5; 10:1–2; 14:13–14). This work is the manifestation of His covenant promises to Abram.

Redemption Defined: God's work to free mankind from slavery to sin.

Why is the theme of redemption important in order to understand the gospel?

_____

_____

In what ways is sin like slavery? How is grace like freedom?

_____

_____

God's redemptive work is not simply limited to the nation of Israel, however. The nations are in view from the outset. The story of God gathering a worshiping people is never meant to end with the nation of Israel. Instead, it is meant to extend to the very ends of the earth through Israel. The circumcision of the male members of Abraham's household (Gen 17:12–14), and the engrafting of outsiders like Ruth, demonstrate that God will gather a people from all the nations.

Since God desires His glory to fill the earth, and since the nations are scattered over the entire earth, the best way to have His glory fill the earth is to gather a people from every tribe, tongue, and nation. The people of the world could know God by becoming a part of His covenant promises to the nation of Israel. The hope that the nations would come to know and rightly worship God is a common theme in the Scriptures. For example, read the following passages and note what they say about the nations:

Genesis 22:18 _____

_____

Joshua 4:24 _____

_____

Jeremiah 12:16–17 _____
_____

Psalm 22:27 _____
_____

Psalm 102:15 _____
_____

Isaiah 2:2 _____
_____

Isaiah 45:22–23 _____
_____

Daniel 7:14 _____
_____

Galatians 3:7–9 _____
_____

A summary of the scriptural plan for the nations is found in Psalm 86:9 "All the nations you have made will come and bow down before You, Lord, and will honor Your name." God's mission to reclaim worshippers from every nation is the story of the Bible. He will use His people, the nation of Israel, to accomplish this majestic purpose by placing them on a land in the center of the nations to serve as a light to those around them. The contours of the Biblical story have now taken shape. We have:

- **The Main Characters:** The Trinitarian God and sinful image-bearers;

- **The Problem:** Sin has made it impossible for man to give glory to God;

- **The Mission:** To reclaim God's worshippers;

- **The Scope:** To reclaim worshippers from the line of Abram who will in turn gather worshippers from all the nations;

- **The Plan:** The sending of a seed who would defeat Satan, sin, and death.

All great stories consist of these same elements. Think about the last movie that you watched. The characters made their appearance and were confronted with a problem. The movie then told the story of the main character's mission to overcome the problem (often involving high-speed car chases and explosives) by executing a plan. God's story works the same way—only this is no Hollywood script, but rather a true story that explains all of life.

The Bible sets out to demonstrate how this mission will be fulfilled. Seen in this light, all of the micro-stories are connected to form one macro-story of God's plan of redemption. As the story develops, the reader is awakened to the ever-increasing demonstrations of the brilliance of God.

> ***Metanarrative Defined***: The grand, unified story of the Bible that tells of God's mission to reclaim worshippers for His glory.

Unfortunately, we rarely read the Bible this way. For most people, the Bible serves as an encyclopedic tool for learning how to obey God. Perhaps you are familiar with the process—You need help in a certain area of life, so you flip to the back of your Bible or do a quick Google search in the hopes of finding the perfect verse to address your problem. Sometimes, it may seem that you are successful. You look up the Word "suffering," and immediately you are met with a lengthy list of verses that promise the help and provision of God. So, after a quick Facebook post, you leave the Bible feeling refreshed and encouraged.

But there are problems:

- There are a host of topics that are simply not addressed in this way in the Bible. For example, try looking up "dating" in a concordance. Nothing. Does this mean that God does not care about your dating decisions?

- An encyclopedia approach to the Bible leads you to conclude that there are vast sections of the Bible that are unnecessary. I mean, how likely is it that your concordance is going to direct your attention to the eleventh chapter of Daniel? As a result, you own a Bible with many pages that still stick together because they have never been read.

- The likelihood that you take the verses out of context is at an all time high. Perhaps the verses that you think are sure-fire promises from God to you are actually not promises at all. Maybe the passages that show up on our Christian t-shirts or coffee mugs actually say something quite different than we think.

Consider Philippians 4:13 (the go-to verse of college athletes the world over). Look it up and read what this verse means in its original context.

_____

_____

What happens when a verse that is meant to be an encouragement for those who are being persecuted for their faith becomes a sign at a college football game?

_____

_____

Pretend for a moment that someone hacked into your emails and read a lengthy note that you sent to a personal friend. Rather than reading the entire note, they simply scanned down to the seventeenth sentence and read that. Then they took that sentence and posted it on their favorite social media feed as a clear indication of your views and opinions. What would you do?

Hopefully you would yell, "STOP! That is not what I said. You have to read the rest of the note!" The same is true of the Bible. Unless we understand the story and the context, it is impossible to understand what God is trying to communicate.

God wrote the Bible as a story.

People are often drawn to stories. Think about how often we use them. Stories capture our attention, connect with our hearts, and engage our actions in ways that other types of information do not.

Consider the last sermon that you heard. What was the pastor's text and main points? If you can't remember you are in good company. Most people can't remember 45 minutes worth of content, but they can remember stories.

What is it about stories that capture your mind and heart?

_____

_____

The Bible is a true story.

Approaching the Bible as a story doesn't mean that the Bible is a fable or fairy-tale. Unfortunately, most modern notions of story equate the Bible with fiction, and our postmodern world assumes that the Bible lacks universally valid truth.[1] The story of the Bible is an authoritative story, a true story, or as Goheen and Bartholomew claim, "The true story of the whole world."[2] The story of the Bible makes sense out of the seemingly random nature of the world in which we live.

What competing stories do people offer to explain the world? How does the Bible compare to those stories?

_____

_____

_____

1. For a thorough treatment of this important people see Kevin Vanhoozer. *Is there a Meaning in the Text?* (Grand Rapids: Zondervan, 1998).
2. Michael W. Goheen and Craig Bartholomew, *A True Story for the Whole World: Finding Your Place in the Biblical Drama* (Grand Rapids: Faith Alive, 2004).

The Bible is a purposeful story.

No events in the story are random if the story is written by God, and it is the true story of the whole world. Everything that happens in the story happens for a purpose and intentionally fulfills God's plan to gather a "chosen race, a royal priesthood, a holy nation, a people for His possession (1 Pet 2:9)." Like any good story, the story of the Bible is always moving towards the author's intended purpose. In this case, with God as the author, not only of the story of Scripture but also of all of life, we can be assured that the Bible and life are moving towards a foreordained conclusion written by the very hand of God (Ps 115:3).

How does God's sovereign implementation of His story enhance your trust and confidence in His work in your own life?

_____

_____

The Bible is a united story.

Stories are connected in chapters. Each chapter provides increased understanding of the movement of the story. The Bible is no different. It, too, moves in stages. Theologians have formulated various schemes, chapters, or stages of the progressive revelation of God. The weekly titles of each section of *Aspire* can be seen as one such way of viewing the chapters of the biblical story. With each subsequent stage, the clarity of the plan and provision of God increases. This progressive revelation serves to take the black-and-white promise of Genesis 3 and bring it into HD clarity.

The Bible is a cosmic story.

God is not content with simply reclaiming *a worshipper*, but rather He is interested in reclaiming *worshippers*. This means that the mission is corporate in nature; it extends to all people who will be given a chance to trust in God's work. Ultimately, the mission extends to all things. All things that were affected by sin are in the process of being reclaimed by the mission of God.

The ability to articulate these aspects of the mission of God will have significant implications for you in a variety of areas. How might this be true of your life?

_____

_____

At minimum the story of the Bible should provide you with the following:

- **Purpose:** Through the gospel story, your life can be punctuated with an exclamation mark rather than a question mark. You can have confidence on what God is doing in the world and how your life fits into that plan. It might go something like this, "God is reclaiming worshippers, and the purpose of my life is to be a worshipper myself. I must live on mission so that other people are drawn to worship God rightly." Without a clear purpose, there is a great danger that your life will be absorbed into some lesser story.

Think about your life right now. Is it telling the same story God is telling in the world? Are you walking in step with His purposes or against them? Explain your answer in the space below.

_____

_____

- **Understanding:** An understanding of the grand story of Scripture helps you understand the Bible. You don't have to open your Bible on a treasure hunt for the perfect passage any longer. Instead you can study any passage of Scripture and ask yourself, "How does this story fit in to God's mission to reclaim worshippers?"

Try your hand at it with the following texts:

Genesis 22:1–19 _____

_____

Exodus 12:1–20 _____

_____

Joshua 6 _____

_____

1 Samuel 17 _____

_____

- **Protection:** Holistic understanding protects you from sin and heresy. It is so easy to miss the point of the text or to cause the text to mean something it never meant. This can lead to all sorts of sloppy practices. For example, what is the point of the story of Hosea? Is it that all God-fearing people should go marry a prostitute? Probably not! Instead, it tells the story of the covenant faithfulness of God to reclaim His wayward nation Israel who have prostituted themselves to idols. You are also protected from poor sermons or Bible studies. You can now "examine the Scriptures daily to see if these things were so (Acts 17:10–12)."

- **Transformation:** Gospel understanding should lead to transformation. As we will see in the sessions that follow, God's purposes have not and will not change. Therefore, we can read the Bible and apply its truths to our lives with confidence. While we may not be Israelites or live under the Old Testament law, we serve the same God and are tempted to choose the same forms of idolatry. We can read the Old Testament for more than developing a "sound-byte faith" that quotes random, isolated Bible verses out of context. Instead, we can read, understand, and apply the Bible to our own walk with God.

Draw some personal application from the following texts in the Old Testament. How does the grand story shape your application? What might you say about these passages if you did not understand the macro-story of Scripture? How does the macro-story of the Bible help you interpret them rightly?

Genesis 17:15–27: The Covenant with Abraham

_____

_____

Genesis 24: The Marriage of Isaac

_____

_____

Exodus 3–4: The Call of Moses

_____

_____

- **Evangelism:** Finally, understanding the Bible as a story should increase your confidence in speaking clearly about the Bible to other Christians and to non-believers. While you may not be able to answer every question that someone may ask, you are now far down the road in your understanding of how the Bible fits together.

Why did God create all things?

_____

_____

What went wrong?

_____

_____

What is His plan to make all things right again?

_____

_____

This allows you to be prepared to give an answer to anyone who asks (1 Peter 3:15). For example, consider the following situations. How would you apply the story of the Bible to these people's lives? Give it some thought and be prepared to discuss it with your mentor when you meet this week.

- A non-Christian co-worker has an insatiable hunger to succeed at work. He is cut-throat; doing any and everything in order to get ahead. One week learns that he has been passed over for a recent promotion. He is devastated and comes to share the news with you. What do you say?

_____

_____

- A person in your small group shares that they are struggling with discouragement and depression. A fellow group member who is a young Christian says, "Be encouraged brother. God wants you to be happy, and He will make sure that you get what you desire. Just be patient." You are sitting in the group and know that this answer is insufficient. What do you say to the discouraged group member and to the man who gave the counsel?

_____

_____

- Your seven-year-old daughter is beginning to ask questions about God. She brought it up again recently when your family pet died. This is the first time your daughter has been close to death, and she is clearly troubled. She asks, "Why does God let things like this happen?" How does the story of the Bible inform your answer to this question?

_____

_____

- You are confronted with the news that you never wanted to hear—"You have cancer." The diagnosis feels like a punch in the face. After several days of stunned silence, you are now faced with the prospect of battling a dreaded disease, and you are feeling the weight of looming death in a way you never have. How do you find encouragement from the story of the Bible?

_____

_____

Trimester 1: Gospel

With the storyline in place we are now positioned to see the execution of the plan of God in spite of the continued sin and rebellion of His people. This will not only serve to help you understand and explain all of the Scripture but also prompt your heart to worship as you see yourself caught up in this glorious story.

Week 5: Kingdom

"Indeed, a king will reign righteously, and rulers will rule justly."
—*Isaiah 32:1*

"Obedience flows from grace: it does not buy it. Obedience is the fruit and proof and sustenance of a relationship with the God you already know."[1]
—*Christopher J.H. Wright*

God's people obey out of gratitude for His grace.

You are four weeks into what may feel like weight training at the gym. Be encouraged. If you have not used these spiritual muscles before, it is natural for you to be sore. Or, if it has been a long time since you have given intentional thought to these matters, you may find that the muscles have begun to atrophy.

How consistent have you been with your time in the Word? What do you find difficult about being disciplined in the Word, particularly as we journey deeper into the historical books of the Old Testament?

_____

_____

These Old Testament books center on the life of holiness required of God's reclaimed worshippers, particularly the nation of Israel. And let's be honest—some of the things God commands the people to do seem downright strange. I mean, what do you do with commands like:

- Don't let cattle graze with other kinds of cattle (Lev 19:19).

- Don't have a variety of crops on the same field (Lev 19:19).

- Don't wear clothes made of more than one fabric (Lev 19:19).

---

1.   Christopher J.H. Wright, *Knowing Jesus through the Old Testament* (Downers Grove: IVP, 1992), 193.

- Don't cut your hair or shave (Lev 19:27).

- If a man cheats on his wife, or vise versa, both the man and the woman must die (Lev 20:10).

- If a man sleeps with his father's wife... both him and his father's wife is to be put to death (Lev 20:11).

- If a man sleeps with his wife and her mother, they are all to be burnt to death (Lev 20:14).

- Psychics, wizards, and so on are to be stoned to death (Lev 20:27).

- People who have flat noses, or are blind or lame, cannot go to an altar of God (Lev 21:17–18).

- Anyone who curses or blasphemes God should be stoned to death by the community (Lev 24:14–16).

Many people give up on reading and understanding the Bible because they simply don't know what to do with large sections of Scripture. And not only that, if they do understand the passage, it is far from clear how the passage relates to Christians today.

Yet, we are told that "all Scripture is inspired by God and is profitable for teaching, for rebuking, for correcting, for training in righteousness, so that the man of God may be complete, equipped for every good work (2 Tim 3:16–17)." A right understanding of God's mission to reclaim worshippers is the key to making sense of all of the Bible and utilizing it so that you may be built up and equipped for the good works that God has prepared for you to do (Eph 2:10).

God is reclaiming His worshippers from foreign oppressors and leading them to the land of His choosing. This is a common refrain—God calls a people to Himself to live in a land that He has made. A large section of the Pentateuch (the first five books of the Bible) contains stories from the time of the Israelites' deliverance from slavery in Egypt to their ultimate conquest of the Promised Land.

During that time, God provides the people with a number of indispensable practices for understanding how He would accomplish His plan of filling the earth with worshippers. Years later, Moses provides the nation of Israel with a succinct summary of God's desire for the nations. Surely, this was a common theme among the people of God in the years following their deliverance.

> *Listen, Israel: The Lord our God, the Lord is One. Love the Lord your God with all your heart, with all your soul, and with all your strength. These words that I am giving you today are to be in your heart. Repeat them to your children. Talk about them when you sit in your house and when you walk along the road, when you lie down and when you get up. Bind them as a sign on your hand and let them be a symbol on your forehead. Write them on the doorposts of your house and on your gates. When the Lord your God brings you into the land He swore to your fathers Abraham, Isaac, and Jacob that He would give you—a land with large and beautiful cities that you did not build, houses full of every good thing that you did not fill them with, wells dug that you did not dig, and vineyards and olive groves that you did not plant—and when you eat and are satisfied, be careful not to forget the Lord who brought you out of the land of Egypt, out of the place of slavery (Deut 6:4–12).*

What does God desire from His people? Why would this be the proper response to God's work?

_____

_____

God wants worship.

That has been His mission since creation. He desires to be rightly revered as the supreme object of joy, affection, and passion for a people that He has saved by His grace. He even provides His people with His covenant name YHWH (Yahweh or Jehovah), derived from the phrase "to be" (Ex 3:14). God says, "I am, I have been, and I will always be God. Worship me. I will be faithful to my promises." And as His people do, He will be their God, and they will be His people (Lev 26:12).

Worship is the key to understanding the confusing terrain of the Old Testament. God is after the worship of His people, and that worship must take a particular form. So He gives them some help.

The Law

A large majority of the Old Testament narrative is law. The people are to be holy as God Himself is holy (Lev 11:44–45). If we are not careful, these laws can obscure the nature of the gospel. Notice how the giving of the law begins in the Sinatic Covenant, "And God spoke all these words: I am the Lord your God, who brought you out of the land of Egypt, out of the place of slavery (Ex 20:1–2)." Before God gave them the law He gave them Himself.

Edmund Clowney warns, "The great mistake of legalism is to detach the law of God from the God who gave it."[1] The law starts with grace. In fact, the law is a response to grace. This has always been the case. In the garden God provided man a bountiful provision. Even there, however, He institutes rules to govern the people's worship. God declares one tree off limits, clearly demarcating the line between good and evil.

This trend continues in the giving of the law. God wants proper worship from His people, and He provides them with the grace-gift of the law so that they do not have to guess at how He desires to be worshiped. It is essential to see the law as a means of rightly responding to the grace of God and not as a tool for earning that grace. In essence, the law was the mark of the community that was already experiencing the grace of God.

A holy God desires a holy people, not in order to be saved, but because they are already saved. Grace is a gift. The keeping of the law is a response to that grace gift.

In the law, God says, "Act like the kind of people I called you to be." Goldsworthy writes that "to claim to have received the gift of friendship with God while persisting in a life marked by alienation and enmity is clearly nonsense."[2] The laws come in different shapes and sizes—some are clear moral laws that are applicable at all times and in all places (do not kill), and some seem to be based on the historical situation of the people of God at the time the law was given (do not mix the fabrics on your clothes). One overriding purpose unites them all.

---

1. Clowney, *Unfolding*, 103.
2. Goldsworthy, *According*, 142.

Read Jesus' words in Matthew 22:36–40. How does Jesus answer when asked about the chief end of the law? Why does this matter?

_____

_____

The law was given to help people know how to worship God and love people. Many theologians point out that the first four laws of the Decalogue (the Ten Commandments) relate to how a person should love God, while the remaining six focus on one's love for other people. Goldsworthy compares the law to the training of a young child. Early in their lives, children need more training; as they mature, however, the parents trust their children to make wise decisions on their own.[1] God knows that His worshippers need help, so He gives them the law. Sadly, what was intended to be a gift of grace is often turned into a form of legalism, guilt, shame, and condemnation. How have you understood the law in the past? How does a misunderstanding of the law lead to a misunderstanding of the gospel?

_____

_____

How do the following statements reflect a misunderstanding of the law of God?

- "I guess I just need to clean up my act and then God will like me."
- "I'm just out of the habit of going to church and reading the Bible. I guess that is why things are going wrong in my life?"
- "Christianity is just a bunch of rules, and I can never keep them all."
- "It just seems to come easier for you. You are a good person, and I'm just a bad person."

_____

_____

---

1. Ibid., 143–44.

Each of these popular statements run counter to the claims of the gospel. Grace comes before law for both the people of God in the Old Testament and for all subsequent worshippers.

How does obedience to God demonstrate whether or not a person truly understands grace?

_____

_____

Obedience fuels mission by putting the transforming grace of God on display. Read Exodus 19:4–6. What is the promise God makes in this text? Why does obedience matter?

> 'You have seen what I did to the Egyptians and how I carried you on eagles' wings and brought you to Me. Now if you will listen to Me and carefully keep My covenant, you will be My own possession out of all the peoples, although all the earth is Mine, and you will be My kingdom of priests and My holy nation.' These are the words that you are to say to the Israelites.

_____

_____

Compare Exodus 19 with 1 Peter 2. What do you note about this text? Whom is it written to, and why does that matter?

> But you are a chosen race, a royal priesthood, a holy nation, a people for His possession, so that you may proclaim the praises of the One who called you out of darkness into His marvelous light. Once you were not a people, but now you are God's people; you had not received mercy, but now you have received mercy. Dear friends, I urge you as strangers and temporary residents to abstain from fleshly desires that war against you. Conduct yourselves honorably among the Gentiles, so that in a case where they speak against you as those who do what is evil, they will, by observing your good works, glorify God on the day of visitation.

_____

_____

God sets His people among the nations and commands them to obey Him. The nations would then see what life looks like when it is lived under the rule of God. The nations should say, "So, that is what the people of God look like!" This behavior should serve as a contrast to the idolatry of the nations.

Why is the obedience of God's people critical for their mission of making worshippers of the nations?

_____

_____

How is this motive for obedience similar to your motive for obedience?

_____

_____

The Sacrificial System

The problem is that humans are inept at obedience. They simply cannot obey God rightly or consistently. The law was set up to prove this. Paul says in Galatians 2:16 that "no one is justified by works of the law." Instead, "All who rely on works of the law are under a curse; because it is written: everyone who does not continue doing everything that is written in the book of the law is cursed (Gal 3:10)."

God's people are unable to approach Him because of their inability to keep the law. They are right back where they started—cut off from God due to their sin. So, God sets up an elaborate sacrificial system in order to further explain the way in which He will deal with sin. The people are told to bring a substitute—a sacrifice that they will offer to God for their sins. They will offer a perfect sacrifice (often an unblemished lamb) to the priest, who will confess the sins of the people over the animal before slaughtering it and offering the blood to God in the tabernacle. In this way the sins of the people are atoned for through the death of a substitute. Again, the story of the garden is on display as God covers the sins of His people through the blood sacrifice of a substitute.

> ***Atonement Defined***: The process by which God makes it possible for sinful humans to have a relationship with Him through the death of a substitute.

Rather than pouring out His wrath on man himself, the wrath of God is poured out upon a substitute. As the author of Hebrews says, "Without the shedding of blood there is no forgiveness of sins (Heb 9:22)." Someone must die because of sin—either the sinner or the substitute.

> ***Propitiation Defined***: The wrath of God fully poured out upon a substitute.

Can you imagine living during the time of the sacrificial system? What would this process have taught you about your sin and God's holiness?

_____

_____

The daily, continual process of offering a substitute will remind God's people of the cost of a relationship with Him. The smell of slaughter would constantly fill the camp with the aroma of sin. The people would have known that their sin is deadly, and that they need a substitute in order to approach God.

These sacrifices will be offered to God in the place of His choosing; first the tabernacle and then the permanent temple (Ex 25–40). In a scene reminiscent of the creation narrative, God creates a new dwelling place for Himself among His people in the tabernacle (Ex 25:1; 30:11; 30:17; 30:22; 30:34). He he makes it clear that people could not haphazardly enter into His presence. They cannot return to relationship with Him by their own merit, but only by grace through the blood sacrifice of a substitute.

In this way they are tutored to Christ. Goldsworthy helps us see that there was salvation in the Old Testament:

> *But the shadow must fade so that the full light of the solid reality may be revealed in its place. In the meantime, those who by faith grasp the shadow are undoubtedly thereby grasping the reality of salvation in Christ.*[1]

How was such a process a precursor to the sending of Jesus?

_____

_____

How was a person saved in the Old Testament? What was necessary for salvation? How is this similar or different from the way in which God saves people today?

_____

_____

The scene looks familiar to a people in relationship with God by His grace; approaching Him by means of a sacrifice; worshiping Him by means of obedience. God sets up His Kingdom among these people. The language of the Kingdom of God is lost on many modern evangelicals, yet it is a prominent theme in the Scriptures.

Kingdom of God Defined: The rule of God demonstrated on the earth among a worshiping people.

The exact phrase "the Kingdom of God" is not used until later in the Bible, but the concept permeates the Old Testament and is a useful way of understanding the entirety of the Bible. Words such as rule, throne, scepter, reign, dominion, sovereign, or almighty are meant to evoke images of the Kingdom. For example, in Genesis 49:10 we see the prophecy of the coming, promised seed in these words: "The scepter will not depart from Judah, or the staff from between his feet." We are now told that this seed, who has been pledged from the beginning, will be a King. He will rule and reign among a people

1. Ibid., 186.

who live in obedience to His character and ways. This is God's plan. His Kingdom is coming on earth as it is in heaven. He will rule and reign over a people forever.

How is the Kingdom of God similar to the shalom of the garden?

_____

_____

How does this inform Jesus' first statements after He began His public ministry: "Repent, for the Kingdom of God is here (Mt 3:2; Mk 1:15)"?

_____

_____

How does the Kingly image of God inform how you should respond to Him?

_____

_____

God, as a King, will rule and reign. His glory will be seen, and His mission in creation will be fulfilled. In order for that to happen, however, He must provide a permanent answer to the problem of human sin. The excruciating process of offering the blood of bulls and goats year after year cannot be His permanent plan. Something more lasting is needed. But, before He provides that lasting means of substitution, He would once again judge human sin, this time by exiling His people from the land of promise.

Week 6: Judgment

"The Lord reigns! Let the earth rejoice; let the many coasts and islands be glad. Clouds and thick darkness surround Him; righteousness and justice are the foundation of His throne."

—Psalm 97:1–2

"When you are edging closer and closer to the abyss, the most progressive direction is backwards."[1]

—Peter Kreeftt

The holiness of God requires that He judge sin.

The theme of the Kingdom in the Old Testament is seen most clearly in the establishment of a king in Israel under Saul, David, and Solomon. The story of the development, rule, and subsequent failure of the kingdom gives shape to an understanding of the final movement of redemptive history demonstrated in the Old Testament.

> ***Theology Defined***: The study of the character and actions of God.

Perhaps you don't see yourself as a theologian, but you are. You are doing theology any time you think thoughts about God or communicate His purposes to other people. I remember my time shortly after conversion. I knew that God had saved me and that He had placed me in His church. But my knowledge of God's character and work was paltry to say the least. I would sit in my pick-up truck in the parking lot at Furman University and listen to Tommy Nelson teach through the Bible book by book. I could not get enough. I was also quickly given the opportunity to speak of God to other people. Not only did I have a responsibility for thinking rightly myself, but now other people's thoughts of God were being shaped by my teaching as well.

---

1. Peter Kreeft, *Back to Virtue* (San Francisco: Ignatius Press, 1992), 13.

Trimester 1: Gospel

Consider the amount of theology that is required to answer the following simple questions:

- How do I make good decisions?

- Why do I consistently make bad decisions?

- Why is there evil in the world?

- What should I do with my life?

How do the answers to these questions reveal what a person thinks about God?

_____

_____

These questions and others like them can come from Christians and non-Christians alike. And yet, their answers require some type of understanding of God's nature and actions in the world. A theologically sound answer requires a view of the world that is informed by the biblical story. Since the answers require you to speak of God, it makes sense to desire to speak rightly about God. However, we must be careful. Theology has a dangerous underside. It can cause you to puff up with spiritual pride (1 Cor 8:1).

Ignorance and arrogance are both deadly.

Which is a potentially greater problem in your life: ignorance or arrogance? What have you seen developing in your own heart as you have begun to think more deeply about God's will and ways?

_____

_____

How do you fight against spiritual pride in your life?

_____

_____

Theology is meant to lead to worship.

The more you know about God the more your heart is drawn to worship Him. Consider the following passages of Scripture and note the effect that the knowledge of God should have on your life:

Mark 12:30; Luke 10:27: _____

_____

Romans 12:1–2: _____

_____

1 Corinthians 13: _____

_____

Ephesians 1:15–23: _____

_____

Before we journey a bit further, take a few minutes to pray that God will expand your capacity for worship as you grow in your knowledge of Him. No really—stop and pray. Journal your prayers in the space below.

_____

_____

We saw in the last session that God is establishing His Kingdom on earth among a people who will approach Him by means of a substitute in order to worship Him by means of obedience. God, in His grace, grants them the land of His choosing. There, they are to worship faithfully.

They are the unworthy recipients of the grace of God; they have the law, the promises, and the presence of God. Yet, they repeatedly fail to allow this knowledge to result in worship. Instead, they are marked by rebellion, the spread of wickedness, the crescendo of folly, the systemic nature of sin, and the inability to deliver themselves from the recurring contours of the narrative. Their rebellion, similar to that of Adam and Eve in the garden, also provides a paradigmatic model for the way in which sinful people like us continue to rebel against God. What is stunning about the failure is that it came in the face of such grace.

What does the ongoing failure of God's people reveal about the nature of sin?

_____

_____

Where sin abounds, grace does much more abound. God's *hesed* (covenant-faithfulness) is seen most clearly in hopeless situations, and the nation of Israel is no exception. The sin-drenched Israelites are still given:

- **The Blessing of the Land:** After 40 years of wilderness wandering, the people are given the bountiful provision of the Promised Land which they do not earn or deserve.

- **The Blessing of Rest:** The land is marked, at least at the outset, by rest from war (Josh 11:23). At the battle of Jericho, God proves that the battle is His. He conquers Israel's enemies and drives them out of the land.

- **The Blessings of God's Presence:** God now dwells among His people in a unique way. No longer does the presence of God travel with the tabernacle. Instead, Solomon establishes a permanent dwelling place for God in the temple. There the people can meet with God and worship Him correctly.

- **The Blessing of the Law:** The nation is given the law and the Sacrificial system in order to worship God, and in addition they are given wisdom literature, which guides the life of the covenant community.

- **The Blessing of the Prophets:** God raises up men who call the people to return to God when they begin to rebel. These prophets warn of the coming judgment of God and cry out to the people to repent from their sins and worship God rightly. Though the people do not ultimately heed these warnings, the people are not without the voice of God during this time.

- **The Blessing of Salvation:** God's *hesed* pursues His people. Everywhere they go, His grace goes with them. Even in the face of outright rebellion, God continues to pursue His people in love (see the book of Hosea). As Clowney comments, "The point of the emphasis on generations is that God has not forgotten His promise. The appointed line of the descendants of the woman must continue. Through the dark and bloody history of human sin and violence, God continues the line of promise."[1] He is, and has always been, on mission to reclaim worshippers.

How is the blessing of God seen in your life in spite of your sin?

_____

_____

How are these blessings similar to those seen in the people of God in the Old Testament?

_____

_____

Cycles of Failure

The people's failure to obey God is exemplified by their worship of the golden calf when Moses was receiving the law of God. From the outset, obedience to God is contrasted with human idolatry.

Read Exodus 32. What are the people doing?

_____

_____

What is their excuse?

_____

_____

Here, the scene of the garden is relived. Man chooses to worship created things rather than Creator God, and as a result, God judges them for their sin. God's presence continues to overshadow the people. There is no hiding from a sovereign God. He dwells among His people and sees all of their sin.

---

1. Clowney, *Unfolding*, 40.

Judgment is imminent. How could those who have ready access to the grace of God respond with such folly? Let's consider the reasons for the failure of the people that are demonstrated throughout their history.

Known Idolatry

God's people are told to drive out the inhabitants of the Promised Land, lest they be tempted to worship their false gods (Jud 2:3). But the people do not obey. They coddle the gods of the nations, and before long, they fall prey to their insidious snare. The end of the book of Judges tells us that the people live by doing what is right in their own eyes (Jud 21:25). The nation is guilty of rebellion always God on a cosmic scope.

> ***Idolatry Defined***: Worshipping as God anything other than God.

Consider the images of sin outlined in week 2. How are these seen in the life of God's people?

_____

_____

In what ways are you tempted to tolerate idols in your own life?

_____

_____

Where are you prone to sin as a result of a close proximity to the idolatry of others?

_____

_____

Distrust in God

In stark irony, the people who have every reason to trust in God's provision are unwilling to do so. They are a stiff-necked people, quick to complain about their situation and circumstances. These complaints draw the anger of God in Numbers 14:11 where God asks Moses, "How long will these people despise me? How long will they not trust in me despite all the signs that I have performed among them?" God promises judgment because of the people's unbelief.

How are you tempted to distrust God in spite of His grace in your life? In what areas are you tempted to complain?

_____

_____

Desire to be like the nations.

The people were created to demonstrate God's glory to the nations. This should mark them as a unique people, distinct from the idolatry of the nations. The nations should then be drawn to the worship of the God that they observe among His people.

Instead, the opposite happens. The people of God watch the actions of the nations and long to be like them. They notice that the other nations have kings. Like an child longing for his friend's toys, the people of God ask Samuel to give them a king too. This is not God's desire; He is the King over His Kingdom. God, however, gives the people over to their desires and gives them a king like the nations around them. This sets the stage for the ongoing conflict between their human kings and their sovereign King.

How are you enticed by the lives of those who live far from God?

_____

_____

Disobedience of Leadership

Three successive kings are appointed to rule God's people. Saul is the first king, who proves to be a total failure in spite of his impressive resume. His insecurity and disobedience led God to remove him from his position as King, and his life ended in shame and defeat.

The appointment of King David, Saul's successor, provides the greatest hope the nation has seen up to this point. Here is the Lord's anointed servant, a man after His own heart, who will lead God's people to an era of unprecedented peace and prosperity. Perhaps the Kingdom would come through David? Was he the seed that had been promised?

The shepherd boy, who is anointed king following his defeat of Goliath, is the recipient of another series of Covenant promises from God.

> *Now this is what you are to say to My servant David: 'This is what the Lord of Hosts says: I took you from the pasture and from following the sheep to be ruler over My people Israel. I have been with you wherever you have gone, and I have destroyed all your enemies before you. I will make a name for you like that of the greatest in the land. I will establish a place for My people Israel and plant them, so that they may live there and not be disturbed again. Evildoers will not afflict them as they have done ever since the day I ordered judges to be over My people Israel. I will give you rest from all your enemies.' The Lord declares to you: 'The Lord Himself will make a house for you. When your time comes and you rest with your fathers, I will raise up after you your descendant, who will come from your body, and I will establish his kingdom. He will build a house for My name, and I will establish the throne of his kingdom forever. I will be a father to him, and he will be a son to Me. When he does wrong, I will discipline him with a human rod and with blows from others. But My faithful love will never leave him as I removed it from Saul; I removed him from your way. Your house and kingdom will endure before Me forever, and your throne will be established forever (2 Sam 7:8–16).*

What do you notice about this covenant? What makes the Davidic covenant similar or different to the earlier covenants that God has made with his people?

_____

_____

The rule and reign of David moves to the center of God's redemptive plan (Is 9:27–7; 11:1–5; 16:5; 55:3–5; Jer 23:1–6; Ez 34:20–24; 37:24–28; Amos 9:11). As Leihart notes, "All the promises of God to Abraham are now delivered to David, so that the future of Israel is bound up with David's household."[1] The hopes the people place in David prove to be misplaced. David is a man after God's own heart, yet he is plagued by adultery, murder, doubt, distrust, fear, and outright rebellion against God. God tells David that he will die. He is not the seed, but we are told that the seed will come

---

1. Peter J. Leithart, *A House for My Name: A Survey of the Old Testament* (Moscow: Canon Press, 2000), 148.

through his kingly line. God extends His Kingdom promises to David's son Solomon, whom He appoints to build a permanent house among the people. Solomon does so and reigns during a period of peace, knowledge, and wealth unlike anything Israel had ever known (1 Kgs 4:20–34). Solomon's kingdom extends far and wide, and the shalom of the garden seems to have returned.

Solomon dies as well, however, and shortly after his death the kingdom divides into two nations (1 Kgs 11:43). The story of the divided Kingdom is a nauseating read. One king arises who does right in the eyes of God and leads the people to worship, yet the very next king rebels against God and capitulates to idolatry (c.f. 1 Sam 8:3). The kingdom that had been united for 120 years under Saul, David, and Solomon now splits, with ten tribes in the north with Samaria as their capital (Israel), and two in the South with Jerusalem as their capital (Judah).

Loss of the Word

Their rebellion is also marked by a loss of God's Word. It's not that He is silent (at least not yet), but that they fail to listen and obey His Word. They try to do it on their own.

A scene from 2 Kings 22:8–20 makes this point clearly. Read that text and note what the people found. What does this say about the role of the Word among the people of God?

_____

_____

David Wells writes, "When the Church loses the Word of God it loses the very means by which God does his work. In its absence, therefore, a script is being written, however unwittingly, for the Church's undoing, not in one cataclysmic moment, but in a slow, inexorable slide made up of piece by tiny piece of daily dereliction."[1] This is true of the people of God, today's church, and your personal life. When the Word of God is neglected, failure is sure to follow.

---

1. David F. Wells, *Above All Earthly Pow'rs: Christ in a Postmodern World* (Grand Rapids: Eerdmans, 2005), 9.

Think about your time in the Word this past week. What are you doing to ensure that you do not lose the Word?

_____

_____

Exile

A just God must judge His idolatrous, sinful people. His name was on the line. Notice the motive for the exile in Ezekiel 36:22–28:

> *Therefore, say to the house of Israel: 'This is what the Lord God says: It is not for your sake that I will act, house of Israel, but for My holy name, which you profaned among the nations where you went. I will honor the holiness of My great name, which has been profaned among the nations—the name you have profaned among them. The nations will know that I am Yahweh'—the declaration of the Lord God—'when I demonstrate My holiness through you in their sight.'*
>
> *For I will take you from the nations and gather you from all the countries, and will bring you into your own land. I will also sprinkle clean water on you, and you will be clean. I will cleanse you from all your impurities and all your idols. I will give you a new heart and put a new spirit within you; I will remove your heart of stone and give you a heart of flesh. I will place My Spirit within you and cause you to follow My statutes and carefully observe My ordinances. Then you will live in the land that I gave your fathers; you will be My people, and I will be your God.*

If the people live in outright rebellion against God, His name will be slandered among the nations. God's holiness will not allow this. Plus, He had long ago warned the people that if they did not obey, He would kick them off the land. God always keeps His promise—even in judgment. Israel is defeated first by Assyria in 722 BC, and Judah is defeated shortly thereafter in 586 BC by the Babylonians. The land that had been given in the conquest is now taken away in the exile. God's people are now a defeated and scattered remnant among the nations.

The scene among the people is eerily familiar. They have been incapable of living under the rule and reign of God. The cyclical pattern of sin and rebellion creates a deep cavern between the people and God. It is clear that all is not well by the end of the Old Testament. The nation is divided, split, and conquered. Even the remnant that has returned to the Promised Land has been unable to walk in obedience. They are a broken and frail people longing for hope and deliverance.

It seems that the hope of the Seed is lost forever. Yet, the prophets continue to speak of the hope of a second Exodus, a day in which the Seed will appear, reclaim the scattered worshippers, and rule and reign over His people (Is 40:1–5; 43:1–7, 15–21; 48:20–21; 49:24–26; 51:9–11; Jer 23:7–8).

The prophet Jeremiah spoke of this day using the language of covenant. Notice his words in Jeremiah 31:31–34:

> *"Look, the days are coming"—this is the Lord's declaration—"when I will make a new covenant with the house of Israel and with the house of Judah. This one will not be like the covenant I made with their ancestors when I took them by the hand to bring them out of the land of Egypt—a covenant they broke even though I had married them"—the Lord's declaration. "Instead, this is the covenant I will make with the house of Israel after those days"—the Lord's declaration. "I will put My teaching within them and write it on their hearts. I will be their God, and they will be My people. No longer will one teach his neighbor or his brother, saying, 'Know the Lord,' for they will all know Me, from the least to the greatest of them"—this is the Lord's declaration. "For I will forgive their wrongdoing and never again remember their sin."*

How does this covenant compare to the other covenants God has made with His people? What is unique about the New Covenant?

_____

_____

These promises stand as the refrain that echoes over a cavern of silence. While a fringe remnant of the people are allowed to return and rebuild the temple under Nehemiah and Ezra, it is clear that the exile is not over. Then, for 400 years God is silent. Nothing. No more prophets. No more promises. How would you have felt during this time of silence? Clearly, you would wonder if God had forgotten you. Have the people finally broken God's will and thwarted His mission?

They are longing for a word from God, to demonstrate that He had not forgotten them. They did not simply get *a* word—they got *the* Word—Jesus (Jn 1:1,14).

Week 7: Incarnation

"Now listen: You will conceive and give birth to a son, and you will call His name JESUS. He will be great and will be called the Son of the Most High, and the Lord God will give Him the throne of His father David. He will reign over the house of Jacob forever, and His kingdom will have no end."

—*Luke 1:31–33*

"All the promises of the kingdom of God are fulfilled in Christ; he is God's people, God's place and God's rule."[1]

—*Vaughn Roberts*

Jesus is God on mission.

As we journeyed through the Old Testament narrative, you may have found yourself thinking, "All of this stuff reminds me of Jesus!" And you are right. In fact, Jesus is the key to understanding the Bible. When I was a kid, we used to sing a song in church with a chorus that said: "Jesus is the answer for the world today." I remember having a clear understanding that Jesus mattered—the problem was I didn't know why.

This is an all-too-common reality that *Aspire* is attempting to counter. You now have a rich understanding of the mission of God in the Old Testament and are positioned to rightly understand both how and why Jesus truly is the answer.

The task of understanding the Bible (hermeneutics) depends on rightly understanding Jesus. As Paul says in 2 Corinthians, "For every one of God's promises is 'Yes' in Him (2 Cor 1:20)." Jesus demonstrates this reality when speaking to the travelers on the road to Emmaus. Luke recounts that Jesus explained to them all that was said in the Scriptures concerning Himself by "beginning with Moses and all the prophets (Lk 24:27)." Everything in the Bible points to Jesus.

---

1. Vaughn Roberts, *God's Big Picture: Tracing the Storyline of the Bible* (Downers Grove, IVP, 2002), 109.

> ***Hermeneutics Defined***: The interpretation of the Bible that exalts Jesus as the true hero.

Try your hand at a few examples. How does the person and work of Jesus serve to explain the following stories?

Genesis 22:1–19 _____

_____

Genesis 49:8–10 _____

_____

1 Samuel 17 _____

_____

1 Kings 10:14–11:3 _____

_____

Isaiah 53 _____

_____

Over the previous six weeks you have been introduced to the central question the Bible seeks to answer: How will God reclaim worshippers in order to fill the earth with His glory?

Jesus' work can most clearly be seen from our time in redemptive history. We are blessed by God to have the full revelation of God's finished work declared to us in the pages of the Scriptures.

The people in Jesus' day, on the other hand, are longing for the promised Savior, yet their view is limited in ways that ours is not. They are attempting to understand the story as it is developing. Seven hundred years before the time of Christ, the prophet Isaiah pictured the day of His coming:

> *For a child will be born for us, a son will be given to us, and the government will be on His shoulders. He will be named Wonderful Counselor, Mighty God, Eternal*

Father, Prince of Peace. The dominion will be vast, and its prosperity will never end. He will reign on the throne of David and over his kingdom, to establish and sustain it with justice and righteousness from now on and forever. The zeal of the Lord of Hosts will accomplish this (Is 9:6–7).

The language is strong—Wonderful Counselor, Mighty God, Everlasting Father, Prince of Peace, Ruler on David's throne.

What would you expect the Messiah to be like if all you had were these descriptions of His coming?

_____

_____

The people in Jesus' day have expectations as well. Perhaps some assume that the Messiah will be a powerful political ruler who will overthrow Israel's enemies. Others assume that He would be the prototypical leader of God's people, who would rightly uphold the Law of God in a way that Saul, David, and Solomon could not. Some may even think that He will never come. It has been four hundred years since they have heard the voice of any prophet. Perhaps God has just gotten tired of the sinfulness of His people and abandoned them completely.

Jesus has been the plan of God all along, however. The stories told by the Gospel writers show that Jesus is the fulfillment of the promises of God. His birth certainly does not seem like the story of a King. Jesus is born to a teenage virgin, in a remote part of the land, and in a stable because His parents could not secure lodging for the night. His birth was attended by a few shepherds. It would have been easy to overlook the fact that this baby in a manger is the Son of God, Immanuel, who will save His people from their sins. He comes in a way that fulfills all of God's promises, but He comes in a way that the people could not imagine.

> *Incarnation Defined*: The coming of God to earth in the flesh as a man, who was both fully God and fully man.

> What expectations do you have of God? How could these expectations cause you to miss God?

_____

_____

Jesus is central to God's mission to reclaim worshippers from every tribe, tongue, and nation. We need to be reminded of the brilliance of God's plan, revealed in the incarnation of His Son, so that we do not miss Jesus.

Jesus is God in Skin

Jesus comes to earth as God in skin. The author of Hebrews introduces his letter with these words about Jesus:

> *Long ago God spoke to the fathers by the prophets at different times and in different ways. In these last days, He has spoken to us by His Son. God has appointed Him heir of all things and made the universe through Him. The Son is the radiance of God's glory and the exact expression of His nature, sustaining all things by His powerful word. After making purification for sins, He sat down at the right hand of the Majesty on high (Heb 1:1–3).*

He is the "radiance of the glory of God" and the "exact imprint of His nature." Jesus is God, and "in Him all of the fullness of God was pleased to dwell (Col 1:19)." The claim that Jesus is God is essential for the Christian faith. It is of little value to us if Jesus is simply an exemplary model for how to obey God. Instead, Jesus claims to be divine.

How would you respond to someone who says, "Jesus is a good man, but He is not God!" Can Jesus be good and not God? Why or why not?

_____

_____

What evidence do we have in the Scriptures that Jesus claimed to be God?

_____

_____

Jesus is the Word Made Flesh

God did not create Jesus; rather, Jesus has existed from eternity past. God sends His Word to earth at the ordained time to accomplish His sovereign purposes. According to John 1, Jesus is the Word of God who has put on flesh:

> *In the beginning was the Word, and the Word was with God, and the Word was God. He was with God in the beginning. All things were created through Him, and apart from Him not one thing was created that has been created. Life was in Him, and that life was the light of men. That light shines in the darkness, yet the darkness did not overcome it (Jn 1:1–5).*

John notes that the incarnate Word came to dwell as light in a world of darkness. God dwells among His people, this time not in the form of a moveable tent, but rather in the very person of His Son. This is a humbling step for the son of God. Paul tells us in Philippians 2 that Jesus willingly laid aside his position with God and took on the form of a servant in order to reclaim worshippers (Phil. 2:6–11).

Take a minute to read this passage for yourself. How is the cross a demonstration of the humility of Jesus? What did the incarnation cost God? What does this tell us about Him?

_____

_____

How is the dwelling of God through the person of Jesus different than His dwelling among His people in the tabernacle and temple?

_____

_____

Jesus is the Seed of Abraham

Matthew begins the story of Jesus in a most unique fashion—with a genealogy. It is not an exhaustive genealogy, but a selective one designed to make a point.

Read Matthew 1:1–17. What do you notice about this genealogy?

_____

_____

Notice the types of people that are forever etched in His lineage. What do you know about these people?

- Tamar _____

- Boaz _____

- David _____

- The Wife of Uriah _____

- Jehoshaphat _____

- Ahaz _____

- Zerrubabel _____

- Mary _____

What does it say about God that these people would be in the genealogy of Jesus? How does this truth encourage you?

_____

_____

Luke makes a similar point but in a different way. He records the interaction of God's angel with Mary, the mother of Jesus.

Read Luke 1:31–33. What does the angel say to Mary? Why does this matter?

_____

_____

Mary's womb would be the home for the promised Seed, who would be the recipient of the covenantal promises of God through Abram and David. He would finally and fully accomplish what others had been unable to do—save the people from their sins (Mt 1:21).

Jesus is the Fulfillment of the Covenant

Jesus also serves as the fulfillment of the covenant promises of God. Not only is He the promised Seed, but He has been sent in order to accomplish the purposes God outlined in Genesis 3. The timing of His coming is no accident either, for "when the time came to completion, God sent his Son, born of a woman, born under the law (Gal 4:4)." Simeon testifies to this reality when he sees Jesus in the temple:

> *Simeon took Him up in his arms, praised God, and said: Now, Master, You can dismiss Your slave in peace, as You promised. For my eyes have seen Your salvation. You have prepared it in the presence of all peoples—a light for revelation to the Gentiles and glory to Your people Israel (Lk 2:28–32).*

God keeps His promise in Christ. Simeon sees what the people of God have been longing to see: the promised one who will declare His glory among the nations through a chosen people. Jesus fulfills the hope of His people.

If God can be trusted to fulfill His promises to send a Savior over thousands of years of redemptive history, what does this say about His trustworthiness in your life?

_____

_____

In what areas are you most tempted to doubt God? How can the incarnation serve as an encouragement to you?

_____

_____

Jesus is the Prophesied Messiah

Jesus will save His people in the way that the prophets predicted. The sacrificial system instituted in Israel is no accident. Rather, it is a foreshadowing of the work of Christ, whose path to redeem His people will come through suffering and sacrifice.

Read Isaiah 53. What does this text say the Messiah will do?

_____

_____

Look up the following list of Old Testament prophecies that pointed to the coming Messiah. What New Testament evidence do we have that these were perfectly fulfilled in the person of Christ?

Old Testament Prophecy	New Testament Fulfillment
Genesis 3:15	
Micah 5:2	
Isaiah 7:14	
Genesis 49:10	
Hosea 11:1	
Isaiah 40:3–5	
Psalm 2:7	
Isaiah 11:1	
Isaiah 9:1–2	
Zechariah 9:9	
Isaiah 53	
Psalm 34:20	
Psalm 16:10	
Psalm 49:15	
Psalm 68:18	

Jesus is the Embodied Mission

The mission of God, as we have seen, is always extended to the nations. His desire has been to use His people to be a means of declaring and demonstrating His glory among His image-bearers, both near and far. Jesus declares that He comes, first and foremost, to gather the lost sheep of the house of Israel (Mt 15:24). His people lay in shambles, a paltry reflection of their former selves. Jesus comes to seek and save that which was lost (Lk 15).

However, God's purposes remain unchanged. He is reclaiming worshippers from the nations. People of all ethnicities are the recipients of God's grace.

Read the following passages. What do you note about the mission of Jesus from these passages?

Matthew 9:35–38 _____

_____

Matthew 14:13–21 _____

_____

Matthew 22:35–40 _____

_____

Mark 2:15–17 _____

_____

Mark 10:35–45 _____

_____

Luke 14:1–24 _____

_____

Luke 15:1–2 _____

_____

Luke 18:15–17 _____

_____

John 3:16–18 _____

_____

Jesus serves as the Kingdom-bearer through His pursuit of wayward worshippers. His heart for the poor, broken, and marginalized demonstrates that God is doing in Christ what God has always been doing—reclaiming worshippers for Himself. Jesus' life mission sets the stage for the worldwide mission that will be inaugurated through His disciples and His church (Mt 28:18–20; Acts 1:8).

Jesus is the Victorious King

The incarnation creates a strong juxtaposition: the King in a manger. However, this King will bring the true Kingdom. John Piper comments on the inbreaking of the Kingdom when he writes:

> *Christmas is not another bend in the river. It is the arrival of the salt water of the kingdom of God which has backed up into the river of history. With the coming of Christmas, the ocean of the age to come has reached backward up the stream of history to welcome us, to wake us up to what is coming, to lure us on into the deep.*[1]

The Kingdom has broken into the world in the person and work of Christ in the same way the ocean water reaches back into the river. The incarnation proves that the Kingdom is on earth and will forever accomplish the promised plan of God. God has never forgotten His people, and He will be faithful to remember you as well.

What aspects of your life seem impossible? How should the hope of the incarnation shape how you view those situations?

_____

_____

Christmas incites celebration, but not the kind you might imagine. This season is marked not simply by time with family and friends, but by the coming of the very Son of God. It is a climactic moment in the mission of God to reclaim worshippers from every tribe, tongue, and nation. Christmas is not something that we simply look forward *TO* but rather it is something that we look forward *FROM*. Jesus' coming informs all of salvation history both before and after. And like the sun breaking through the clouds on an overcast day, the inbreaking of the rays of the Kingdom is only just beginning.

---

1. John Piper, "Christmas as the End of History" online at http://www.desiringgod.org/sermons/christmas-as-the-end-of-history.

Week 8: Life

"In the beginning was the Word, and the Word was with God, and the Word was God... The Word became flesh and took up residence among us. We observed His glory, the glory as the One and Only Son from the Father, full of grace and truth."

—*John 1:1,14*

"But the whole point of the gospels is to tell the story of how God became king, on earth as it is in heaven."[1]

—*N.T. Wright*

Jesus is the epicenter of the Kingdom of God.

Marriages never begin at the wedding ceremony. While the ceremony serves as the focal point of much longing and anticipation, there is a much broader and richer story in play. Every couple has a story of how they met, dated, and got engaged, which is often full of twists and turns, hurts and failures, romance and love. The wedding makes little sense without the story.

The same is true for the life of Christ. Much focus is rightly given to His birth, death, and resurrection; however, this may lead to a neglect of the life of Christ itself. If Jesus' life did not matter, than why did He live for over three decades? If he was simply to come and die as a substitute for the sins of His people, then why was He not killed on His first birthday, or His first day of life for that matter?

The good news of the gospel is more than that Jesus was born and died. Rather, it is the sum total of the news of His birth, life, death, resurrection, and ascension. Each of these aspects of the person of Christ is essential to understanding the good news of the gospel.

The gospel writers tell us little about the events between Jesus' birth and the beginning of His public ministry. These years are a season of silence, but they are not marked

---

1. N.T. Wright, *How God Became King: The Forgotten Story of the Gospels* (New York: Harper Collins, 2012), 34.

by inactivity. Jesus is preparing to publically announce the arrival of the Kingdom and demonstrate His reign for all to see.

When the time comes, Jesus does just that. He enters the temple, takes up the scroll, and reads from the prophet Isaiah of the things that will accompany the coming of the promised Messiah (Lk 4:18–19). He reads these words:

> *The Spirit of the Lord is on Me, because He has anointed Me to preach good news to the poor. He has sent Me to proclaim freedom to the captives and recovery of sight to the blind, to set free the oppressed, to proclaim the year of the Lord's favor.*

Jesus calls the people to repent because the Kingdom of heaven is near (Mt 3:1–2). Why would repentance be the proper response to the inbreaking of the Kingdom of God?

_____

_____

His life shows what it looks like when God's Kingdom breaks into the world. Sadly, most people in Jesus' day missed it. The Pharisees, at the end of Jesus' life, continued to badger him with questions about the coming Kingdom. Jesus replied, "The Kingdom of God is not coming with something observable; no one will say, 'Look, here!' or 'There!' For you see, the Kingdom of God is among you (Lk 17:20–21)." The Kingdom was with them in the person of Jesus, and yet they missed it by missing Him.

The religious leaders are the very ones who should anticipate Jesus' coming. All of the Messianic signs point to Jesus as the one who would full the promise of Genesis 3. He is the promised Seed who will finally and fully defeat Satan, sin, and death. All of this is easier for us to see from our perspective in time and with the full counsel of God's revealed Word. Not so for those in Jesus' day. His Kingdom does not come with the expected fanfare, but with the obscure life of a Jewish carpenter.

How are you most tempted to miss Jesus?

_____

_____

What good things might cause you to miss Jesus (such as the Pharisees' keeping of the law)?

_____

_____

Jesus' life paints a glorious picture of the mission of God as He spends His life *declaring and demonstrating* the Kingdom.

Jesus Declares the Kingdom

Jesus' Kingdom is consistently proclaimed—from the words that announced the beginning of His ministry to the sign that hung over His head at the crucifixion. Jesus boldly announces the Kingdom and calls people to repent. His sermons are short and sweet, often told in the form of concise parables meant to reveal the nature of the Kingdom.

The prophets had a long history of proclaiming the reality of the Kingdom of God and the need for people to repent of their sins and trust in God. Jesus, as the truer and greater prophet, can not only call people to repent, but He invites them to trust in His work as the Kingdom-bearer (Mk 1:14–15; Lk 4:16–21; Heb 1:1–2). The Kingdom is not simply an abstract concept; it is a concrete reality. People can leave their way of life, enter the Kingdom, and follow Jesus.

Consider the following stories Jesus tells about the Kingdom. What is the main point of each story? Based on each passage, what attitudes and actions would mark a Kingdom citizen (someone who has repented of their sins and followed Jesus)? What attitudes and actions would mark someone who has rejected the Kingdom?

Matthew 7:24–27

Main Point: _____

Repentant Response:_____

Rejection Response: _____

Trimester 1: Gospel

Matthew 13:1–9

    Main Point: _____

    Repentant Response:_____

    Rejection Response: _____

Mark 13:34–36

    Main Point: _____

    Repentant Response:_____

    Rejection Response: _____

Matthew 19:16–30

    Main Point: _____

    Repentant Response:_____

    Rejection Response: _____

Mark 4: 26–34

    Main Point: _____

    Repentant Response:_____

    Rejection Response: _____

Luke 13:22–30

    Main Point: _____

    Repentant Response:_____

    Rejection Response: _____

Throughout His life, Jesus functions as a prophet, declaring the mystery of the Kingdom in these and other stories.

Where do you see yourself in the above stories? Does your life reflect repentance or rejection of the King's rule?

_____

_____

Jesus Demonstrates the Kingdom

Jesus not only speaks of the Kingdom, but also demonstrates what form the Kingdom takes when it comes to earth. His life is the picture of worship as He always does what is pleasing to God. He lives to bring God glory. He does what Adam, and all subsequent humanity, cannot do—He faithfully and fully keeps the law of God (Mt 5:17). Note the following people in the Scriptures. How does Jesus accomplish, in His life, what the following individuals were incapable or unwilling to do?

- Adam _____

- Noah _____

- Abraham _____

- Israel _____

- Moses_____

- Job_____

- David_____

- Jonah _____

Jesus, in contrast to all those who have come before, exemplifies what it means to live in the Kingdom. His spotless and unblemished life establishes Him as the Son of God.

Righteousness Defined: Perfect moral conformity to the law of God.

Jesus not only defeated sin with His death, but He defeated it with His life.

Peter says that Jesus "did not commit sin, and no deceit was found in His mouth (1 Pet 2:22; c.f. 2 Cor 5:21; Heb 4:15; 1 Jn 3:5)." In so doing, He can indeed be called the "lamb of God who takes away the sins of the world (Jn 1:29)." He is the embodiment of the Old Testament sacrificial system, a spotless and unblemished lamb that will qualify as a substitutionary sacrifice for sins.

It is not as if Jesus is somehow immune to sin, however, like some bionic superfigure. He experiences temptations as a man and emerges victorious (Heb 4:15).

Read the story of the temptation of Jesus in Matthew 4:1–11. How does Satan tempt Jesus? How does Jesus fight these temptations?

_____

_____

What encouragement does this bring to your battle with temptation and sin?

_____

_____

The author of the book of Hebrews says that the reality of the temptation of Jesus uniquely qualifies Him to serve fallen humanity.

> *Therefore, since we have a great high priest who has passed through the heavens— Jesus the Son of God—let us hold fast to the confession. For we do not have a high priest who is unable to sympathize with our weaknesses, but One who has been tested in every way as we are, yet without sin. Therefore let us approach the throne of grace with boldness, so that we may receive mercy and find grace to help us at the proper time (Heb 4:14–16).*

In light of this text, how should those who know Christ respond to temptation and sin?

_____

_____

Why are people more likely to run from God than to God with their sin?

_____

_____

Jesus' life of perfect righteousness also serves as an example for those who follow Him in His Kingdom mission. They are to embody characteristics that they observe in Jesus. We can look to Jesus to observe the nature and character of God. This is a much more tangible approach than trying to observe the nature of God and His Kingdom from general revelation alone. Jesus is God in the flesh, and He serves as the perfect picture of a life lived to please God.

What do we observe about the nature of God from the example of Jesus in the following passages of Scripture? How does the example of Christ challenge you to live a life that is pleasing to the Lord?

Matthew 4:1–11 _____

_____

John 13:1–17 _____

_____

Luke 15 _____

_____

1 Peter 2:21–22 _____

_____

What other passages of Scripture demonstrate Jesus' life of worship?

_____

_____

A word of caution is warranted at this point, however. Before Jesus can be our example, He must be our substitute. It will not suffice simply to note the marks of righteous living seen in Jesus and then attempt to copy them. Human sin, as we have seen throughout our study, will thwart our attempts at such obedience. If you attempt this, you will find yourself crumbling under the frustration and failure of your inadequacies.

Those who are able to follow Christ do so through a radical acknowledgement of their own inability. They fling themselves wildly on the mercy of God, declaring themselves to be sinners in constant need of God's sustaining grace. The path to obedience is worship.

Reclaimed worshippers follow Jesus in order to declare and demonstrate His glory among the nations. We see a group, albeit a small one, that seems to grasp this. Jesus begins this work by gathering a new Israel, twelve rag-tag disciples, including one whom He knew would betray Him (Mk 1:16–20; 2:13–14). This initial group of twelve, reminiscent of the twelve tribes of Israel, is called to worship God rightly and declare His glory to the nations.

> ***Disciple Defined***: A person who worships God rightly because of the work of Jesus.

The word disciple, a common word in the ancient Near East, referred to a learner or student. Jesus' disciples are unique, however. They are the beginning of the fulfillment of the plan of God to reclaim worshippers through Christ. This was quite a massive task for a disjointed and often faithless group of men.

Consider the following people. What do we know about them and their efforts to follow Jesus? How does this serve as an encouragement to you in your attempts at worshiping God?

Matthew

_____

_____

John

_____

_____

Peter

_____

_____

The twelve are not alone. Others respond in worshiping God, though most of those who meet Jesus oppose His mission and message. Those who do decide to follow Him receive a great call: the call to live a life of worship. This will require them to leave everything to follow Christ (Mt 8:18–22; 10:16–25). The cost is great. He then commissions them to live as His Kingdom ambassadors to the world, declaring and demonstrating that He is the promised Son of God (Mt 10:1–14). They have little idea that what lies ahead is not a path of glory—it was a path to the cross (Mt 16:24–26).

They are sent with a message of good news. The spotless lamb has been prepared by God and is ready to declare victory over Satan, sin, and death. The word gospel is derived from the Greek, _euangelion_, or "good news." The word is not religious in its orientation; it is used to describe a good news announcement. For example, a messenger might run to a town to deliver news of the victory of the King in battle. He would announce, "The battle is over, and the King has won." The disciples were commanded to announce good news as well (Mt 28:18–20). Their news was even better—"The King of the Universe is here, and He will win the battle forever" (Mt 28:18–20).

Back in week one of _Aspire_ you were asked to define the gospel. Flip back now and consider your answer. What would you add or change about your answer based on your work so far?

_____

_____

What does it mean to be a disciple of Jesus in today's world? In what ways is it easier to be a disciple today? In what ways is it more difficult?

_____

_____

Trimester 1: Gospel

The gospel is good news for disciples today, just like it was then. Jesus has come to perfectly fulfill God's plan to reclaim worshippers among the nations—including you. May a fresh awareness of the truth of the gospel propel you to live a life of worship.

Week 9: Cross

"For Christ our Passover has been sacrificed."

—1 Corinthians 5:7

"The gospel is an invitation to receive a gift. But many people hear it as a summons to do better. Paul makes it clear that the gospel is not about something we do. It is about what God has done for us in Jesus Christ." [1]

—Sinclair Ferguson

God fulfills His covenant promises through the life, death, burial, and resurrection of Jesus.

The cross is the most recognizable symbol of the Christian faith. The fact that an implement of torture and death would serve to define one of the world's largest religious groups is steeped in irony. The cross was reserved only for the most heinous of criminals in the first century. In fact, the Old Testament declares that anyone who hangs on a cross is cursed of God (Deut 21:23). Yet, this is the fate of the Son of God. How can this be?

It is crucial that we do good theology here. Sloppiness at this point can be deadly. The cross of Jesus is one of the most important and divisive theological truths. The truth of Christianity is bolstered and substantiated by it. Without it, everything falls apart.

What are some examples of insufficient explanations for the cross of Christ (For example, "Jesus died a martyrs death on the cross because He remained true to His beliefs.")?

_____

_____

How might an inadequate understanding of the cross of Christ lead to faulty conclusions about God?

_____

_____

---

1. Sinclair B. Ferguson, *By Grace Alone: How the Grace of God Amazes Me* (Lake Mary, FL: Reformation Trust Publishing, 2010), 40.

The apostle Paul, an amazing theologian, argues in 1 Corinthians 15:3–4 that "I passed on to you as most important what I also received: that Christ died for our sins according to the Scriptures, that He was buried, that He was raised on the third day according to the Scriptures." This passages reveals two essential truths:

- First, Paul says that the *singular thing* that is most important is the death, burial, and resurrection of Jesus. This unit is linked together as the core of the good news announcement. It is not simply the death or resurrection that matters, but all of these aspects of the gospel working together. The centrality of this gospel message is substantiated by the fact that these realities are repeated throughout the New Testament.

- Second, the death, burial, and resurrection of Jesus happened "according to the Scriptures." This was not some random and unexpected tragedy, but rather the fulfillment of the predetermined plan of God as revealed in the Scriptures.

That this is the clear plan of God is demonstrated by the fact that Jesus willingly allows himself to be killed. In a very real sense, God kills Jesus, and Jesus willingly lets Him. No person or group of people, no matter how powerful or destructive, could kill the Son of God. Jesus makes this same claim in John 10 when He says, "This is why the Father loves Me, because I am laying down My life so I may take it up again. No one takes it from Me, but I lay it down on My own. I have the right to lay it down, and I have the right to take it up again. I have received this command from My Father (17–18)." Jesus humbles Himself to death on the cross in order to fulfill the predetermined plan of God (Acts 2:23; Phil 2:7–8).

The story of the death of Jesus may be familiar, but it is no less stunning. The gospel writers record the events leading up to His death and his horrific murder in vivid detail. Read the crucifixion story as told in Matthew's gospel in chapters 26–27. What do you observe about the death of Christ from this passage?

_____

_____

Now read the prophetic word of Isaiah foretelling the role of the suffering servant in Isaiah 53. What do you observe from this text? How are the prophecy of Isaiah 53 and the death of Christ in Matthew 26–27 related?

_____

_____

Why would God's Messiah, the one we are told would emerge as the victorious King, willingly lay down His life in this fashion? The answer to this question is clear—He is reclaiming worshippers from the horrific condition their sin has created. All mankind has willingly disobeyed God, and they are therefore the rightful targets of His righteous wrath.

> **_Wrath Defined_**: The righteous anger of a Holy God towards sin.

Wrath is not a popular subject in the church. It is far easier (and safer) to talk about the love of God than it is to consider His wrath.

> What evidence do you have that God's wrath is not a popular concept in our culture?

_____

_____

The cross simply cannot be understood apart from the wrath of God. It is reasonable to assert that wrath is not only acceptable for God, but necessary. Consider a man who confesses to his wife a long-standing adulterous relationship. How would you expect her to react? With anger, right? To not react in anger would demonstrate a lack of love. What if she said, "Oh, it's no big deal, but thanks for telling me," or "Go ahead, I hope the relationship works out for you." This would not be love; rather it would reflect apathy and hate. Her flippant attitude towards the behavior would demonstrate a lack of love.

In a similar way, God's love for people is demonstrated _by_ His wrath, not _in spite_ of His wrath. God's holiness demands that He must judge sin. God cannot look the other way and pretend that sin does not exist. He must judge sin in order to retain His holiness (Rom 3:26).

The just judgment for sin is death (Rom 6:23). God cursed humans in the garden with this fate, which included both spiritual and physical death. *Spiritually* all people are born in a state of separation from God, alienated from His presence like Adam and Eve who were cast out of the garden. Not only are people separated from God, but also they are unable to do anything to make their way back into relationship with Him. *Physically*, all people die and face an eternal continuation of their separation from God in hell, forever separated from His grace.

Death is easily ignored in our modern world by the fact that God delays one's physical death in order to allow people time to repent of their sin and trust in Christ. At times He may demonstrate His wrath through active consequences and punishment for sin, thus alerting people of their sinful state (active wrath).

What are some examples of the active wrath of God toward sin?

_____

_____

At other times, He simply lets sin run it course, giving people over to the natural consequences of their sinful choices (passive wrath).

What are examples of the passive wrath of God? What is particularly frightening about the passive wrath of God?

_____

_____

Whether it be active or passive, the clear implication is that someone must pay for sin. This picture was clearly established in the Old Testament worship system, as the sins of the people were symbolically placed on a spotless animal. It was then slaughtered, and the blood was poured on the altar of God (Lev 16:29–30; 23:27–28). We read in Leviticus 17:11 that "the life of a creature is in the blood, and I have appointed it to you to make atonement on the altar for your lives, since it is the lifeblood that makes atonement." The people of God would have clearly understood that "without the shedding of blood there is no remission of sin (Heb 9:22)." Clearly, the most obvious person to pay for sin is the sinner himself.

BUT GOD.

Praise be to God that this is not the end of the story. The prophet Ezekiel foretold a day when the covenants God made with His people would be fulfilled.

> *For I will take you from the nations and gather you from all the countries, and will bring you into your own land. I will also sprinkle clean water on you, and you will be clean. I will cleanse you from all your impurities and all your idols. I will give you a new heart and put a new spirit within you; I will remove your heart of stone and give you a heart of flesh (Ez 36:22–26).*

Notice the first person pronouns in the text. God pledges to do the work that was necessary in order to save His people. The prophet spoke of a day when the deadened hearts of depraved men and women would pulsate with life. Their hearts would be cleansed from idolatrous worship and renewed in order to rightly declare the glory of God. The cross of Jesus is the God-appointed means of reclaiming worshippers.

God takes the initiative to cleanse His people from their sin and make them alive by granting them a new heart. The glorious promises of Romans 5:8–10 ring true:

> *But God proves His own love for us in that while we were still sinners, Christ died for us! Much more then, since we have now been declared righteous by His blood, we will be saved through Him from wrath. For if, while we were enemies, we were reconciled to God through the death of His Son, then how much more, having been reconciled, will we be saved by His life!*

The amazing thing about the cross of Jesus is that it all happens at the initiative of God. He authors a way for man to be restored to Himself, and He does the work to make that relationship possible.

> How does the role of God in the salvation of mankind prompt your heart to worship?

_____

_____

The work of Jesus on the cross is too massive for scholars to describe in one word (imagine that—something too big for scholars to define succinctly). The word atonement is most often used to speak of the process by which God grants salvation to people through the death of His Son. The concept of atonement has components, all of which are essential for the right understanding of the cross of Jesus.

Sacrifice

On the cross, Jesus is the sacrifice for the sins of the people. The key word here is the word "for." Jesus came to "give His life as ransom *for* many" (Mt 20:28), and "He, Himself is the propitiation *for* our sins (1 Jn 2:2)." He is the sacrifice *for* His people.

Only God could live a perfect life of holiness, and only a man could suffer the wrath of God while paying the price for sin. The incarnate Son of God, Christ Jesus, is the only one who could do both. Read the following Scripture passages and note what Jesus does *for* his people:

Galatians 1:3–4 _____

_____

Galatians 2:20 _____

_____

Galatians 3:13 _____

_____

Ephesians 5:2, 25 _____

_____

Jesus' death pays the penalty which sin deserves. For this reason many evangelicals refer to the atonement as the "penal" atonement, meaning Jesus paid the penalty for sin. Edmund Clowney notes that "Jesus had come, not to bring judgment, but to bear it."[1] He takes the full brunt of God's wrath against sin.

---

1. Clowney, *Unfolding*, 185.

God tells us how He responds once the debt for sin has been paid. Read the following Scriptures and note how God responds to sin for those who love and fear Him:

Psalm 103:11–13 _____

_____

Isaiah 43:25 _____

_____

1 John 1:9 _____

_____

God forgives sins through the cross of Jesus. The biblical word for this act is justification. It is a legal term that refers to the formal declaration of a verdict of "not guilty." The text that we read earlier from Romans 5 made this point clearly, "We have now been declared righteous by His blood (5:9)." God proclaims the not guilty verdict for the sins of His people from the cross.

> ***Justification Defined***: The formal act whereby God declares a person not guilty for sin.

Substitute

God does not simply pay the penalty for sin in a detached way, but rather He paid the penalty for the sins of His people *by taking their place*. Like the ram caught in the thicket when Abraham went to sacrifice Isaac, Jesus is offered up "instead of" fallen humanity (Gen 22:1–13). Paul says in 2 Corinthians 5:21, "He made Him who knew no sin to become sin for us so that in Him we might become the righteousness of God."

This sovereign exchange fully covers the sinful exchange man has made since the garden. We all exchange the worship of God for the worship of created things. Jesus makes a far more glorious exchange. He takes on our sin and gives us the righteousness that His life earned as a gift (Is 53:6). John Stott says that "the essence of sin is man substituting himself for God, while the essence of salvation is God substituting himself for man."[1]

The center of the Christian faith rests in the *penal, substitutionary atonement* of Jesus. Go ahead, you burgeoning young theologian, try your hand at defining this weighty theological phrase. What is penal, substitutionary atonement, and why does it matter?

_____

_____

How is this doctrine related to the idea of worship?

_____

_____

The cross is the path to restored worship. All mankind finds themselves on one of two sides of the cross. Read Romans 5:12–19 and attempt to summarize this passage below:

_____

_____

> ***Gospel Defined***: The announcement of the good news of Jesus' work to restore idolatrous image-bearers to rightful worship through the substitutionary death of Jesus Christ.

All people are born *in Adam*—bound by idolatrous worship and are the rightful object of God's wrath. Others are saved to be *in Christ*—restored by faith as worshippers because the full wrath of God has already been poured out upon Christ.

This is wonderful news! Yet, worship is not found simply by embracing good news, but rather by embracing *the one* who made the good news possible. God is the one who deserves worship for salvation, and you have been saved for Him. Peter says that "Christ also suffered for sins once for all, the righteous for the unrighteous, that *He might bring you to God* (1 Pet 3:18)." God Himself is the gift of the gospel. Christians get to worship

---

1. John Stott, *The Cross of Christ* (Downers Grove: IVP, 2006), 159.

the one true God. They do not simply believe a set of doctrines. They get God. As John Piper writes:

> *The ultimate good of the gospel is seeing and savoring the beauty and value of God. God's wrath and our sin obstruct that vision and that pleasure. You can't see and savor God as supremely satisfying while you are full of rebellion against Him and He is full of wrath against you. The removal of this wrath and this rebellion is what the gospel is for. The ultimate aim of the gospel is the display of God's glory and the removal of every obstacle to our seeing it and savoring it as our highest treasure. 'Behold Your God!' is the most gracious command and the best gift of the gospel. If we do not see Him and savor Him as our greatest fortune, we have not obeyed or believed the gospel.*[1]

Worship is the mark of the Christian life. Remember back to week one—the mission of creation is that God would be preeminent among all things. God's preeminence is declared among His people by faith and repentance, which is made possible through the cross of Christ.

Faith

Faith is a declaration of the preeminence of God. It boldly declares that Jesus is who He says He is and has done the work necessary to accomplish salvation. As in the Old Testament, those who are saved must place their faith in the substitute. They must trust that He is God and has accomplished the work of salvation. Paul says in Ephesians 2:8 that man is saved "by grace through faith." Clearly, grace is not something that people do—it is something that is done for them. The appropriate response to the gift is faith.

Faith and trust are cousins. Faith is not some blind leap into the unknown, but rather a fixed trust in a sure object. For example, a person may have faith that a chair will support his weight, but this faith is demonstrated when a person actually sits in the chair.

The same is true with the gospel. Faith means that a person puts their trust in what Jesus has done for them. They rest in it. This rest is possible because salvation does not depend on the level of the person's faith, but on the object of that faith. Jesus is a

---

1. John Piper, *God is the Gospel: Mediations on God's Love as the Gift of Himself* (Wheaton: Crossway, 2005), 56.

supremely trustworthy object of faith, and He can be trusted to save all those who come to Him in faith, because "whoever believes should not perish, but have everlasting life (Jn 3:16)."

Write a definition of faith.

_____

_____

What would you say to a person who felt like God was calling them to be saved? What form should their faith take?

_____

_____

How about a person who was wrestling with whether or not they were ever saved? How do you know if someone has faith?

_____

_____

Repentance

Repentance professes that you are not God. Repentance means turning from sin and to Jesus. The word implies a 180-degree life change in which a person renounces all false forms of worship and runs towards Christ. The image of the prodigal from Luke 15, or the cry of the broken in Luke 18:13, exemplifies this heart attitude: "God, turn your wrath from me—a sinner."

Define repentance. Use the following passages to help you develop your definition:

Acts 3:19 _____

_____

Romans 2:4 _____

_____

Luke 17:3–4 _____

_____

2 Corinthians 7:9–10 _____

_____

Romans 2:4–5 _____

_____

How would you apply the truth of the gospel and the necessity of faith and repentance to someone who professed faith in Jesus and had:

- A live-in girlfriend _____

  _____

- An alcohol addiction or eating disorder _____

  _____

- A massive amount of credit card debt _____

  _____

- A past of immoral living resulting in a criminal record _____

  _____

Thankfully, God tells us how He responds to the cry of repentance and faith from all people, even those mentioned in the case studies above. He grants salvation. Jeremiah prophesied of a day when God would make a New Covenant with His people. He writes:

> *"Look, the days are coming"—this is the Lord's declaration—"when I will make a new covenant with the house of Israel and with the house of Judah. This one will not be like the covenant I made with their ancestors when I took them by the hand to bring them out of the land of Egypt—a covenant they broke even though I had married them"—the Lord's declaration. "Instead, this is the covenant I will make*

with the house of Israel after those days"—the Lord's declaration. "I will put My teaching within them and write it on their hearts. I will be their God, and they will be My people." (Jer 31:31–33)

The New Covenant dawned in the person of Jesus. God, through faith and repentance, takes out the heart of stone marred by idolatry, and puts in its place a heart of flesh marked by worship. He makes the dead to live, the broken to be made whole, the slave to be free, and the rebel to be a son.

In one sense, this process is complete in a moment; in another sense, it takes a lifetime. It may be helpful to think of salvation in three tenses:

Past Tense—"I am saved"

Jesus' cry from the cross that "it is finished" reveals that the atonement is fully complete. The sacrifice which Jesus offered to God has been accepted, and He has finished the work. The author of Hebrews demonstrates the finality of the sacrifice of Jesus when he says, "After making purification for sins, he sat down at the right hand of the Majesty on high (Heb 1:1–4)." The work is done, and Christ sat down because there was nothing left to do.

As a result, guilty sinners are *redeemed from the penalty of sin*. Paul declares that sinners "have redemption in Him through His blood, the forgiveness of our trespasses (Eph 1:7)." They do not earn this forgiveness, nor receive it in progressive stages. It is a present possession for the Christian. This reality means that a Christian can trust that they are saved. Since a person did not earn his or her salvation by good works, salvation cannot be lost by sinful works either (Eph 2:1–10).

Have you ever doubted your salvation?

_____

_____

Rate your confidence in your own salvation on the scale below, (with 1 being a sign that you are unsure and a 10 being an indication of total confidence). What reason would you give for your choice?

1 2 3 4 5 6 7 8 9 10

God marks those who are His by giving them His Spirit, whom He pledges as a down payment on their eternal salvation. The Spirit is a guide into all truth and a constant companion on whom the Christian can depend. The Spirit's task is to guide the Christian to make much of Jesus and worship Him rightly.

What is the role of God's spirit in the following passages?

John 14:15–17 _____
_____

John 14:26 _____
_____

John 16:7–15 _____
_____

Acts 1:8 _____
_____

Galatians 5:22–23 _____
_____

Romans 8:26 _____
_____

Present Tense—"I am being saved"

Justification leads to sanctification. It is the process whereby a child of God progressively conforms to the image of Christ by renouncing idolatry and pursuing worship.

> ***Sanctification Defined***: The work of God to conform fallen sinners into faithful worshippers.

Paul tells the church in Philippi to "work out your own salvation with fear and trembling. For it is God who is working in you, enabling you both to desire and to work out His good purposes (Phil 2:12–13)." God is at work in sanctification, yet Christians are given a task. God is at work propelling grace-driven effort in the heart of the Christian so he/she may act in light of His justification (2 Cor 4:16). As a result, the Christian is increasingly *freed from the power of sin* and able to live the life God desires.

Believers are to respond to grace through daily, active, sacrificial worship that encompasses their whole lives. This worshipful obedience is marked publically by the act of baptism (Rom 6:3–4). Here, a Christian publically professes faith in Jesus and is incorporated into the church.

Read the following passages. Why do they say that baptism matters?

Acts 2:41; 10:44–48 _____

_____

Romans 6:3–4 _____

_____

Have you been baptized following your repentance from sin and your profession of faith in Christ? Describe your baptism experience. What significance has it played in your life?

_____

_____

_____

If you have yet to be baptized following your salvation, stop now and talk to your mentor about baptism. This is a vital and God-honoring first step of obedience. From there, life is a constant process of growing in grace in order to worship God rightly.

Future Tense—"I will be saved"

One day our faith will be sight, and we will perfectly and forever be conformed to the image of Jesus. We will be able to rightly worship Him forever. At the end of time, humans will be freed from *the presence of sin*. Imagine that—a time when sin will be gone. You will no longer be crushed under the weight of your sin. You will not have to look at the implications of sin in disease, disaster, or war (Rev 21:1–4). All things, including Christians, will be renewed and restored in order to worship Him forever. All of creation longs for the day when we will be changed to be like Him (Rom 8:23; 1 Cor 15:52; 1 Jn 3:2).

Conclude this session by writing a prayer in light of these three tenses of salvation. First, thank God for Jesus and for His work on the cross, using the language of Scripture and the foundational understanding this session has provided you.

_____

_____

_____

_____

Second, ask Him to grow your heart to worship Him rightly. Repent of those things that you do which still reflect faulty worship, and beg Him to transform your heart by His Spirit.

_____

_____

_____

_____

Third, pray that He will finish His mission and bring salvation to people from every tribe, tongue, and nation, so that the day will appear when all things will be restored!

_____

_____

_____

_____

Week 10: Resurrection

"And if Christ has not been raised, your faith is worthless; you are still in your sins."

—1 Corinthians 15:17

*"If Jesus rose from the dead you have to accept all he said, if he
didn't rise from the dead then don't worry about anything he said…
If Jesus rose from the dead it changes everything."*[1]

—Tim Keller

The resurrection proves that God keeps His promises.

Everyone has faith. Life requires it. Even the claim that "there is no God" takes tremendous faith. Similarly, it takes faith to affirm that Jesus is the Son of God, who lived a perfect life and died a substitutionary death in order that idolatrous men and women could once again worship Him rightly. In our day this claim may appear crazy. In the world of the first century such a claim would get you killed.

This is the fate of most of the early followers of Jesus. They were killed for professing the message of the gospel. Something profound must have happened in order for them to risk their lives for this message. No one makes that kind of sacrifice for something they *might* believe. Rock solid confidence is necessary.

The resurrection was the fuel for such confidence. Twice in the same chapter Paul says, "If Christ has not been raised, then our preaching is in vain and your faith is in vain (1 Cor 15:14)." He continues, "If Christ has not been raised, your faith is futile and you are still in your sins (1 Cor 15:17)." Clearly, the resurrection of Jesus is an important fact.

Think about the last sermon you heard on the resurrection? What was the main point of the sermon?

_____

_____

_____

1. Tim Keller, *The Reason for God* (London: Hadder and Stoughton, 2008), 202.

Have you ever heard a sermon on the resurrection that was *not* given on Easter Sunday? What does the modern neglect of the resurrection say about most people's understanding of the gospel?

_____

_____

The first resurrection Sunday certainly looked different than our modern celebrations. This is not the way His followers thought it would end. It seems that the promised Messiah has failed. There are no tailgating tents or breakfast. There is little joy and much sadness. Jesus' followers do not expect the resurrection. They do not show up at the tomb with party poppers and streamers waiting for Jesus to come out. Instead we read in Matthew 28:2–7:

> *Suddenly there was a violent earthquake, because an angel of the Lord descended from heaven and approached the tomb. He rolled back the stone and was sitting on it. His appearance was like lightning, and his robe was as white as snow. The guards were so shaken from fear of him that they became like dead men. But the angel told the women, "Don't be afraid, because I know you are looking for Jesus who was crucified. He is not here! For He has been resurrected, just as He said. Come and see the place where He lay. Then go quickly and tell His disciples, 'He has been raised from the dead. In fact, He is going ahead of you to Galilee; you will see Him there.' Listen, I have told you."*

"He is not here" and "He is risen" are two great statements that change everything.

The resurrection of Jesus the Messiah changes the shape of the world, and the validity of Christianity depends on it. It proves that God is doing what He said He was doing, and it proves that Jesus is who He says He is.

Paul says in Romans that "Jesus…through the Spirit of holiness was declared with power to be the Son of God, by his resurrection from the dead: Jesus Christ our Lord (Rom 1:4)." The resurrection proclaims that Jesus is who He says He is.

1 Corinthians 15 recounts six different groups of people to whom Jesus appears after his resurrection, validating that this was not a hoax, but the real Jesus: really dead and then really resurrected. This reality becomes the core message of the gospel and the climax

of redemptive history. Peter concludes his first Easter sermon by saying, "Therefore let all Israel know with certainty that God has made this Jesus, whom you crucified, both Lord and Messiah (Acts 2:36)." Jesus is Lord and Messiah. The resurrection stamps this claim into the history books for all ages. While the cross looks like defeat, it results in the validation of the divinity of Jesus.

Why does the resurrection matter?

_____

_____

Paul answers that question in 1 Corinthians. He has spent the majority of this letter defending his credentials, answering questions, and challenging the overt sin in the church. He ends the letter by placing His hope, and in turn the church's hope, in the resurrection of Jesus. He writes, "Brothers, I tell you this: flesh and blood cannot inherit the Kingdom of God, and corruption cannot inherit incorruption. Listen! I am telling you a mystery (1 Cor 15:50–51)."

Paul reveals a mystery to the church. This does not mean something that is a cryptic secret but rather something that has been hidden in the past and is now revealed through the person and work of Christ. What is the mystery?

> *We will not all fall asleep, but we will all be changed, in a moment, in the blink of an eye, at the last trumpet. For the trumpet will sound, and the dead will be raised incorruptible, and we will be changed. For this corruptible must be clothed with incorruptibility, and this mortal must be clothed with immortality. When this corruptible is clothed with incorruptibility, and this mortal is clothed with immortality, then the saying that is written will take place: Death has been swallowed up in victory. Death, where is your victory? Death, where is your sting? Now the sting of death is sin, and the power of sin is the law. But thanks be to God, who gives us the victory through our Lord Jesus Christ (1 Cor 15:51–57)!*

The message of the resurrection is the chant of victory. But, victory over what? Paul points to three enemies that Jesus defeated through His resurrection:

The resurrection proclaims victory over death.

Everyone dies and no one likes it. In fact, though death is a 100% certainty, everyone seems shocked when it happens. Death is always an unwelcomed intruder into the world. In spite of modern advances, no one has sedated the shocking reality of death. Sure, we invent different language (passed away, moved on, left us) but the reality remains. You may postpone it for a while, but you will not beat it permanently. It is certain and unalterable.

And yet, Jesus defeated death. Paul cites two Old Testament texts to show how God has defeated death (Isa 25:8 and Hos 13:14). Jesus confronted death, not by running from it, but by running through it. He defeated death by absorbing it fully for us. Death's victory has been overcome by Christ's victory. Death's deadly sting has been abated. Indeed, the stinger itself has been removed through Christ's resurrection.

Paul says that Jesus' death defeats death for the Christian and guarantees a future resurrection. He says, "For as in Adam all die, so also in Christ all will be made alive. But each in his own order: Christ, the firstfruits; afterward, at His coming, those who belong to Christ (1 Cor 15:22–23)." What happened to Christ in his resurrection will happen to those who are in Christ. Jesus' resurrection is not a random, one-time event; rather, it is the precursor to what will happen to all of God's people. Currently, we are perishable and mortal, but one day those who are in Christ will be resurrected imperishable and immortal.

How does Jesus' victory over death offer you hope?

_____

_____

How would you utilize the good news of the resurrection in your care for someone who had recently lost a loved one or who was battling a terminal illness?

_____

_____

The resurrection proclaims victory over sin.

Jesus' victory over death also proclaimed a victory over sin. Why? Because sin is at the root of death. James notes the natural procession towards death, "Then after desire has conceived, it gives birth to sin, and when sin is fully grown, it gives birth to death (Ja 1:15)." Sin is the deadly poison that leads to death. Death is the outworking of sin and not simply the outworking of normal human processes. The defeat of death proclaims the defeat of sin.

Christ's defeat of sin guarantees forgiveness of sins for those who are united to Christ by faith. Not only does He forgive sin, but also He empowers those whom He saves to fight sin in their lives. Sin has no power over those who are in Christ. They can fight sin knowing that it is a defeated foe.

As I write these words, I have just finished a conversation with a group of university students in a predominantly Muslim part of the world about sin and the afterlife. When asked about forgiveness, these men described their vague hope that they would merit forgiveness based on their good deeds outweighing their evil deeds. In contrast, we recounted the work of Jesus on the cross to these men and spoke of the firm and fixed confidence we could have that our sins were forever forgiven. Sadly, these men said that they could have no such confidence.

Such a scale method is often the way people think of forgiveness. As a result, they live with a steady sense of shame and guilt based on their ongoing sin. We often forget that the person and work of Christ has fully settled the weight of the scales. You are forgiven.

How does the death of sin aid you in your battle against sin?

_____

_____

How does this gospel truth speak to issues of shame and guilt?

_____

_____

The resurrection proclaims victory over the law.

The resurrection proclaims the defeat of the law. What does the law have to do with death and sin? The law is an external means of controlling behavior to mitigate against sin and death. Paul argues that "Christ is the end of the law for righteousness to everyone who believes (Rom 10:4)." The Christian is no longer ruled by law. The resurrection changes the Christian from law-abiding to gospel-believing. No longer does self-righteousness and moral achievement rule the heart. Instead, a deep and abiding trust in the work of Christ takes its place. The resurrection frees us from the death that the Law requires to the eternal life that Jesus purchased! The resurrection frees us from sinful slavery to glad hearted worship.

Paul concludes:

> *More than that, I also consider everything to be a loss in view of the surpassing value of knowing Christ Jesus my Lord. Because of Him I have suffered the loss of all things and consider them filth, so that I may gain Christ and be found in Him, not having a righteousness of my own from the law, but one that is through faith in Christ—the righteousness from God based on faith. My goal is to know Him and the power of His resurrection and the fellowship of His sufferings, being conformed to His death, assuming that I will somehow reach the resurrection from among the dead (Phil 3:8–11).*

Today, praise God that the three mortal enemies of all of humanity are defeated. In fact, Paul says that their sting is removed. A wasp without a stinger is one that we could swat away playfully. It's no threat at all. Neither are death, sin, and the law. The long chain of decay and death initiated by the first Adam will finally and irrevocably be broken by the last Adam. Do not be afraid: death need not have the final word; sin need not have the final word; the law need not have the final word; the victory has been won!

Christians can take heart knowing that Jesus has won the victory and triumphed over the great enemies of Satan, sin, and death (Col 2:15; Jn 16:33). The result of this glorious truth is hope. Hope is the defining virtue of a person who truly grasps the message of the resurrection. Paul uses this same language in Colossians 1:23 where he writes, "If indeed you remain grounded and steadfast in the faith and are not shifted away from the hope of the gospel that you heard. This gospel has been proclaimed in all creation under heaven, and I, Paul, have become a servant of it." The Christian life is to be marked by gospel-driven hope. Paul says that this reality means we need not grieve when we encounter death as those who have no hope (1 Thes 4:13), and it should be so counter-cultural that people ask us to give a "reason for the hope that lies within us (1 Pet 3:15)."

Is your life marked by hope? What worries, frustrations, or fears reveal your lack of hope in the gospel?

_____

_____

To be a disciple of Jesus is to be hopeful—*full* of hope. The resurrection is not a static, historical fact, but the basis for the Christian life in a fallen world. It fills each day with hope until the day when the King returns and permanently eradicates Satan, sin, and death forever.

Week 11: Church

"This grace was given to me—the least of all the saints!—to proclaim to the Gentiles the incalculable riches of the Messiah, and to shed light for all about the administration of the mystery hidden for ages in God who created all things. This is so that God's multi-faceted wisdom may now be made known through the church to the rulers and authorities in the heavens."

—Ephesians 3:8–10

"The Church is the community that experiences in the midst of life the power of God's renewing work and thus embodies the comprehensive and restorative salvation of the kingdom for the sake of the world."[1]

—Michael W. Goheen

The church is God's community of reclaimed worshippers.

Words are like a paintbrush. Whenever they are used they bring certain images to our minds. This is true of all words, particularly words that are used to speak of God. Consider the following words that are commonly used among Christians and pastors. What comes to your mind when you hear these words? What do you think comes to the mind of those who are not Christians?

Word	What comes to your mind?	What do you think comes to the mind of those who are not Christians?
God		
Jesus		
Father		
Spirit		
Cross		
Faith		
Salvation		
Bible		

---

1. Michael W. Goheen, *A Light to the Nations: The Missional Church and the Biblical Story* (Grand Rapids: Baker, 2011), 19.

If you are curious about what a non-Christian might think, ask them. Take a minute and ask someone you know who does not know Jesus what they think of when they hear these words.

The church, at its essence, is the community of reclaimed worshippers.

The word "church" is loaded with stereotypes. Millions upon millions of people worship Jesus Christ every week and do so at a church. Yet, if you walk into various churches and ask people what the word "church" means, the odds are that you will get either a blank stare or a series of conflicting definitions. It will be even worse if you ask those who are outside of the church. Their perception is often jaded by a host of negative presuppositions.

What events or ideas shape how people view the church?

_____

_____

What has been most instrumental in shaping how you view the church? Are these ideas positive or negative?

_____

_____

The string of popular adjectives used to describe the church reveal the confusion found in defining the church: liquid church, emerging church, organic church, missional church, multi-site church, externally-focused church, house church, future church, ancient-future church, blogging church, and prevailing church. It seems that even those who lead the church have a hard time defining it correctly. So long as a few people are doing something spiritual, it appears that we can call it a church.

Biblically, the church is not a thing or a place where people go. The church is made up of all people in all places who have called upon the name of the Lord for salvation (the universal church). Thus the modern church, when understood correctly, finds itself in the lineage of those whom God has saved throughout all human history among all peoples. God gives some of His most beautiful promises to the universal church. For example, Jesus promises to build His church in a way that "the gates of hell shall not prevail against it (Mt 16:18)."

Yet, the Scriptures more often speak of the church in concrete terms. It refers not to abstract notions about the church but to specific, local expressions of the people of God who worship Him together at a singular point in time and cultural context (the local church).

The church is so marvelous that the biblical authors struggle for words to describe it. Wouldn't you? I mean, how do you describe the group of people that are the culmination of God's promise and plan since the beginning of creation? The Scriptures describe it through a series of pictures; images that paint a panoramic picture of the splendor of the church.

The church is like a family.

The very idea of the church requires more than one person. You (singular) are not the church, but you (plural) are the church. This runs counter to the most common ways of thinking about Jesus' work. We say, "Jesus died for me." Now of course, there is an element of truth in this claim. Jesus did die for every single one of His children. No one is saved based on the faith of someone else.

You must trust Christ personally. However, you never trust Christ alone.

When a person repents and places faith in Christ that person is adopted into a family— a really large family at that (Eph 1:5). This family will be much like a biological family. It is imperfect and broken as a result of sin. The reality of the gospel is that Jesus died and rose again to create a single new humanity; not only to redeem us from sin but also to adopt us into God's family; not only to reconcile us to God, but also to reconcile us to one another. The church is an integral part of the gospel.

How should the view of the church as a family change the way that you view the church?

_____

_____

Do you relate to your church as you would a family?

_____

_____

The church is like a body.

This metaphor functions in the context of local churches, made up of real people who commit to worship God together at the same place and time. In some ways, it is far easier to love the universal church, because it is comprised of people that you do not see on a regular basis. Loving real life people in the context of the local church is real work, however.

Thankfully, this work is also made possible by the death of Christ. Notice Paul's words in the book of Ephesians:

> *For He is our peace, who made both groups one and tore down the dividing wall of hostility. In His flesh, He made of no effect the law consisting of commands and expressed in regulations, so that He might create in Himself one new man from the two, resulting in peace. He did this so that He might reconcile both to God in one body through the cross and put the hostility to death by it (Eph 2:14–16).*

Jesus died for both Jews and Gentiles. These people were united into one new Body by virtue of Christ's work. As a result, unity in the church is something you work *from* rather than simply something you work *for*. Jesus united his people, and the church is given the glorious task of living in light of this unity.

How does the good news of Jesus shape the way people are related to one another? Why should the good news be a basis for love and service to fellow Christians in the church?

_____

_____

Paul also uses gift language to speak of the uniqueness of the members of the church body. Unity need not require uniformity. In fact it must not. Paul writes,

For as the body is one and has many parts, and all the parts of that body, though many, are one body—so also is Christ. For we were all baptized by one Spirit into one body—whether Jews or Greeks, whether slaves or free—and we were all made to drink of one Spirit. So the body is not one part but many…Now you are the body of Christ, and individual members of it (1 Cor 12:12–14, 27).

The church can function as an effective body because of the uniqueness of its members. The members do not have the same function, but they leverage their unique spiritual gifts in ways that build up the Body of Christ (Rom 12:4–8; Eph 4:11–16).

> ***Spiritual Gifts Defined***: Unique ways that the Holy Spirit gives believers to serve to build up the church.

How has the Spirit of God gifted you to serve the church?

_____

_____

How are you currently using those gifts? Where are you seeing gospel fruit?

_____

_____

The church is like a bride.

Paul says that the church is also like a bride—the very bride of Christ. Paul uses the picture of marriage to describe the church. He writes, "For this reason a man will leave his father and mother and be joined to his wife, and the two will become one flesh. This mystery is profound, but I am talking about Christ and the church. To sum up, each one of you is to love his wife as himself, and the wife is to respect her husband (Eph 5:31–33)."

This image is stunning in its beauty. Paul says that God created marriage as a means of displaying the mystery of the gospel. It was not as if God was in heaven saying, "I need a way to show my people how I love them…marriage…Yeah, marriage is just the right picture." Rather, God intentionally created marriage as a way of declaring and demonstrating the mystery of the gospel to the world.

Marriage does this for the gospel. It takes good news and makes it tangible. A marriage that is tender and patient demonstrates to the world that God's love is not flighty and selfish. A marriage that perseveres through steady covenant commitment demonstrates that God's love is not fickle and easily broken. A marriage that is selfless lovingly declares that God's love is humble and kind, even to the point of taking Him to the sacrifice of the cross.

God loves the church like a husband loves his new bride. Have you ever stropped to watch the face of a groom as he watches his bride walk down the aisle on their wedding day? It is one of my favorite moments. The smile is unmistakable as he cranes his neck to catch a glimpse of his bride walking towards him. She is a treasure. This is how God sees His redeemed worshippers in the church.

John Stott contrasts this perspective with the earthly picture that we often have of the church:

> On earth she is often in rags and tatters, stained and ugly, despised and persecuted. But one day she will be seen for what she is—holy and without blemish, beautiful and glorious. It is to this constructive end that Christ has been working and is continuing to work. The bride does not make herself presentable; it is the bridegroom who labors to beautify her in order to present her to himself. His love and self-sacrifice for her, his cleaning and sanctifying of her, are all designed for her liberation and her perfection, when at last he presents her to himself in full glory.[1]

How does seeing the church as a bride shape how you view the church? How should it affect how you talk about the church and act towards it?

_____

_____

---

1. John Stott, as quoted by Josh Harris, *Why Church Matters* (Portland, OR: Multnomah, 2011), 31.

The church is like a temple.

The next image makes little sense apart from an understanding of the Old Testament. Peter writes, "Coming to Him, a living stone—rejected by men but chosen and valuable to God—you yourselves, as living stones, are being built into a spiritual house for a holy priesthood to offer spiritual sacrifices acceptable to God through Jesus Christ (1 Pet 2:4–5)." Paul utilizes the same imagery of a building, but defines it more specifically. He says that the church functions like the Old Testament temple.

> *So then you are no longer foreigners and strangers, but fellow citizens with the saints, and members of God's household, built on the foundation of the apostles and prophets, with Christ Jesus Himself as the cornerstone. The whole building, being put together by Him, grows into a holy sanctuary in the Lord. You also are being built together for God's dwelling in the Spirit (Eph 2:19–22).*

Two factors are of chief importance about the temple imagery. First, since the church is like a temple, it is the place of God's dwelling. God dwells among His people by means of His Spirit. Jesus tells His followers that once He returns to heaven the Spirit would come and "guide them into all truth" (Jn 14:1–3, 18–20; 15:26–27; 16:4).

How does the daily obedience of God's people serve as a means of declaring the glory of God in the places that they live, work, and play?

_____

_____

The church is like a picture.

Finally, the church functions like a picture. As you may have noticed, many of the images used to speak of the church are used in the book of Ephesians. Here we find these words:

> *I was made a servant of this gospel by the gift of God's grace that was given to me by the working of His power. This grace was given to me—the least of all the saints—to proclaim to the Gentiles the incalculable riches of the Messiah, and to shed light for all about the administration of the mystery hidden for ages in God who created all*

things. This is so God's multi-faceted wisdom may now be made known through the church to the rulers and authorities in the heavens. This is according to His eternal purpose accomplished in the Messiah, Jesus our Lord (Eph 3:7–11).

Paul says that the manifold wisdom of God is put on display through the church. It is designed to paint a picture of the multifaceted beauty of God as He reclaims worshippers. The heavenly realms and the nations are meant to see in the church the realization of the eternal purpose and plan of God.

What type of picture is your local church painting?

_____

_____

What is your role in this painting?

_____

_____

Let the beauty of the local church fill your heart with worship. You stand in the long line of reclaimed worshippers whom God is calling to Himself. The promise of Genesis 3 finds its fulfillment in the people of your church. Amazing grace indeed.

Week 12: Consummation

"Then comes the end, when He hands over the kingdom to God the Father, when He abolishes all rule and all authority and power. For He must reign until He puts all His enemies under His feet. The last enemy to be abolished is death."

—*1 Corinthians 15:24–26*

God made everything in the beginning and he will redeem everything in the end. The Bible is heading towards a conclusion in heaven because that is the culmination of God's plan for the world."[1]

—*Vaughn Roberts*

Worship is the theme of heaven.

Endings are rarely happy occasions, whether it's the end of a friendship, a job, a season in a certain home, or even the end of life. Conclusions are often met with sadness, remorse, and even fear. Even when the end is necessary, such as a bad job or a failed romance, the transition to the next stage of life is often met with apprehension.

I heard a number of sermons as a child about Jesus' return with the basic premise: "You better be ready, He could come back tonight." I vividly remember thinking, "I sure hope not. I've got a big basketball game this weekend," or "That stinks. He better wait until I can get married. That would be totally unfair for him to end things now." As silly as those responses seem to me now, they accurately represent the misunderstandings that many have when it comes to the way in which God will finish His story.

What makes it challenging to properly understand the way the world will end?

_____

_____

What are some secondary matters that tend to dominate this discussion?

_____

_____

_____

---

1. Roberts, *Picture*, 28

With God's story, the beginning and the end are often met with the most speculation. For instance, we often spend massive amounts of time discussing the scientific mechanisms by which God created the world. How did he do it? How long did it take? Were the days literal 24-hour days or some other period of time? How does all of this square with the process of evolution? While these are interesting questions, they may miss the main purpose of the creation narrative. God exists. He created all things. He created all things for His glory. These are the dominant realities that the creation story is meant to answer.

The same is true for the end of the story. Speculation abounds as people debate the timing of the end of the world and the exact process by which God will make all things new. This is aided by the complexity of the scriptural writings about the end times (such as much of Daniel or the entirety of Revelation). To combat this temptation, it is vital that we focus on the main, dominant realities that the Scriptures clearly affirm concerning the end times. This will help us avoid the distracting speculation that can divert us from seeing that God will do what God has always been doing—reclaim worshippers.

God Wins.

The promise of Genesis 3:15 is fulfilled through the sacrificial and substitutionary death of Jesus Christ. While it may seem that life is filled with the shrapnel of sin, the reality is that the victory is already won. The Seed of the woman crushed the head of the serpent, forever defeating Satan, sin, and death. And, as a result of His victory, God "also highly exalted Him and gave Him the name that is above every name, so that at the name of Jesus every knee should bow—of those who are in heaven and on earth and under the earth-and every tongue should confess that Jesus Christ is Lord, to the glory of God the Father (Phil 2:9–11)." All people will bow the knee in worship to the King—either in this life through faith and repentance or in the next life in wrathful judgment.

Think about a movie or sports game that you have re-watched numerous times. How does knowing the ending of the story shape how you experience the story when you watch it again?

_____

_____

How should knowing that Satan, sin, and death will be proven to be defeated on the last day shape how you respond to these realities now?

_____

_____

God Recreates.

Sadly, the church is often guilty of having a myopic view of God's restorative work. We see the cosmic restoration of all things as simply a free pass to heaven for those who have professed faith in Jesus. Instead, the biblical notion of the restoration of all things is holistic in nature.

This idea of restoration and renewal forms the basis of the biblical notion of the end times. In contrast to views that picture the world being eradicated through fire, the Bible pictures the world being cleansed of the effects of sin and recreated according to its original design (2 Pet 3:11–13). For example, the prophet Isaiah writes, "For I will create a new heaven and a new earth; the past events will not be remembered or come to mind (Is 65:17)."

All of the created order that is now groaning under the tyranny of sin and longing for redemption will be made new (Rom 8). The world will be made right, perfectly declaring the glory of God through all created things without the brokenness of natural disasters and destruction. Everything, even the created world, that has been marred by the effects of sin will be made right again.

Think for a moment about the most beautiful thing you have ever seen. Perhaps it's the Rocky Mountains, the Grand Canyon, or a tropical beach. The most beautiful thing you have ever seen is still contaminated by sin and will pale in comparison to the beauty that will be seen when God makes all things new. How should this prompt your heart to worship?

_____

_____

The human body will also be made new (1 Cor 15:35–45). Bodies broken and marred by the distortion of sin will be perfectly remade, never again to be ravished by sin. God will triumph over death, disease, and all forms of human despair. Throughout the gospels, Jesus' miracles make this point clear, as people get a glimpse of the way in which God seeks to restore and heal a world broken by sin. Miracles in the gospels serve as a foretaste of heaven when all things will be made right again—the lame will walk, the deaf will hear, the mute will speak, and the dead will be raised.

God Rules.

In the end, it is heaven that comes to earth and not Christians that go to heaven. The Kingdom of God fully and forever comes to earth.

Theologians have historically referred to this reality as the "already/not-yet" tension of the Kingdom of God. In a sense, the inbreaking of the Kingdom of God was seen at the incarnation of Jesus. However, even after his death, resurrection, and ascension, His rule and reign is still veiled in many ways. Evidence of his coming restoration abound. Yet this work is not yet fully consummated. The residue of sin remains. This reality could be picture as follows:

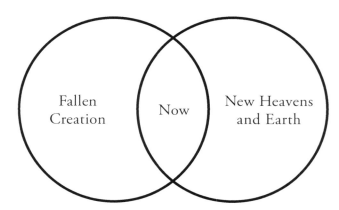

The work of Christ on the cross inaugurated his Kingdom, yet that Kingdom will not be fully consummated until some point in the future, when all things are made new. Here the twin themes of the nature and character of God will be seen once again. God, as a just judge, will banish those who have been unwilling to submit to Him in faith and repentance to an eternal separation apart from Him in hell. To those who have bowed the knee to worship of the King in this life, He will grant an eternal life of worship in His presence.

Talk of heaven and hell is sure to make most modern believers uncomfortable. Based on your understanding of God's redemptive mission through what you've read in *Aspire*, how would you respond to the statement, "A loving God would never send anyone to hell"? Why is hell essential for a holy God?

_____

_____

How does the "already/not-yet" tension of the Scripture shape the following areas of your life? Attempt to provide scriptural support for your answers. An example is provided for you below:

- Your pain and suffering

  Example: *I should view my pain and suffering as light and momentary considering the glory that will be revealed in me (2 Cor 4:17).*

  _____

  _____

- Your prayer life

  _____

  _____

- Your fight for holiness

  _____

  _____

- Your school/vocation

  _____

  _____

- Your relationships

  _____

  _____

- Your church

  _____

  _____

God is Worshipped.

Poor views of earthly worship lead to poor views of heavenly worship. If we think of earthly worship as just singing another verse to yet another praise chorus, the thought of unending worship in heaven may seem a bit unappealing. However, heavenly worship will be holistic in nature. Restored image-bearers will do forever what they were created to do—rule and reign over God's good creation. This life of worship will be the theme of heaven.

Revelation 7:9–12 reads:

> _After this I looked, and there was a vast multitude from every nation, tribe, people, and language, which no one could number, standing before the throne and before the Lamb. They were robed in white with palm branches in their hands. And they cried out in a loud voice: Salvation belongs to our God, who is seated on the throne, and to the Lamb! All the angels stood around the throne, the elders, and the four living creatures, and they fell facedown before the throne and worshiped God, saying: Amen! Blessing and glory and wisdom and thanksgiving and honor and power and strength be to our God forever and ever. Amen._

In heaven, for the first time, it will be impossible for men and women not to worship. Even in the pristine nature of the creation design, man had the freedom to abandon the worship of God, which they did. After the fall, mankind could no longer worship God rightly. The cross makes authentic worship possible through the finished work of Jesus. In the new heavens and the new earth, worship will be the only choice; sin will not be an option.

How should you prepare now knowing that you will worship God forever?

_____

_____

How should the worship of God shape your longings for him to return (Rev. 22:20)?

_____

_____

We have come full circle: God created a world in order to be worshiped; that worship was marred by human sinfulness; Jesus paid the penalty that sin deserved making worship possible again; one day the world will be renewed and filled with the worship of God.

Let's worship Him rightly as we long for the day when we will worship Him fully.

Trimester 1: Top Ten List

What are the top ten take-aways that you have from this trimester of *Aspire*? How is God is bringing transformation in your life?

1. _____

2. _____

3. _____

4. _____

5. _____

Trimester 1: Gospel

6. _____

7. _____

8. _____

9. _____

10. _____

Suggested Reading List

Bartholomew, Craig G. and Michael W. Goheen. *The Drama of Scripture: Our Place in the Biblical Story*. Grand Rapids: Baker, 2004.

Bridges, Jerry and Bob Bevington. *The Great Exchange: My Sin for His Righteousness*. Wheaton: Crossway, 2007.

Buzzard, Justin. *The Big Story: How the Bible Makes Sense Out of Life*. Chicago: Moody, 2003.

Carson, D.A. *The God Who is There: Finding Your Place in God's Story*. Grand Rapids: Baker, 2010.

Chandler, Matt. *The Explicit Gospel*. Wheaton: Crossway, 2012.

Clowney, Edmund. *The Unfolding Mystery: Discovering Christ in the Old Testament*. Phillipsburg: P&R, 1988.

Dempster, Stephen. *Dominion and Dynasty: A Biblical Theology of the Hebrew Bible*. Downers Grove: IVP, 2003.

Fee, Gordon and Doug Stuart. *How to Read the Bible for All Its Worth*. Grand Rapids: Zondervan, 2003.

Gentry, Peter J. and Stephen J. Wellum. *Kingdom Through Covenant: A Biblical-Theological Understanding of the Covenants*. Wheaton: Crossway, 2012.

Goldsworthy, Graeme. *According to Plan: The Unfolding Revelation of God in the Bible*. Downers Grove: IVP, 1991.

Greear, JD. *GOSPEL: Recovering the Power that Made Christianity Revolutionary*. Nashville: B&H, 2011.

Leithart, Peter J. *A House for My Name: A Survey of the Old Testament*. Moscow: CanonPress, 2000.

Morris, Leon. *The Atonement: Its Meaning and Significance*. Downers Grove: IVP, 1983.

Packer, J.I. and Mark Dever. *In My Place Condemned He Stood: Celebrating the Glory of the Atonement*. Wheaton: Crossway, 2007.

Plantinga, Jr. Cornelius. *Not the Way It's Supposed to Be: A Breviary of Sin*. Grand Rapids: Eerdmans, 1995.

Plantinga Jr., Cornelius. *Engaging God's World*. Grand Rapids: Eerdmans, 2002.

Piper, John. *God is the Gospel*. Wheaton: Crossway, 2003.

Roberts, Vaughn. *God's Big Picture: Tracing the Storyline of the Bible*. Downers Grove: IVP, 2002.

Sailhamer, John H. *The Pentateuch as Narrative*. Grand Rapids: Zondervan, 1995.

Sproul, RC. *The Holiness of God*. Carol Stream, IL: Tyndale, 1985.

Stott, John R. *The Cross of Christ*. Downers Grove, IVP, 2006.

Thompson, Jim. *A King & and Kingdom: A Narrative Theology of Grace and Truth*. Tigerville: Auxano, 2011.

Vincent, Milton. *A Gospel Primer for Christians: Learning to See the Glories of God's Love*. Focus Publishing, Minnesota, 2008.

Wolters, Albert M. *Creation Regained: Biblical Basics for a Reformational Worldview, 2nd ed*. Grand Rapids: Eerdmans, 2005.

Wright, Christopher J.H. *Knowing Jesus through the Old Testament*. Downers Grove: IVP, 1992.

Wright, N.T. *Jesus and the Victory of God*. Minneapolis: Fortress Press, 1996.

TRIMESTER 2
Ministry

Week 1: Worship

"Therefore, brothers, by the mercies of God, I urge you to present your bodies as a living sacrifice, holy and pleasing to God; this is your spiritual worship. Do not be conformed to this age, but be transformed by the renewing of your mind, so that you may discern what is the good, pleasing, and perfect will of God."

—Romans 12:1–2

"God is most glorified in us when we are most satisfied in him. The fight of faith is a fight to feast on all that God is for us in Christ. What we hunger for most, we worship."[1]

—John Piper

Gospel understanding is not enough. Transformation is the goal, both for your life and for those you love and lead.

The process is similar to attempts to lose weight. It is not enough to simply understand your own weight issues, the dietary content of the foods you eat, an intentional workout routine, and the regime for developing healthy eating habits. You have to apply that information to your life by going to the gym, lifting the weights, and eating properly. Information alone is insufficient.

The same is true of a person's spiritual life. What about you? In what seasons of your life have you seen the greatest amount of transformation? What was true of your life at that time? How did the first trimester of *Aspire* shape the way that you worship?

_____

_____

We've all had experiences of trying to change and failing. There is nothing more frustrating. The cause of this futile effort is often the result of attacking the wrong problem —the negative behavior itself. Behavior modification may work for a season, but it is insufficient to produce lasting change.

---

1. John Piper, *A Hunger For God: Desiring God Through Fasting and Prayer* (Wheaton; Crossway, 2007), 10.

The second trimester of *Aspire* is designed to aid you in applying the richness of the gospel message to your daily life. This process will require deep thought and intentional choices as you seek to apply information about the gospel to personal transformation by means of the gospel.

In their book *How People Change*, Tim Lane and Paul Tripp claim that people have gospel gaps that hamper their ability to truly change.[1] These gaps are found in the space between a person's affirmation of the gospel and their application of the gospel to their daily lives.

What are some examples of these gaps in your life currently?

_____

_____

> ***Worship Defined***: A whole-life response to the glory of God seen in the gospel of Jesus Christ.

Maybe you find yourself thinking that worship is simply something that happens when the church gathers to sing, pray, or listen to a sermon. The reality is, however, that all of life is meant to be worship. How so?

God designed the human heart to respond to the person or thing that it finds most valuable. Think about it for a minute. How do you know what a person loves? You check their behavior, right? People give themselves to those things that they love such as their favorite sports team, hunting club, or health craze. Behavior follows our affections, so the way to change behavior is to address the affections. It's seemingly counter-intuitive, but it is the only way to consistently produce a heart of godly character.

You must fall increasingly in love with God in order to live a life of worship.

---

1. Timothy S. Lane and Paul David Tripp, *How People Change* (Greensboro: New Growth Press, 2008), 1–17.

God designed His world to do this. In *The Happiness of God*, John Piper writes,

> *All the different ways God has chosen to display his glory in creation and redemption seem to reach their culmination in the praises of His redeemed people. God governs the world with glory precisely that he might be admired, marveled at, exalted and praised. The climax of his happiness is the delight he takes in the echoes of his excellence in the praises of the saints.*[1]

We have already seen from Colossians 1 that this was God's motive in creation, His accomplishment in redemption, and the outcome of the new heavens and the new earth. He will be seen as preeminent.

The fall, as we saw last trimester, altered our ability to do this. Man tried to be his own god, rebelling from the authority and care of God. Instead of rightly worshiping God, man has chosen to worship created things. The result was catastrophic. Sin introduced death into the world and contaminated all that God had made (Rom 1).

However, through Christ's person and work, man can once again respond rightly to God. Allow your heart to ponder the beauty of the gospel Paul declares to the church at Ephesus. His gospel message comes in three parts.

The Painful Truth

Paul describes the process of gospel transformation in his marvelous summary in Ephesians 2:1–10. There he begins:

> *And you were dead in your trespasses and sins in which you previously walked according to the ways of this world, according to the ruler who exercises authority over the lower heavens, the spirit now working in the disobedient. We too all previously lived among them in our fleshly desires, carrying out the inclinations of our flesh and thoughts, and we were by nature children under wrath as the others were also (Eph 2:1–3).*

---

1.   John Piper, *Desiring God* (Portland, OR: Multnomah, 1986), 34.

139

What does Paul affirm about the plight of humanity apart from Christ? What words does he use? Why do you think he chooses those words?

_____

_____

A right understanding of sin is essential for a proper understanding of the gospel because unless you rightly understand sin you will never be able to comprehend grace. Paul uses a number of descriptive words in this passage—none more all-encompassing than the word "dead." That is what sin makes you. Your sin separates you from God (spiritual death) and leads to permanent separation from God (physical death). Sin is deplorable, deadly and, even worse, the rightful target of God's righteous judgment. While sinful fruit may take numerous forms, it is always an affront to a holy God. Thus, it must be dealt with severely.

As a disciple of Jesus and leader of others, it is vital that you see sin rightly. Write a simple definition of sin using the language of Ephesians 2.

_____

_____

Apply this language to your own life. What do you see in your own life that fits this definition?

_____

_____

If you could snap your fingers right now and be freed from sin, what would be some of the most notable changes?

_____

_____

The Glorious Grace

The depth of sin found in Ephesians 2:1–3 is superseded by the grace demonstrated in verses 4–9. Here Paul writes:

> *But God, who is rich in mercy, because of His great love that He had for us, made us alive with the Messiah even though we were dead in trespasses. You are saved by grace! Together with Christ Jesus He also raised us up and seated us in the heavens, so that in the coming ages He might display the immeasurable riches of His grace through His kindness to us in Christ Jesus. For you are saved by grace through faith, and this is not from yourselves; it is God's gift— not from works, so that no one can boast.*

How does Paul speak of God's grace in this passage? What does this reveal about God?

_____

_____

Death comes through sin, and life comes through Christ. Christ's work was an act of grace, whereby God fulfilled his covenant promise to conquer Satan, sin, and death forever.

Grace is difficult to define. It is sheer…well…grace. But give it a try. How would you define grace?

_____

_____

Grace is impossible to define apart from Christ. Jesus is grace personified. By seeing Christ we see grace. Particularly here in Ephesians 2, Paul points to the death, burial, and resurrection of Christ as defining features of the grace of God. God gives his children what they do not deserve by living the life they could not live, dying the death that they should have died, and exchanging His perfect righteousness for their sin-tattered ways.

However, we do not worship a doctrine. We worship a person. The person of Jesus, and not simply His redemptive work, is the focus of the church's worship. Paul writes to the wayward Corinthian church that:

> *In their case, the god of this age has blinded the minds of the unbelievers so they cannot see the light of the gospel of the glory of Christ, who is the image of God. For we are not proclaiming ourselves but Jesus Christ as Lord, and ourselves as your slaves because of Jesus. For God who said, 'Let light shine out of darkness,' has shone in our hearts to give the light of the knowledge of God's glory in the face of Jesus Christ (2 Cor 4:4–6).*

This helps us see that our worship crescendos in the person of Christ (Heb 1:2–3). He is the object to which grace points. And what does Christ do?

> *Christ also suffered for sins once for all, the righteous for the unrighteous, that he might bring you to God (1 Pet 3:18).*

> *In Christ Jesus you who were far away have been brought near by the blood of the Messiah…that he might…reconcile both to God in one body through the cross… For through him we both have access by one Spirit to the Father (Eph 2:13–18).*

Grace brings us to Christ. Christ brings us to God. God gets our worship.

How does a right understanding of Jesus motivate life change?

_____

_____

The Life of Worship

Grace meets truth and leads to worship. Note Paul's concluding exhortation to the church at Ephesus in this passage.

> *For we are His creation, created in Christ Jesus for good works, which God prepared ahead of time so that we should walk in them (Eph 2:10).*

Good works are a response to the good news of the gospel and not a way to earn God's favor. They do not merit salvation, but they are essential nonetheless. They demonstrate that a person is rightly captivated by the reality of their own sinfulness and their desperate need for God's grace.

Imagine for a moment that you are a parent with a young child. You take care of the child—providing food, water, shelter, and an assortment of fun activities because this is your child. You do not do those things in order to make him your child. But because he already is your child, you will do those things.

Worship works like this. God brings you into relationship with Himself. This is a pure and inalterable relationship. From the sure foundation of that relationship you are then commended to offer your life as an act of worship (Rom 12:1–2).

Worship happens at the intersection of TRUTH and GRACE.[1]

Why do you need both truth and grace in order to rightly worship God?

_____

_____

Without a right understanding of the truth of your sin you will never understand your need for Jesus' work on the cross. Without a right understanding of the grace of God you will believe that there is no way for your sins to truly be forgiven. Walking the path of worship is a daunting undertaking, however. Two ditches loom on either side of the path that result from an overemphasis on either truth or grace.

The Truth Ditch

Those that overemphasize truth become religious legalists. No one has to convince them of their sin or the sin of others. They see it clearly. And they work to avoid it. This produces a rule-based religion whereby they attempt to prove and validate their worth. Rules are normative. Actions are supreme. Repentance amounts to a redoubled effort to try harder. And the heart is neglected. The danger for those who fall into the truth ditch is not only that they end up there but that they lead others there as well. Leaders with

1. This understanding of Ephesians 2:1–10 is heavily influenced by the teaching of Dr. Mark Liederbach, professor at Southeastern Baptist Theological Seminary.

an overdeveloped "truth muscle" prod more than lead, dominate rather than invest, criticize rather than care.

The Grace Ditch

The other, and equally destructive ditch, is the grace ditch. In this ditch, people forget their need for the gospel, presume upon the provision of Christ, and allow grace to become an excuse for continuing to sin. Emotions reign supreme and repentance is inconsequential. God's love is all that matters. There's no need to concern oneself with sin and judgment.

Leaders will fail to lead well if they operate out of the grace ditch. They will communicate a gospel of "easy believism" that undermines the radical nature of discipleship. In which of these ditches are you most likely to find yourself?

_____

_____

Let's consider a fictitious scenario to allow you to apply these principles to the lives of others. A person comes to you struggling with homosexual desires and infrequent sexual activity. Sin has built up a head of steam in this person's life and is threatening to destroy everything.

What would your Biblical counsel be in this situation if you were operating from the truth ditch?

_____

_____

How would your counsel change if you were leading out of the grace ditch?

_____

_____

Let's move one step closer to home. Consider a situation in which you find yourself frustrated with your spouse. In your mind, she has sinned against you and demonstrates little willingness to change. You feel like she is overly demanding in your home and is unwilling to submit to your leadership. You have tried to address this issue in the past, but it has only led to a painful conversation and greater distance in your marriage.

What is the voice from the truth ditch in this situation? What is the voice from the grace ditch?

_____

_____

And finally consider your own heart. Imagine that you assume your first position as the pastor of a local church, only to discover that you are not nearly as skilled and gifted as you once thought. Instead you struggle to make decisions, to lead a team, preach effective sermons, provide Biblical counsel, and even manage your own time.

What would you say to yourself from the truth ditch? What would you say to yourself from the grace ditch?

_____

_____

The Path of Worship

The path of worship navigates the balance of grace and truth and allows one to lead himself, his family, and his church as an act of worship. A person walking the path of worship readily acknowledges his sinfully depraved heart and inability to earn the favor of God. Therefore such a person humbly and willingly places his faith in the finished work of Jesus to both satisfy the wrath of God towards his sin and to grant him the perfect righteousness of Christ. As a result, Jesus becomes the supreme treasure of life, and life is lived for his glory (1 Cor 10:31).

Consider the above case studies one final time. How does the path of worship speak to the man struggling with homosexuality?

_____

_____

How does the path of worship speak to your family?

_____

_____

How does the path of worship address your own sinful heart?

_____

_____

Gospel transformation starts from a heart of worship. You may have a cognitive grasp of the truths found in the first trimester of *Aspire*, yet, if they do not cause you to love, treasure, and worship Jesus, they are futile. However, if these truths effectively permeate your heart, the result will be lasting transformation.

Week 2: Transformation

"And when you were dead in trespasses and in the uncircumcision of your flesh, He made you alive with Him and forgave us all our trespasses. He erased the certificate of debt, with its obligations, that was against us and opposed to us, and has taken it out of the way by nailing it to the cross."

—*Colossians 2:13–14*

"The Lord Jesus has undertaken everything that His people's souls require; not only to deliver them from the guilt of their sins by his atoning death, but from the dominion of their sins, by placing in their hearts the Holy Spirit; not only to justify them, but also to sanctify them."[1]

—*JC Ryle*

Personal transformation is the path to discipleship and leadership in the church.

At this point, you may find yourself thinking: "What a waste of time. This is JV Bible stuff, when are you going to help me become a mature Christian or leader in the church?" These questions reveal a lack of insight into the centrality of the gospel in the life of a Christian. The terrain of the gospel must become a well-trodden path for someone to lead himself, his family, or a church. No one, not even a pastor, is beyond the need for the gospel.

Consider the demands of a basketball player. Of course, practicing layup drills and free throws is essential. Without them a player would be useless on the court. However, very rarely does a basketball player run a layup drill in the middle of the game. Instead he must navigate unique defenders, a depleting shot clock, a noisy crowd, and his own adrenaline to accomplish the goal—scoring a basket.

Growth in discipleship and leadership in the church presents a similar challenge. No two circumstances are alike. People are challenging and you are a mess (even on your good days). As a result, you must first become an expert at applying the truth of the

---

1. JC Ryle, *Holiness: Its Nature, Hindrances, Difficulties, and Roots* (Moscow: Charles Nolan Publishers, 2001), 20.

gospel to yourself and then discern how best to communicate it to others. The Biblical authors use a number of words and concepts to describe the work of Jesus on their behalf. None of these words in and of themselves capture the full splendor of the gospel, but together they help us understand the height, depth, length, and width of the love of Christ.

How do you think the average attendee of your local church would define the gospel?

Is the gospel something for non-Christians or for Christians? Why?

_____

_____

The need for gospel clarity is why Paul could begin his massive corpus on the gospel to the church at Rome by saying, "so I am eager to preach the good news to you also who are in Rome (Rom 1:15)."

He says the same thing to the church in Corinth:

> *Now brothers, I want to clarify for you the gospel…For I passed on to you as most important what I also received: that Christ died for our sins according to the Scriptures, that He was buried, that He was raised on the third day according with the Scriptures (1 Cor 15:1–4).*

This seems quite strange. The church has already heard and responded to the gospel. Why would Paul need to remind them of it again?

For the same reason that you need to be reminded of it. Because we are quick to forget that the beauty of the gospel is the only truth sufficient to address the sinful depravity of our hearts and the hearts of those we love. In our day, the evangelical community has been reminded of our need to recover the centrality of the gospel for all of life. However, we must be careful lest this idea simply becomes another buzzword. The gospel must lead to transformation.

For this to happen you must be able to apply the implications of the gospel to the mountain of sin that lies in each of our hearts. In order to do so, the truths of the gospel must become sticks of dynamite that you place in strategic positions to detonate recognizable rocks in the mountain of sin. Thankfully the Biblical authors provide numerous sticks of dynamite that each express unique truths about the gospel. Let's consider some of these main sticks of dynamite that the gospel message provides:

Propitiation

On the cross, Jesus substituted for your sins and fully took the wrath that sin deserved. As a result Paul says, "They are justified freely by His grace through the redemption that is in Christ Jesus. God presented Him as a propitiation through faith in His blood, to demonstrate His righteousness, because in His restraint God passed over the sins previously committed (Rom 3:24–25)." Like the spotless lamb of the Old Testament sacrificial system, the pure and spotless Lamb was sacrificed on behalf of God's children. This truth, which we looked at in depth in the last trimester of *Aspire,* reveals that I do not have to atone for my sins by earning God's favor. Rather, on the cross, the penalty for my sin was paid in full.

> How do you deal with your sin? What would change about your life if you truly believed that the penalty for sin had been fully paid through the cross of Christ?

Justification

The cross also declares that you are no longer held guilty for your sins. Paul writes in Romans, "Therefore, since we have been declared righteous (justified) by faith, we have peace with God through our Lord Jesus Christ (Rom 5:1)." Justification is a legal verdict declaring you not guilty for your sin because Jesus has taken your place. You are fully loved by God and do not have to live under the tyranny of shame, guilt, or fear. There is no need to fear. God is not going to learn something about you that makes Him love you less. His love for you is a fixed and final reality.

What things are currently causing you shame and guilt? What would change if you believed that you were justified?

Union

Paul writes that, "For as *in Adam* all die, so also *in Christ* all will be made alive (1 Cor 15:22)." The finished work of Christ transforms you from being in Adam (dead in my sin) to being in Christ (alive by grace). As a result, all that is Christ's is now yours—including His perfect righteousness and His victory over death.

What do you get by virtue of being "in Christ"?

_____

_____

Adoption

Because you are in Christ, you are permanently adopted into His family. Paul reminds the Ephesian church that "In love He predestined us to be adopted through Jesus Christ for Himself, according to His favor and will, to the praise of His glorious grace that He favored us with in the Beloved (Eph 1:5)." You are, by virtue of your adoption, grafted into the people of God as an heir of His promises to Abraham, Isaac, and Jacob, and made brothers and sisters with all of those who are in Christ.

What does it mean to be an heir to the promises of God? What promises are yours in Christ?

_____

_____

Reconciliation

The gospel reveals that all barriers that separate you from God have been destroyed. Paul writes, "Therefore, if anyone is in Christ, he is a new creation; old things have passed away, and look, new things have come. Everything is from God, who reconciled us to Himself through Christ and gave us the ministry of reconciliation (2 Cor 5:17–18)." All people, because of their sin, are out of relationship with God—in fact, they are His enemies. Through Christ, those who were enemies are now friends. How amazing to consider that fallen humanity can be a friend of a sovereign God!

What should you see in the life of someone who is a friend of God? Is this true of your relationship with God? Do you tend to see God as a friend or a foe?

_____

_____

Redemption – "free"

God has also provided "redemption in Him through His blood, the forgiveness of our trespasses, according to the riches of His grace (Eph 1:7)." Redemption is the language of freedom. Those who were slaves have been made free through the cross, in a similar fashion as God freed his people from slavery in Egypt. The good news of Christ frees you from all things that enslave. You can be free from sin and live a life pleasing to God by the power of the Holy Spirit.

How are you still living in slavery to sin?

_____

_____

Imputation

Jesus' offering for sin provided you with the perfect righteousness of Christ. The author of Hebrews notes that "For by one offering He has _perfected forever_ those who are sanctified (Heb 10:14)." The gospel announces that his children are given the righteousness of Christ (imputation) through no work of their own, and that now God sees them like He sees Christ. This means that you can avoid the hypocrisy that comes from trying to look good without being good and can instead rest in the righteous standing of Jesus.

Where are you masking unrighteousness in your life? What corners are you cutting? What "minor" sins are you rationalizing?

_____

_____

Sanctification

God promises to progressively conform a person to be holy like Jesus. This will not happen in a moment. Rather, it is the work of the Spirit, the Word, and the church over the totality of one's life, only to be fully realized in heaven. In 2 Thessalonians Paul says, "But we must always thank God for you, brothers loved by the Lord, because from the beginning God has chosen you for salvation through sanctification by the Spirit and through belief in the truth (2 Thess 2:13)." As a result you should fight sin with all vigor knowing that it is not a trivial matter.

Where do you find yourself apathetic to sin? How should the gospel stir you to action? How does this process crush your pride?

_____

_____

Glorification

The promises of the gospel exist in the past, remain in the present, and persist in the future. The future is sure as well. Paul writes, "For I am persuaded that not even death or life, angels or rulers, things present or things to come, hostile powers, height or depth, or any other created thing will have the power to separate us from the love of God that is in Christ Jesus our Lord! (Rom 8:38–39)." The gospel shouts victory over Satan, sin, and death and provides the ultimate assurance of new heavens and a new earth, where righteousness dwells. Those who are in Christ can live with confident, forward-facing hope, knowing that God always keeps his promises.

In what areas of your life have you lost hope? How should the gospel inform this area of your life?

_____

_____

Churchification

Sure, it's a made-up word. But it is an essential, though neglected, reality of the gospel message. Paul writes, "There is one body and one Spirit—just as you were called to one hope at your calling—one Lord, one faith, one baptism, one God and Father of all, who is above all and through all and in all (Eph 4:4)." The church is not some arbitrary option for those who are saved by Christ, but rather the outcome of the gospel itself. You are placed in the church. As a result you, in Christ, must renounce individualism and pursue unity, love, and burden-bearing relationships with others.

Are you meaningfully connected to the local church? Why does this matter?

_____

_____

The same dynamite that detonates the mountain of sin in your life is sufficient to accomplish the same purpose in the lives of others. For a leader of the church, these gospel truths will become the tools in your tool belt. You will use them over and over again in your counseling, teaching, preaching, and leadership. Without them, you may provide people a self-help guide to overcome their present problems, but you will never truly minster to others unless you help them understand and apply the beauty of the gospel to their lives.

Let's try our hand at this now. Think about the following people in your life right now. What gospel truth would be helpful for them to hear at this point in their lives?

- Your spouse, girlfriend or boyfriend, or best friend;

  _____

  _____

- The person you are discipling;

  _____

  _____

- Your small group, Bible study class, or church community.

  _____

  _____

Now consider the following case studies. How would you use the dynamite of the gospel to provide meaningful help to people in these situations? Discuss your thoughts with your *Aspire* mentor this week. Not only will this process be helpful for you to bring encouragement to others, but it will also deepen your understanding and appreciation for these truths in your own life.

- A Christian teenage girl battling an eating disorder;

  _____

  _____

- An apathetic middle-aged church attendee who professed faith at a young age;

  _____

  _____

- A retiree who professes faith in Christ but is not meaningfully involved in the local church because of wounds from his past;

  _____

  _____

- A divorced Christian man whose wife left him following his extra-marital affair;

  _____

  _____

- A young mom who just had a miscarriage.

  _____

  _____

Welcome to the life of a disciple and disciple-maker. You will spend the rest of your life working to apply the above truths to your life and to the lives of those you love. The result, by God's grace, will be transformational.

Week 3: Idolatry

"But that is not how you learned about the Messiah, assuming you heard Him and were taught by Him, because the truth is in Jesus: you took off your former way of life, the old man that is corrupted by deceitful desires; you are being renewed in the spirit of your minds; you put on the new man, the one created according to God's [likeness] in righteousness and purity of the truth."

—Ephesians 4:20–24

"God is the absolute reality that everyone in the universe must come to terms with… To ignore him or belittle him is unintelligible and suicidal folly."[1]

—John Piper

Idolatry comes in two forms—the kind you can see and the kind you cannot.

Transformation is a slow and often painful process. It is slow because you and I are far more sinful than we often admit. And it is painful, because all along the way our sin is exposed, causing transformation to be a progressive work rather than a linear ascent.

I remember when God saved me. There was, in a moment, clear transformation in my life. Certain sinful actions disappeared from my life with little to no effort on my part. I simply did not desire various facets of the life of sin I lived prior to God converting my heart. But then there were other areas that did not seem to change. I found that I was confessing the same sins week after week and seeing little transformation. It is easy to grow frustrated in those situations. It seemed that it would be easier if God just took away all sin when he provided me with the gift of salvation.

Such transformation does not happen in a moment, however. It takes the arduous and time-consuming process of repenting of idolatry and reminding yourself of the gospel over and over again. The Scriptures are replete with examples of the idolatry of God's people. They were consistently susceptible to the lure of idols, and the prophet Ezekiel locates these idols in the heart (Ez 14:1–8). Since the fall, humanity is prone to run after such idolatrous God replacements. Their insidious presence makes them a target of the

1. John Piper, *Let the Nations Be Glad* (Grand Rapids: Baker, 1993), 14.

Christian's warfare. As John affectionately concludes his first epistle, we are to guard ourselves from idols (1 Jn 5:21).

Fruit Idols

Fruit idolatry is seen in the things we commonly refer to as sin: lying, cheating, stealing, sexual immorality, alcoholism, anger, and the like. These sins are public—visible to both the perpetrator and to those around him. Romans 1 describes them in lured detail:

> *And because they did not think it worthwhile to acknowledge God, God delivered them over to a worthless mind to do what is morally wrong. They are filled with all unrighteousness, evil, greed, and wickedness. They are full of envy, murder, quarrels, deceit, and malice. They are gossips, slanderers, God-haters, arrogant, proud, boastful, inventors of evil, disobedient to parents, undiscerning, untrustworthy, unloving, and unmerciful. Although they know full well God's just sentence—that those who practice such things deserve to die—they not only do them, but even applaud others who practice them (Rom 1:28–32).*

Throughout the Bible, these sinful vices are described using the language of fruit. Jesus points out that you can tell the type and quality of a tree by its production of fruit. A quick glance at this list of sinful fruit and one would be tempted to think that the fruit was the basis of the problem. But it is not. A few verses earlier Paul places the blame at a deeper level:

> *Therefore God delivered them over in the cravings of their hearts to sexual impurity, so that their bodies were degraded among themselves. They exchanged the truth of God for a lie, and worshiped and served something created instead of the Creator, who is praised forever. Amen (Rom 1:24–25).*

The blame is placed squarely on the shoulders of faulty worship. Paul says that mankind made a fundamental exchange—they chose to worship created things rather than worshiping the Creator. This worship disorder is the basis of the second form of idolatry.

Root Idols

Root idols are lodged deep in the heart. They are the source of faulty worship. There are not many of them, but they are deadly. Root idols are those characteristics of a sinful and depraved heart that drive people to fruit idols. They are seen in what people trust, make sacrifices for, prioritize, esteem, place value in, daydream about, and long for. Take one of the most basic root idols—pride. Pride is difficult to see and it easy to ignore when we speak of sin; yet, it is at the root of every sin.

For example, anger is rooted in pride—"I want what I want, when I want it, and in the way I want it. If you don't do it that way then I get angry." What is this if not pride? Pride propels anger. Or consider another root idol—unbelief. Unbelief says that I do not trust that God is going to be true to His Word and meet my needs. Put fruit on unbelief and you have the sin of worry.

The heart consistently churns out idols and our fallen culture coddles them, making them more difficult to see and weed out. In fact, we have an entire society built around the celebration of our idols.

Make a list of the primary root idols that we see in our culture:

_____

_____

_____

_____

Which of these are the main root idols that you battle? How do you notices these idols in your life (fruit idolatry)?

_____

_____

_____

_____

Fruit to Root[1]

The process of transformation happens as a person recognizes and kills idolatry. You, and those you lead, will have to consistently travel the path of fruit to root. Let's consider a couple of fictitious case studies to allow you to try your hand at this process.

- **Case Study 1:** Every Sunday you see a married mother of two sitting in church alone. She is there consistently, with kids in tow, but never with her husband. You've met him a couple of times at special church events such as Easter Sunday, but you haven't had more than a casual conversation with him. One Sunday after preaching you notice her sitting, quietly crying. You offer to pray with her and inquire about how you can help her. She tells you through broken sobs that her husband admitted to an affair the night before. She has suspected it for some time, but he finally came clean. Surprisingly, she says that he seems broken over his decisions and does not want his marriage and family to fall apart. Their kids, ages 10 and 8, do not know at this time. The lady tells you that she has moved out and is trying to process all that is going on. She asks if you would be willing to meet with her husband the next day.

  What "fruit idolatry" is clearly visible in her husband's life?

  _____

  _____

  What would you suspect about the "root idolatry" in this case?

  _____

  _____

  What questions would you ask to move from visible fruit to root?

  _____

  _____

---

1. The various authors of the Christian Counseling & Educational Foundation emphasize this point. The work of Paul Tripp and Tim Lane highlight the effect of root idols in shaping human behavior.

How would you use Scripture in your conversation with the husband?

_____

_____

- **Case Study 2:** An area pastor invites you out to lunch one Monday. The two of you are good friends so the meeting is not abnormal. The conversation begins as expected, but quickly takes a sharp turn. "I just submitted my letter of resignation," your friend says. He continues, "I am frustrated, exhausted, and think I made a mistake even entering pastoral ministry. My church is hopeless, and I have given up." Over the next few minutes, you ask a few questions to discern if there is clear immorality that is prompting the decision. Did he have an affair? Did he steal money? Each answer reveals that the culprit is not simply one of these predictable causes. It is something deeper in his heart.

What is the "fruit idolatry" that is clearly visible?

_____

_____

What would you suspect about the "root idolatry" in this case?

_____

_____

What questions would you ask to move from visible fruit to root?

_____

_____

How would you use Scripture in your conversation with the pastor/minister/your friend?

_____

_____

Share your comments with your *Aspire* mentor this week and ask for feedback on how you moved from fruit to root. Another great way to develop this skill is to model it in your own life. No one knows you better than you, so you should be able to see your own fruit and root sins very clearly.

What is a common fruit sin in your life? What might lie at the root of that sin?

_____

_____

Common Idols for Developing Disciples

By this point in *Aspire,* you should be moving into some areas of strategic ministry and leadership in the life of the church. This may be as a small group leader or apprentice, youth ministry leader, or child care assistant. As you do, you will quickly note that leadership in the church is a greenhouse for the growth of idolatry. Here are a number of root idols that are common in the life of growing disciple:

Work Idolatry

Ironically enough, the very work of the ministry can become a source of idolatry. Subtly, leaders can become lured by the thrill of doing something great for God and no longer see their service as an act of worship. They may know that they are not saved based on their works, yet find that they evaluate God's perception of them based on their performance.

How are you tempted to see your obedience as a means of earning God's favor?

_____

_____

Gift Idolatry

A disciple's gifting can quickly become a seedbed for idolatry. Whether it is achievement in a singular domain of ministry, such as preaching, or simply the need to be seen as successful, talented, or useful, leaders can fall prey to performance idolatry. The celebrity culture of modern evangelicalism leads to the increasing need for leaders to compare themselves to other "successful" pastors or leaders. The results are often discouragement and doubt.

How might you be able to detect performance idolatry in your life? Where are you "faking it" as you serve in the church?

_____

_____

Knowledge Idolatry

Developing disciples should see themselves growing as adept thinkers. Often these young, idealistic disciples pride themselves in their ability to be theologically precise and nuanced. Their exegetical understanding, theological perspectives, or philosophical orientation can easily become idolatrous. It could be based on right thinking or right practice—"This is the right way to think about this issue," or "This is the only way to grow the church." It could be a way of reading the Scripture, a theological orientation (i.e. Reformed theology), or a method of doing church (i.e. church growth only happens if Sunday services are done with excellence). Either way, disciples who base their maturity around their specialized knowledge, can find that their knowledge is a tool that results in false worship.

What "knowledge" are you most committed to as a disciple? How could this knowledge become an idol?

_____

_____

People Idolatry

People idolatry rears its head when a disciple has an unnecessary longing to be liked or needed. People trump God as the center of the leader's affections. Perhaps it is found in an inability to make decisions because of a fear of what others might think. Or, it might be the desire to hear people say, "We don't know what we'd do without you." When this happens the fear of people becomes greater than one's fear of God and understanding of the gospel.

Whose opinion of you matters too much? What people in your life affect your emotions based on how they treat you? If you are currently leading, are you doing so out of a desire to be needed or out of a desire to honor God?

_____

_____

Family Idolatry

Service to God can quickly lead to compromise with one's primary context for discipleship—their family. Disciples must find the healthy balance between prioritizing their family and also faithfully fulfilling serving God and the church. If the leader is not carful, his marriage, children, or work can become gods in his life. And, as always, people and things make lousy gods.

How are you doing at balancing your family and your leadership roles in the church? Which are you more likely to drift towards: workaholism or slothfulness?

_____

_____

Comfort Idolatry

A final root idol that regularly makes an appearance in a leader's life is that of comfort. Safety and stability become the goal of life, and any decision that compromises that comfort is avoided at all costs. The host of challenging decisions and people that confront a leader make it quite easy to embrace this idol.

What hard family or leadership decisions do you need to make that you have been avoiding because of your desire to be comfortable?

_____

_____

Idolatry Unmasked

Idols do not come one-size-fits-all. They vary according to people based on their personalities, life history, or sin tendencies. Not only that, but idols can change at different seasons of life. For example, a disciple may struggle more with ministry idolatry at an early age and comfort idolatry later in life. One word of caution: Idols will harden with age. They function like cement. If they are not leveled early in life, they will require a jackhammer to dislodge later in life. Finally, idols may vary according to the context in which a person is serving. A large, megachurch ministry may fan the flames of performance idolatry, whereas a rural church context may foster family idolatry. The multifaceted nature of idolatry means that one must consistently be on the offensive.

So, what questions might you ask yourself consistently to diagnose your idols? Lane and Tripp, in their book, *How People Change*, provide a helpful list of x-ray questions, which they believe help to get to the heart of idolatry.[1] Look over the list and compile your own top ten questions that would be helpful in seeing whether or not you were worshiping things other than God.

1. _____

2. _____

3. _____

4. _____

5. _____

6. _____

7. _____

8. _____

9. _____

10. _____

---

1. Lane and Tripp, *People*, 163–65.

What person should have access to these questions and ask them to you on a regular basis?

_____

_____

Share the list with your *Aspire* mentor this week as you meet. Ask him to hold you accountable to growth in these areas and seek to allow worship to explode idolatry from your life.

Week 4: Character

"Therefore, God's chosen ones, holy and loved, put on heartfelt compassion, kindness, humility, gentleness, and patience."

—*Colossians 3:12*

"My iniquities are great and numberless, but thou art adequate to my relief, for thou art rich in mercy; The blood of thy Son can cleanse from all sin; The agency of thy Spirit can subdue my most powerful lusts."[1]

—*The Valley of Vision*

The formation of a disciple is an inside-out process.

Transformation is a work of God applied to the heart of His children. There is no way to short-cut the hard work required to allow the good news of the gospel to progressively change your life. This work is also quite dangerous because the heart is wicked and deceitful. Thus, the extent of your sinful depravity will be exposed when you begin an exploration of your heart.

Several years ago, I led a youth mission trip to a coastal region to work with a partner church plant. One of our assignments was to serve a local park by cleaning up debris on the nearby playground. The students went about this task with all the energy that a middle-schooler can muster. However, with every successive attempt to scrape up and remove cigarette butts, broken beer bottles, and candy wrappers, another layer of filth was exposed. After some time, and seemingly little progress, I went and asked the park director if we were doing something wrong since it seemed as if we were never going to finish the work. It was then that she told me the news—the playground had been built over an abandoned landfill. No wonder we weren't making any progress.

Heart change has much in common with this local park. The layers of sinful filth that have built around your heart over years of rebellion will not be unearthed quickly. And every time you think you are making progress, it will often only expose another issue

---

1. Arthur Bennett, ed. *The Valley of Vision: A Collection of Puritan Prayers and Devotions* (East Peoria, IL: The Banner of Truth Trust, 1975), 109.

that needs to be addressed. Do not lose heart. This is a reality for all sinners who are being transformed by the gospel. Heart change is a requirement for leadership fruitfulness, however.

What have you learned about your heart as you have begun to explore the gospel through *Aspire*?

_____

_____

What is the heart according to the Scriptures? What happens there and why does that matter? What Scripture would you use to support your ideas?

_____

_____

The heart is difficult to assess because it is hidden from view. Others can't see your heart, and because of hypocrisy and blind spots in your own life, it is difficult for you to see and understand your heart rightly either. Thankfully, the Scriptures provide a tool for heart diagnostics. Last week, we considered the necessity of disciples to locate, expose, and remove idolatry at every turn. This week we will consider the positive character that should take its place. In the Old Testament, such righteous life was seen in a person who walked in the ways of the Lord. In the New Testament, as we have seen, such a holy life is demonstrated by godly fruit. This fruit is the external demonstration of a life of worship. Jesus says:

> *Beware of false prophets who come to you in sheep's clothing but inwardly are ravaging wolves. You'll recognize them by their fruit. Are grapes gathered from thornbushes or figs from thistles? In the same way, every good tree produces good fruit, but a bad tree produces bad fruit. A good tree can't produce bad fruit; neither can a bad tree produce good fruit. Every tree that doesn't produce good fruit is cut down and thrown into the fire. So you'll recognize them by their fruit (Mt 7:15–20).*

The Bible is filled with examples of fruit that should be evident in the life of a disciple and leader. Jesus' most famous sermon, the Sermon on the Mount recorded in

Matthew 5–7, contrasts the righteous living of a pious Israelite with the life of a disciple. Here He does not abrogate the law—He deepens it.

Read Matthew 5–7 and note the characteristics that God expects from His people.

_____

_____

_____

_____

Rather than simply avoiding murder, His people are to avoid anger. Rather than not committing adultery, His people are to avoid lust. Certainly this high standard should reveal that all people are incapable of keeping the commandments of God. That is why we all need Jesus. The marks of a godly life serve as a mirror, consistently revealing our need for the gift of righteousness provided by Jesus (Rom 3:19; Js 1:22–25).

Such standards should not render us passive, however. Grace propels obedience; it does not make obedience obsolete. Paul knows that a proper teaching of the gospel will draw the ire of religious legalists. They would think that since God had freely forgiven sins (past, present, and future) apart from works then people would live a licentious life. He argues that this should not be: "What should we say then? Should we continue to sin so that grace may multiply? Absolutely not! How can we who died to sin still live in it (Rom 6:1–2)?"

Peter helps us see the role that our obedience should play. He writes:

> _For this very reason, make every effort to supplement your faith with goodness, goodness with knowledge, knowledge with self-control, self-control with endurance, endurance with godliness, godliness with brotherly affection, and brotherly affection with love. For if these qualities are yours and are increasing, they will keep you from being useless or unfruitful in the knowledge of our Lord Jesus Christ (2 Pet 1:5–8)._

Why should Christians strive to obey God based on this passage?

_____

_____

Worship is the motive for obedience. You obey—not because you have to but because you get to. Grace propels obedience from your life. And this keeps you from being useless and unfruitful in the good work that God has prepared in advance for you to do (Eph 1:10). All the while, God's grace is still playing a vital role. The Spirit is at work to do for you and in you what you cannot do on your own. As He does, Paul writes, Godly fruit will begin to develop in your life to take the place of the rotten, corrupt fruit of your former self.

> *But the fruit of the Spirit is love, joy, peace, patience, kindness, goodness, faith, gentleness, self-control. Against such things there is no law (Gal 5:22–23).*

Here Paul provides a list of the types of fruit that should be seen in the life of a person indwelt by His Spirit. As we have seen, these traits are not ways of meriting God's favor; however, they are a response to the favor that God has already granted through Christ. These marks are not that of super-spiritual leaders, but should define all disciples of Jesus. However, if a leader is not producing these fruits in abundance, then he is certainly unqualified to lead in the church. Consider the following definitions of the traits found on this list:

- **Love:** A life of sacrificial service to God and all people modeled after the servanthood of Jesus

- **Joy:** A life of delight in God and hopeful optimism rooted in the finished victory of Christ

- **Peace:** A life of trust and confidence in the wisdom and care of God

- **Patience:** A life of humble perseverance through trials and adversity

- **Kindness:** A life marked by genuine benevolence towards others in word and in deed

- **Goodness:** A life characterized by moral uprightness

- **Faithfulness:** A life defined by the keeping of promises

- **Gentleness:** A life of care towards others

- **Self-Control:** A life free of excess

Two things are worth noting here. First, these traits are fruits *of the Spirit* and not simply fruits of religious behavior. They are the outcome of the Spirit's work in your life. Secondly, the list, in its totality, is the *fruit* (singular) of the Spirit. This is not a pick-and-choose list, as if you can have love and kindness, but not gentleness and self-control. Instead, a worshipper of God should see the fruit as a mark of a righteous life.

How are the fruit of the Spirit seen in your life currently?

_____

_____

Which of these fruit are more apparent in your life right now? Which are lacking?

_____

_____

What happens if someone is placed into leadership in the church who is not growing in exemplifying the fruit of the Spirit?

_____

_____

The fruit of the Spirit provides a way for you to assess your heart. Additionally, in two places in the Pastoral Epistles Paul provides a list for those who qualify for the office of deacon or pastor in the church. These qualifications are not a linear progression, as if one grows the fruit of the Spirit, then moves on to develop the fruit of a deacon and then on to the fruit of an elder.

Whether you are a new Christian, a small group leader, or a future pastor, these lists provide a valuable diagnostic tool for your growth and conformity to the image of Christ. The lists, as we will see, are not unique to the office of pastor, but are the expected marks of a disciple of Jesus. For example, Paul writes that pastors must not be addicted to much wine. This does not mean that all Christians have free reign to be drunkards. Rather, all Christians are to avoid addiction to wine, and pastors are to lead the way. Thus, these lists should be seen as marks of all Christians, and pastors should be seen as exemplary in each of these areas.

Space does not permit a thorough explanation of each of these Biblical offices, nor is that the desire of *Aspire*. Use the reading list provided at the end of this trimester to dig deeper into the marks of elders and deacons. Let's briefly look at the qualification lists for the lead servants in the church—the deacons. Paul writes:

> *Deacons, likewise, should be worthy of respect, not hypocritical, not drinking a lot of wine, not greedy for money, holding the mystery of the faith with a clear conscience. And they must also be tested first; if they prove blameless, then they can serve as deacons. Wives, too, must be worthy of respect, not slanderers, self-controlled, faithful in everything. Deacons must be husbands of one wife, managing their children and their own households competently. For those who have served well as deacons acquire a good standing for themselves, and great boldness in the faith that is in Christ Jesus (1 Tim 3:18–15).*

A number of new character qualities emerge from this list that should mark a servant in God's church. The list includes some fruits to avoid and some to pursue. Paul mentions three things that should be avoided and would serve to disqualify a potential leader:

- **Dishonest Speech:** A servant-leader needs to say what he means and do what he says and not lack integrity or purity in conversation.

- **Addiction to Wine:** A servant-leader must avoid addictive behavior and demonstrate an ability to control his passions and pursuits.

- **Greed or Dishonest Gain:** A servant-leader must avoid a worldly pursuit of fame, privilege, position, power, or possessions and learn to be satisfied by God and God alone.

Additionally, Paul writes of a number of things that should be pursued by a leader:

- **A Dignified and Blameless Life:** A servant-leader's public and private life should be exemplary in Christian virtue and conduct. He should be the type of person that can say, "follow me as I follow Christ," and do so with integrity.

- **A Clear Affirmation of the Faith:** A servant-leader should know the gospel and be able to personally affirm and appropriate it to his life.

- **An Honorable Marriage and Family:** A servant-leader should demonstrate the fruit of the Spirit in his home through loving service and discipleship. Such careful leadership of one's home provides a model of the type of leadership that God desires for His church.

The list also places a high value on the person's family. This is not the place to discuss whether Paul intends the list to include a discussion of the wives of deacons or of female deacons. If the list is meant to include qualifications for the wives of deacons, then it certainly highlights the role one's wife plays in serving the church. However, even if the list is in reference to female deacons, it is still clear that Paul places a high value on the faithfulness of the leader to his marriage, and his care and management of his home.

How is marriage and parenting a healthy diagnostic tool for the life of a leader?

_____

_____

This list provides a valuable tool for assessing one's growth and maturity as a follower of Jesus. In contrast to the fruit of the Spirit, this list is measurable. One can ask, "Am I addicted to much wine?" more readily than "Does my life demonstrate joy?" These concrete metrics allow for internal and external assessment for the leader.

Your journey through *Aspire*, particularly your personal mentorship, is providing your church with the tools necessary to assess your character and gifting.

What do you think your church is observing as they watch your life?

_____

_____

So, give it a shot. Rank yourself on the following characteristics on a scale of 1 to 5, with 1 being an indication that you DO NOT exemplify that characteristic and 5 being an indication that you excel in that area. Try to be honest with yourself and allow the Scriptures to expose your heart through this process.

Dignified

1   2   3   4   5

Not Double-tongued

(Here a 1 would mean that you are double-tongued,
a 5 would mean that you are not double-tongued)

1   2   3   4   5

Not addicted to much wine, self-controlled

1   2   3   4   5

Not greedy for dishonest gain

1   2   3   4   5

Holding the mystery of the faith with a clear conscious

1   2   3   4   5

Tested

1   2   3   4   5

Blameless

1   2   3   4   5

Wives who are dignified, not slanderers, but sober minded, faithful in all things

1   2   3   4   5

Faithfulness to one's spouse

1   2   3   4   5

Managing household well

1   2   3   4   5

Once you have assessed yourself, provide the scale to someone with whom you are close (your wife, the person you're dating, or best friend) and to your mentor. Ask them to rank you on the same scale and then discuss their assessment together.

What did you learn about yourself from the assessment of someone close to you?

_____

_____

What did you learn about yourself from the assessment of your mentor?

_____

_____

There is one final list that is helpful in assessing the character of a disciple. Paul provides a list of qualifications for those who aspire to the office of pastor/elder/overseer in the church. Men who aspire to lead, and are planning to journey on toward pastoral ministry or church planting should reflect on the following two lists provided by the apostle Paul:

> *This saying is trustworthy: "If anyone aspires to be an overseer, he desires a noble work." An overseer, therefore, must be above reproach, the husband of one wife, self-controlled, sensible, respectable, hospitable, an able teacher, not addicted to wine, not a bully but gentle, not quarrelsome, not greedy—one who manages his own household competently, having his children under control with all dignity. (If anyone does not know how to manage his own household, how will he take care of God's church?) He must not be a new convert, or he might become conceited and fall into the condemnation of the Devil. Furthermore, he must have a good*

reputation among outsiders, so that he does not fall into disgrace and the Devil's trap (1 Tim 3:1–7).

The reason I left you in Crete was to set right what was left undone and, as I directed you, to appoint elders in every town: one who is blameless, the husband of one wife, having faithful children not accused of wildness or rebellion. For an overseer, as God's administrator, must be blameless, not arrogant, not hot-tempered, not addicted to wine, not a bully, not greedy for money, but hospitable, loving what is good, sensible, righteous, holy, self-controlled, holding to the faithful message as taught, so that he will be able both to encourage with sound teaching and to refute those who contradict it (Titus 1:5–9).

Two new factors emerge from this list:

- **Able to Teach:** A pastor must be able to communicate the truth of the Scriptures and refute those who teach falsehood.

- **Above Reproach:** A pastor must demonstrate a life that is above reproach. This serves as an overarching, umbrella term for all of the fruits we have discussed in this lab. He must demonstrate consistent faithfulness (not perfection) in each of these areas and repent and fight for holiness when he falls short.

Consider these two areas and rank them below using the same scale:

Able to Teach

1   2   3   4   5

Above Reproach

1   2   3   4   5

Again, your close friends or your *Aspire* mentor will be helpful in this process. Ask them to rank you in the two areas above and assess yourself in light of these comments.

You may find that you end this week's workshop frustrated or discouraged. Looking at your heart will do this to you. This is why we have spent a vast amount of time assessing the contours of the gospel through *Aspire*. Were we to have started with this week's content, you would have been tempted to see discipleship and leadership in the church as something that you do. And, you would likely have begun the painful process of trying to bring yourself in conformity with the lists of behaviors above, thinking that if you just tried harder to be good then you would live a life that is pleasing to God. This is not the case. Discipleship isn't primarily something that you do—it is something that you are.

Look back at the dynamite provided in week 2. Where do you need to place dynamite in light of the fruit you have seen in your life this week?

_____

_____

Where is idolatry hindering fruit production in your life?

_____

_____

Praise God that, as Jonathan Edwards writes, "The saints' love to God is the fruit of God's love to them; it is the gift of that love."[1] The richness of the gospel is sufficient motivation to encourage you in your fight for holiness.

1. Jonathan Edwards, *Religoius Affections: A Christian's Character Before God* (Vancouver, BC: Regent College Publishing, 1984), 95.

Week 5: The Spirit

"But thank God that, although you used to be slaves of sin, you obeyed from the heart that pattern of teaching you were entrusted to, and having been liberated from sin, you became enslaved to righteousness."

—Romans 6:17–18

"You are constantly preaching to yourself some kind of gospel. You preach to yourself an anti-gospel of your own righteousness, power, and wisdom, or you preach to yourself the true gospel of deep spiritual need and sufficient grace."[1]

—Paul Tripp

The Spirit serves as the guide to a life of worship.

The gospel is so deep that it is impossible to "hit bottom." You will spend your life attempting to plumb the depths of the magnificent scope of the gospel announcement. Additionally, the process of transformation will not be complete this side of heaven. You will consistently see the residual effects of sin in your life and need to confront them with reckless abandon.

Thankfully, you are not left alone in this work. Transformation is made possible through the work of Christ and the application of the Holy Spirit. Sadly, the Spirit of God is the most neglected person of the Godhead and also one of the most underestimated catalysts for gospel transformation. We have already seen that the fruit of the Christian life is produced by the Spirit (Gal 5:22–23). But how does this process work, and what is the Spirit's role?

---

1. Paul David Tripp, *Dangeorus Calling: Confronting the Unique Challenges of Pastoral Ministry* (Wheaton: Crosway, 2012), 21.

Consider the way that Jesus speaks of the Spirit in the gospel of John:

> *But the Counselor, the Holy Spirit—the Father will send Him in My name—will teach you all things and remind you of everything I have told you (Jn 14:26).*
>
> *When the Counselor comes, the One I will send to you from the Father—the Spirit of truth who proceeds from the Father—He will testify about Me (Jn 15:26).*
>
> *I still have many things to tell you, but you can't bear them now. When the Spirit of truth comes, He will guide you into all the truth. For He will not speak on His own, but He will speak whatever He hears. He will also declare to you what is to come. He will glorify Me, because He will take from what is Mine and declare it to you. Everything the Father has is Mine. This is why I told you that He takes from what is Mine and will declare it to you (Jn 16:12–15).*

What does Jesus say that the Spirit will do in these verses?

_____

_____

The Spirit is a valued companion in the process and is appointed by the Father to make much of Jesus. The Sprit is the main worship leader for the church. Paul gives two explicit commands to the Christian in terms of his relationship with God's Spirit.

Command 1: And don't grieve God's Holy Spirit. You were sealed by Him for the day of redemption (Eph 4:30).

You grieve the Spirit when you allow indwelling sin to fester and grow. Such a life, marked by unrepentant rebellion, is sure to hinder the work of the Spirit in producing worship.

Are you currently grieving God's Spirit by tolerating known sin in your heart?

_____

_____

Command 2: Don't stifle the Spirit (1 Thess 5:1

Stifling the Spirit happens when a believer cuts himself o' means of the Spirit's work. We are all prone to forget the g disciplines to aid in our remembering. Think of it like a Spirit is flowing through the hose, and the Christian ' kinks in the hose. Transformation will result if the water flows .. of common places where kinks in the hose are likely to appear:

Scripture Intake

The Spirit flows through God's Word. Thus, a Christian desiring to be transformed by the gospel must consistently feast on the Word of God. Even in seasons of spiritual drought, you must allow God's Word to flood your heart and mind on a regular basis. As we have already seen in the book of John, the Spirit is called the Spirit of truth and is the one who leads people to discern God's word (1 Cor 2:13).

The process of Scripture intake is aided by the development of a simple hermeneutic (Bible study tool) that you can use to discern God's intended meaning from any passage of Scripture. One such example is provided below. It asks you to consider seven directions, or arrows, to which each Scripture points. This process can be applied to any passage of Scripture and aid you in discerning God's voice through His Word.

Arrow 1: What does this passage say?

Start by summarizing the central meaning of the text in one sentence. What is the main point of the text? Consider a headline in your local paper. The story may share numerous quotations, stories, or illustrations, yet there is one main point (i.e. Residents need to be aware of a proposed tax increase that will be voted on in three weeks). This is true for the Bible as well. There may be many subpoints or illustrations, but each passage has a headline or main point.

What does this passage mean to its original audience?

Then, ask what the text meant to the original audience. Clearly the first hearers or readers of the passage had a far different cultural context than do modern readers. However, a text of the Bible cannot mean what it never meant. If we hope to arrive at the meaning of the text, we must first ask why the author wrote the passage in the first place. To answer this question you may need to consult a commentary or online resource. Ask your pastor for a recommendation of a good resource to help you discern the intended meaning of a text because not all commentaries are equal in terms of quality. Also, you can consult a study bible, such as the ESV Study Bible, for helpful introductions to books of the Bible and commentary throughout the text.

Arrow 3: What does this passage tell us about God?

Next, seek to discern what the text tells you about the nature and character of God and specifically His work through the person and work of Jesus Christ. For some texts, this is going to be clear, such as Paul's famous run-on sentence in Ephesians 1:4–13. This text gives clear descriptions of the person and work of Christ. Other passages will be more challenging, such as the Wisdom Literature found in books like Proverbs. As we have seen in *Aspire*, Jesus is the hero of every passage of the Scriptures so you can rest assured that there is always a path to Jesus.

Arrow 4: What does this passage tell us about man?

Continue by seeking to discover what the text reveals about the sin of mankind. Again, some passages will be clear, such as Jesus' Sermon on the Mount. There you will clearly be confronted by the fallenness of man in areas such as lust, anger, and worry. The Old Testament historical books will require a bit more work on your part. You will have to ask yourself hard questions about how God's people provide a prototype for the sin of all humanity.

Arrow 5: What does this passage demand of me?

Now that you are rooted in the meaning of the text, you are positioned to rightly apply its meaning to your life. Arrows 3 and 4 provide a basis for your application. You can be rest assured that God's character does not change, so whatever you see of Him in the passage will be true for you as well. Additionally, the sin of mankind doesn't change so you can see your own sin in every passage of Scripture. Based on these realities, ask what form obedience to the passage would take.

Arrow 6: How does this passage change the way I relate to people?

Specifically focus on the way in which the text encourages you to love other people. Throughout *Aspire*, we have sought to demonstrate that the gospel is corporate by its very nature. As a result, every passage of Scripture is going to provide a corporate application. Ask how the passage shapes your love for your church, your family, and non-believers.

Arrow 7: How does this passage prompt me to pray?

Finally, allow the text to kindle the fire of prayer in your heart. Praying the Scriptures back to God is one of the primary ways that you can pray in line with God's promises and purposes. The truths of the Scripture you have found using the first 6 arrows should remind you of needs for which to pray. For example, if you just read a passage from Matthew 19 where Jesus discusses divorce and remarriage, then you should take time to pray for your own marriage or the health of the marriages of other people in your church family.

These arrows can help you grow in your confidence to read and understand God's word. Apply the seven arrows of Bible reading to Matthew 6:25–34. Write out your thoughts below to share with your mentor this week:

Arrow 1: _____

_____

Arrow 2: _____

_____

Arrow 3: _____

_____

Arrow 4: _____

_____

Arrow 5: _____

_____

Arrow 6: _____

_____

Arrow 7: _____

_____

What did you find helpful about the process? How can you apply this tool to aid in your Scripture intake on a daily basis?

_____

_____

A growing disciple of Jesus should meet with God in His Word every day (Phil 3:8–10; Mt 22:37–38; Prov 15:8; Ps 119:105; Rom 12:2). This is not something that you have to do, but rather something that you get to do. It is a stunningly beautiful reality that the sovereign God of the universe would want to spend time with people like you and me. You should set aside a time each day where you can spend time reading and reflecting on God's Word. This time should be free from distractions and set apart for God. It should also be the best part of your day, and not the time in which you know that you will be weary and unable to focus.

When would be the best time during your day for you to begin spending consistent time with God? It may be a good idea to start with a short time each day and seek to grow from there (for example, 15 minutes).

_____

_____

Prayer

A relationship with God grows in intimacy the same way every relationship does—through ongoing conversation. Take away the process of talking and listening, and the relationship will not grow, much less lead to transformation. Thankfully, the Spirit is an aid in prayer. As Paul says in Romans 8:26, "In the same way the Spirit also joins to help in our weakness, because we do not know what to pray for as we should, but the Spirit Himself intercedes for us with unspoken groanings."

Prayer does not just happen. You must be intentional and allocate time to develop a thriving prayer life. Such a practice will be one of the greatest joys of your Christian life and one of the most effective means of leading people in the church.

Daily prayers should include an affirmation of the nature and character of God, a reflection on the truths of His Word, a personal admission of sin and need for the gospel, and prayers of hope for God's transformative work in your own life. In addition, you should seek to find a rhythm of intentional, intercessory prayers for others.

How is your current prayer life? What hinders your prayers?

_____

_____

Your prayer life will be enhanced if you take the time to write them in some type of journal. You will be thankful if you do. Write down the needs, the dates, and the evidences of God's grace that you see as you pray. When you finish one journal, file it away and continue in another one. This legacy of prayer will be a lifelong testimony to God's faithfulness in your life and will serve as a great testimony to your friends and family.

Community: A third means of transformation that is forged by the Spirit is that of Biblical community. Paul affirms that Christians are united in one body and one Spirit in the family of God (Eph 4:4–6). Thus, others who are engaging God through Scripture and prayer are in a position to be a conduit of grace to your life as well. This is a welcomed tool, since everyone is susceptible to blind spots in their battle with sin and need the encouragement that comes through their brothers or sisters in Christ. At times, prayer and Scripture reading may be masked by the residue of sin, thus it takes someone from the outside to point out those things that are obvious to everyone. Change is a community project undertaken in the context of the church.

Growing disciples are often guilty of isolating themselves from genuine community. This may be the result of their being ashamed of their sin or fearful of others' perceptions.

As a result, they often have a steady string of casual relationships while maintaining a safe distance from the depth of relationship necessary for true life change to result.

You must be intentional to personally counter this individualistic temptation as you grow as a leader in the church. Consider who currently fills the following roles in your life.

- A Mentor (a person you aspire to be like)

  _____

- A Friend (a trusted confidant and fellow life-traveler)

  _____

- A Disciple (a protégé that you have taken spiritual responsibility for)

  _____

- A Community (a group of diverse people with whom you are living on mission)

  _____

You should work to make sure you have someone in each of those roles *within* the local church of which you are a member. Technological advances have made it possible for many to claim that they have these relationships with people who live hundreds of miles away. While this may be a reality, the type of relationship that you can have with someone via phone, email, or Skype is always significantly less than you could have with a person in your local church context. Often, the amount of time that is spent on developing technological relationships mitigates the development of local relationships. There is no substitute for having these roles filled by people in your local church who are sitting under the same elders, teaching, and local church mission.

Now, think through how you can assist those that you love in doing the same. Start with your spouse (if you are married). If not, substitute someone you are dating or a close friend. Do they have someone in each of those blanks? What can you do to assist them in finding community to aid in their transformation?

Mission

The last means of transformation made possible by the Spirit is that of mission. The sending of the promised Spirit was meant to power "witnesses in Jerusalem, in all Judea and Samaria, and to the ends of the earth (Acts 1:8)." The Spirit powers mission to the ends of the earth, and it is in this mission that God works to transform the heart. God transforms people *in* mission not *before* mission. Thus, a steady regimen of humble, servant-hearted mission is essential to lasting change. The entirety of trimester 3 of *Aspire* will focus on your personal mission, but for now it is sufficient to note that a life of mission requires:

- Meaningful relationships with non-believers in your personal circle of relationships;

- Intentional service to recognized needs in and through those relationships;

- Outspoken witness to the person and work of Jesus Christ;

- Thoughtful stewardship of time, treasures, and talents to make this service possible.

Where are you regularly living on mission?

_____

_____

Transformation will be produced slowly and progressively by the Spirit in the crockpot of life, using the ingredients of Scripture, prayer, community and mission. As Paul writes, "We all, with unveiled faces, are looking as in a mirror at the glory of the Lord and are being transformed into the same image from glory to glory; this is from the Lord who is the Spirit (2 Cor 3:18)." The Spirit will use these means of grace to produce transformation that far exceeds anything you could do alone.

Week 6: Discipleship

"If you love Me, you will keep My commandments."

—John 14:15

"Consumption is detrimental to discipleship."[1]

—Alan Hirsch

Discipleship is simply the act of walking with another person as they learn to apply the gospel to their lives.

Disciples make disciples. Unless you are consistently applying the gospel to your own life and seeing transformation, it will be difficult if not impossible to serve others in this process. But, be encouraged, for the inverse is true as well. If you are consistently becoming a disciple yourself, it will become easier to disciple someone else. If God is truly transforming your heart, then you will long for him to do the same for others. Thankfully, you are well on your way to becoming a reproducing disciple-maker already. The work God is doing in your life can be a catalyst for the life change of others around you. Jesus set this agenda before all of His followers in His final and Great Commandment:

> *Then Jesus came near and said to them, 'All authority has been given to Me in heaven and on earth. Go, therefore, and make disciples of all nations, baptizing them in the name of the Father and of the Son and of the Holy Spirit, teaching them to observe everything I have commanded you. And remember, I am with you always, to the end of the age' (Mt 28:18–20).*

Jesus' disciples are commanded to do one main thing in this text—make other disciples. The means for such disciple-making is clear as well. They are to go, baptize, and teach others to follow Jesus. As the sovereign King, Jesus has the full authority to command them to do this and promises His presence will accompany them in this great work. The

---

1. Alan Hirsch, *The Forgotten Ways* (Grand Rapids: Brazos Press, 2006), 45.

mission cannot fail if the mission is to make disciples. This is the task that lies before you as a disciple in the church. At its most basic element, leadership in the church is the act of multiplying disciples. Nothing more and nothing less.

We need not over think this process. You have already seen this at work through the first trimester of *Aspire*, as you have been meeting with a mentor and learning to apply these truths to your life. Now it's your turn.

If you do not invest in the work of discipleship, you will become spiritually stagnant. You simply cannot continue to consume the meat of the gospel without applying it to others. Think about your physical body. If all you do is eat, you will grow lethargic and obese. You have to give yourself to work in order not to grow sedentary.

The same is true in your spiritual life. If all you do is consume, you will become spiritually obese, stagnant, and prideful. Do not wait until you have it all figured out to begin the process of discipling other people. Start now.

How would you define a disciple of Jesus?

_____

_____

How would you measure the progress of yourself or another person in discipleship?

_____

_____

A proper Biblical definition should include both salvation and sanctification. Discipleship is the total process by which people move from being dead in their trespasses and sins to being fully conformed to the image of Jesus. Clearly, God is responsible for this process. He saves. He brings life from death. He sanctifies. And, He perfectly glorifies people into His image.

Yet, we all have a role to play. We are responsible for applying the God-given means of transformation to our lives, as we saw in session 5, and the lives of others—Scripture, prayer, relationship, and mission. So, now that you know how to apply these tools to your own life, let's consider how you might apply them to the life of someone else.

Scripture

Find someone in your relationship network and ask him or her to meet with you regularly in order to read the Bible together. Each week, both people in the discipleship relationship should agree to read the text together and be prepared to discuss it. There is no set length for reading, but three options seem advisable:

- Read from major heading to the next major heading (i.e. the prologue of John: 1:1–18);

- Read one chapter (Genesis 1);

- Read an entire book (The book of Ephesians).

The approach may depend on the people involved, or you may find it best to vary the length. Perhaps read through a Pauline epistle at a slower pace (major header to next major header) and a gospel at a faster pace (chapter by chapter or book by book).

Warning: Do not read topically. This is confusing to new believers and is unhelpful in developing a holistic framework for the Scriptures. Rather than looking up all the verses on a topic and discussing them, select a book of Scripture and discuss the topics that you find in the book you are reading. You will be amazed at how God's Spirit selects and applies the needed Scriptures at the right times.

This does not mean that you should not be wise in your choice of book to study. Think through the main themes of the Scriptures, and pick a book that best fits the needs of the person you are discipling. For example, what book might be wise to study with:

- A non-Christian struggling with whether or not he believes that Jesus is God;

  _____

  _____

- A young Christian living in a hard marriage;

  _____

  _____

- A non-Christian struggling to understand God's grace;

  _____

  _____

- A young Christian living in unrepentant sin with a weak view of God's judgment.

  _____

  _____

Once you have selected a book of the Bible to read, you can use the seven arrows provided in the last session to guide your reading together. Set up a time to make sure the other person has a copy of the arrows, and then use them to guide your discussion when you are together. Good discipleship is not simply a regurgitation of information, so don't enter each conversation with a truck-load of research and material. Simply read the Bible together, discuss the arrows, and allow the Spirit to guide you both into all truth.

Prayer

Transformation is a work of the Spirit. Applying the God-given means for discipleship will not produce lasting fruit in others unless it is accompanied by the Spirit's work. As a result, prayer is an essential component of the discipleship process. You should:

- Pray that God would transform your heart to make you fruitful in disciple-making.

- Pray that God would provide guidance in leading you to the person(s) that you are best suited to disciple.

- Pray that God would open meaningful avenues for you to enter into a discipleship relationship with those people.

- Pray that God would guide you both into a right understanding of the Scriptures that you are studying.

- Pray that God would pierce your hearts with the truth of the Scriptures and bring about transformation.

- Pray that you would repent and believe the gospel together.

- Pray that God would open your eyes to others in need of discipleship.

Record your prayers in the space below or in your journal. Discuss these prayers with your mentor this week and invite them to partner with you in these prayers.

_____

_____

The seven arrows Bible study tool provides a natural transition to prayer. The seventh arrow asks you to consider how the text in question that week prompts you to pray. This will allow you and the person you are meeting with to learn to pray as a response to meeting with God through His Word. For example, if you are reading Matthew 6 with your discipleship partner, you might consider what things cause you to worry and ask God to expand your confidence in His sovereign care.

Relationship

Discipleship requires relationships. So, how do you find and enter into a disciple-making relationship? Since discipleship is a holistic process we need not distinguish between those who are already Christians and those who are not yet saved. Both are in need of discipleship.

Two types of people make prime candidates for disciple making:

1. Non-believers that live near you, work with you, or enjoy some of the same hobbies that you do: these people are in need of discipleship as a precursor to salvation. They need to see and understand the hope of the gospel message through your life. You will be surprised at how many people who do not claim faith in Jesus would be willing to meet with you regularly for the purpose of Bible reading and prayer. You might say to a co-worker—"Every day I use my

lunch break to read a passage of Scripture and think about its implications for my life. Would you be interested in joining me for lunch once a week to talk about the Bible together?"

2. Young and spiritually immature believers that are a part of your church community: these people need to see, understand, and apply the gospel message to their lives. Most of them, by virtue of their recent conversion, are hungry for the Word and waiting for someone to invite them into an intentional relationship.

Who are these people in your life? Put five potential names in each group.

	Group 1 (non-Christians)	Group 2 (young or immature Christians)
1		
2		
3		
4		
5		

Hint: If you find one of these columns more challenging to complete than the other, it may alert you to a deficiency in your life. If the non-Christian column is barren, then you are doing a poor job in building relationships with the lost. For this to change, you need to work to find ways of meeting them and engaging with their lives.

Think about the general circles of your life (work, school, home, play). How do those areas present opportunities for engagement with those far from Christ?

_____

_____

Do you need to change something about your life in order to meet some non-Christians? If so, consider the following suggestions:

- Leverage your hobbies and invite others to participate with you. For example, if you are a biker, go to city-wide events or rides that allow you to meet other bikers.

- Prayer-walk your neighborhood and map the homes of those you know and don't know.

- Host a party in your home for your neighbors. Use hospitality to develop lasting relationships.

- Find ways to serve those around you that seem to have needs. This may be through financial provision or simply by helping with a need (such as fixing a car, painting a fence, or providing a meal when a new baby is born in your neighborhood).

- Frequent the same stores and restaurants and get to know the employees.

- Do things in public that you could do in private. For example, if you have a choice between working out in your garage or joining a gym, it may be wise to join a gym simply to meet other people.

- Engage in church-wide mission events, keeping an eye out for those that you could personally form a relationship with.

What do you need to start doing in order to develop these relationships?

_____

_____

If you find that you have few young believers in that column, it likely means that you are doing a poor job building community in your local church. Every church, regardless of its size, presents a steady stream of immature Christians. Few of them have ever had anyone engage them in a strategic discipleship relationship. Here are some tips on connecting with some young believers in your church:

- Take time to stop and introduce yourself to people that you do not know.

- Use church-wide fellowship events to meet new people.

- Show hospitality to new people, either by inviting them out to lunch or to your home for dinner.

- Sit in new places when the church is gathered, and introduce yourself to those around you.

- Mix up your patterns at church. Go a different way in the halls and between events, attend a different class, or stand in a different place before or after the worship service.

- Listen for needs in your small groups or Sunday school classes. See if you hear of anyone that has a life story similar to yours or lives or works near you.

- Ask your pastors for the names of people in the church that they know are in need of a discipleship relationship.

What do you need to start doing in order to build these types of relationships?

_____

_____

Your list of both non-believers and fellow Christians should give you a pool of people to choose from for potential discipleship relationships. The most difficult part of the process often lies in the next step—simply inviting them to hang out. Don't over-think this process or make it more awkward than it needs to be. You are not inviting them into a life-long bond of friendship. You are simply inviting them to spend some time with you. At the outset, you should refrain from asking them into a long-term commitment. A simple time to get to know one another is all you need. This could be an invitation to lunch or coffee where you take the lead in asking them questions about their life story and share your own. You may want to talk with a couple of people to try and find a person who is willing to connect, whom you connect well with, and who is open to being discipled. Once you have met for a time or two, you could then ask if they would like to connect weekly and read some Scripture together and talk about life. It can be that causal.

Don't say: "After hearing your story I feel like I have many things I could teach you. Would you like to become my disciple and learn what it looks like to follow Jesus?"

Do say: "I am learning what it means to follow Jesus and would love to meet regularly to talk about what God is teaching us through His Word and how we can more faithfully live the life He desires for us."

Mission

The beauty of the combination of Scripture, prayer, and relationships is that they naturally lead to mission when rightly applied. To see this clearly, you will need a simple tool to aid in your understanding of the Scriptures. The seven arrows plan provided earlier in session 5 should provide you with a simple tool to discern the author's intent from any text of Scripture. Take this tool, or something like it, and use it for each week's reading.

Arrows 1–3 help you discern what the text says, what it meant, and what it tells you about God and fallen humanity. The final arrows (5–7) are meant to drive you toward application.

The Scriptures will present numerous ways that non-Christians and young believers need to change in light of the gospel. Obviously, the most basic change needed for a non-Christian is the change wrought by God's Spirit. They need to repent and believe the gospel. For young Christians, the changes are countless. Whatever the text demands should be the application for the person in question (and the discipler for that matter). Thus, if the text discusses worry, then you should spend your time applying the gospel to the area of worry. If it talks about money, then apply transformation to the area of finances. If it is about marriage, then apply the gospel there. This process works for any and every passage of Scripture, though for some they may be a bit harder to see.

The two individuals currently meeting should ask whether there are other people in their circles of influence that they could invite into the group. This allows the process to continue to grow. Over time, a person can branch off and form a new discipleship relationship with another non-believer or young Christian.

Warning: Don't try to disciple more than two people at the same time. You will spread yourself too thin, and the personalization will break down.

Who are you currently discipling? How is it going? What evidences of God's grace are you observing?

_____

_____

Where do you find yourself frustrated?

_____

_____

The process of discipleship allows the gospel to work *in* and *out* of your life. This is why it is vital. You will see yourself transforming as you walk through this process with others. It will also protect you from becoming puffed up with spiritual pride. The work of disciple-making is hard work and will be an additional tool that God will use to expose your idolatry and prompt you to worship.

Week 7: Gifting

"Based on the gift each one has received, use it to serve others, as good managers of the varied grace of God."

—*1 Peter 4:10*

"Creation is not something that, once made, remains a stale quality. There is, as it were, a growing up (though not in a biological sense), an unfolding of creation. This takes place through the task that people have been given of bringing to fruition the possibilities of development implicit in the work of God's hands…We are called to participate in the ongoing creational work of God, to be God's helper in executing to the end the blueprint of his masterpiece."[1]

God is a gift-giver.

So, how does all of this talk of worship, idolatry, and disciple-making help you serve the church? Simply put—it is the most important thing you can do in the church. Forget the big stage, popular books, and conference speaking engagements. If you are not a disciple and you don't know how to make other disciples, you will not be an effective leader in God's church. But, if you can do those things, you are well on your way to a fruitful ministry, regardless of the exact form that leadership calling takes.

Be encouraged. You are developing the primary tools that shape all effective Christian leaders. In many ways, *Aspire* is the journey I wish I had taken. God saved me at 20, and within 9 months I was on my first church staff (not a good idea for them or for me). I had no clue what I was doing. So, I tried to mimic the godly leaders I observed in the culture, without truly learning to apply the gospel to my own walk with Jesus. At that point, I would have loved someone to take me through a systematic process of growth as a disciple of Jesus. Instead, I tried to figure it out on my own.

By God's grace, this does not have to be your experience. You are learning how to grow as a disciple, and as you do God will provide you ample opportunities to grow in serving the church, maturing as a disciple, and teaching others to do the same. Over

---

1. Wolters, *Regained*, 43–44.

time, you will find that God has uniquely gifted you in certain ways that are needed for the building up of the church.

Your gifting is often defined in and through the work of disciple-making. God clarifies your own gifting as the Spirit transforms you into a disciple and you play a role in helping other people move towards intimacy with God. Discernment of the Spirit's gifting need not be a mystical process or the logical outcome of a spiritual gift inventory. Two things are clear from the outset:

THAT You are Gifted

The essence of salvation is to receive a gift. You have been given the gift of salvation. You have been given the gift of the Spirit. You have been made a part of the church. All of this is from God, who serves as the giver of all that is good and perfect.

You have also been given gifts by the Spirit. Paul writes to the church at Corinth:

> A demonstration of the Spirit is given to each person to produce what is beneficial: to one is given a message of wisdom through the Spirit, to another, a message of knowledge by the same Spirit, to another, faith by the same Spirit, to another, gifts of healing by the one Spirit, to another, the performing of miracles, to another, prophecy, to another, distinguishing between spirits, to another, different kinds of languages, to another, interpretation of languages. But one and the same Spirit is active in all these, distributing to each person as He wills (1 Cor 12:7–11).

God's Spirit gives good gifts to God's people. How amazing is that? The sovereign God of the universe not only saves you, but also equips you with unique and personalized gifts that serve His community of reclaimed worshippers. Since this is true, it is vital that you learn how you are gifted and steward that gift in order to produce the maximum amount of fruit.

WHY You are Gifted

The Scriptures are also clear on the outcome of the gifts of the Spirit. They are not for you, but rather, Paul says:

> *And He personally gave some to be apostles, some prophets, some evangelists, some pastors and teachers, for the training of the saints in the work of ministry, to build up the body of Christ, until we all reach unity in the faith and in the knowledge of God's Son, growing into a mature man with a stature measured by Christ's fullness. Then we will no longer be little children, tossed by the waves and blown around by every wind of teaching, by human cunning with cleverness in the techniques of deceit. But speaking the truth in love, let us grow in every way into Him who is the head—Christ. From Him the whole body, fitted and knit together by every supporting ligament, promotes the growth of the body for building up itself in love by the proper working of each individual part (Eph 4:11–16).*

There we see it quite clearly. God gives the church leaders the task of equipping the saints to do the work of ministry so that they too (and not simply the pastors) cause the church to grow. In context, this growth refers to the process of conforming to the image of Christ, such that we increasingly reflect his image to the world. All reclaimed worshippers are to invest their lives in the task of causing others in the church to grow.

So, whatever gifts the Spirit has given, and He has certainly given you something, are to be used to make disciples who more and more perfectly conform to the image of Christ. Now that we have a foundation for gifting, let's consider how you are gifted.

HOW You have been Gifted

Unfortunately, discerning one's giftedness is often only sought through objective tools like Spiritual gift inventories. These tools, and other leadership surveys, are helpful for systematizing the various giftings that the Scripture mentions. However, it is clear that the discussions of gifting in the Scripture do not mention every gift, nor do they provide a conclusive method for determining which gift you may possess. Discernment happens through a lengthy process of prayer and seeking. Let's think about gifting as four intersecting circles, which are each vital for determining your specific ministry fingerprint.

Warning: the terrain ahead is going to require a good bit of introspection on your part. So, find a quiet place to pray and process each of these four circles.

Circle 1: Your Imago Dei

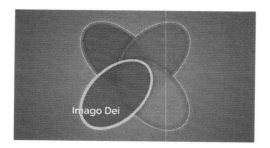

Creation is the place to start for understanding the Spirit's gifting. Your very existence is a gift of grace, and with it comes certain factors that God has uniquely and specifically determined. For example, the time and location of your life will radically shape the way that you are used to make disciples. In Acts 17:26, Paul says that "He made from one, every nation of mankind to live on all the face of the earth, having determined their appointed times, and the boundaries of their habitation." Therefore, God sovereignly places mankind and their cultures on the earth at specific seasons and at specific times for reasons we may not fully know.

The fact that you live during a time of fast global expansion may make it possible for you to use your gifts as a mission worker among an unreached people group that would have been impossible to engage 200 years ago. Additionally, God has knit you together in some specific ways that will shape the life you live: your gender, your personality, and your health will all be tools that God uses. The wonderful words of the Psalmist ring true in this discussion:

> *For it was You who created my inward parts; You knit me together in my mother's womb. I will praise You because I have been remarkably and wonderfully made. Your works are wonderful, and I know this very well. My bones were not hidden from You when I was made in secret, when I was formed in the depths of the earth. Your eyes saw me when I was formless; all my days were written in Your book and planned before a single one of them began (Ps 139:13–16).*

Clearly, you had no choice over where or when you were born, your gender, your personality, or your health. God chose them for you. And God does not make mistakes. Certainly, there are life factors that will influence these, such as the changes in your personality that come from life experiences. And yet, many of them are hardwired from birth. Therefore, as we attempt to analyze the gifting of the Spirit, this is the place to start.

I remember early in my discipleship process being discouraged by the fact that I did not think my personality was well suited for being a pastor in a local church. I was quite introverted—a personality trait that did not seem to fit with pastoral ministry. Aren't pastors supposed to love being around people? I mean, that is all pastors do, right? They are constantly with people and all those that I observed seemed to love it. This all changed for me when I met my first introverted pastor. I asked a member of this man's congregation to tell me about their pastor and he replied, "Matt, he is the holiest man I know." Holiest man I know? I have heard pastors described in many ways—visionary leader, great preacher—but never holiest man I know. It turns out this man was right. This pastor was holy, and he was faithfully leading a local church with an introverted personality. God used this experience to confirm that it was okay to be me and that God could use the way in which He had built me to serve his church. He wanted me to be myself and not try to copy someone else.

- How does the time and place of your life shape the ways in which you can use your gifting?

  _____

  _____

- How does your gender, personality, and health shape how you are most useful in making disciples?

  _____

  _____

Circle 2: Your Life Experience

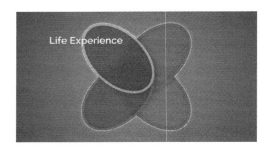

The progressive journey of life, defined by wounds, successes, loves, losses, pain, discouragement, and thousands of decisions, shapes your gifting as well. Some of these experiences are a natural byproduct of life in a fallen world, which create real and lasting wounds. Things like losing a parent, getting fired from a job, struggling with an ongoing sin habit, and a host of other issues shape the person one becomes.

In addition, God saves all people using the same means (the substitutionary death of Jesus) but not in the same way. Your pre-Christian experience with sin and rebellion shape your life today as does the process that God used to save you. And finally, the progressive work that He is doing in your life now is vital to shaping your gifts. We know that God "works out everything in agreement with the decision of His will (Eph 1:11; c.f. Ps 115:3)." Therefore, He has and is orchestrating all of the events and circumstances of your life, even those that are seemingly negative, to accomplish His perfect plan in and through your life (Gen 50:20).

For example, I have never had the experience of grieving a miscarriage or the loss of a child. This is not a part of the process that God has used to shape my life up to this point. For many it is, however. This experience allows those who have traveled this path to empathize with others and serve the church in a way that I will never be able to do myself.

Consider your life:

What are the top three negative life experiences that have shaped the person you are today? How have they changed you? Since God does not waste pain, how might these wounds be tools that are used to encourage or minister to others?

_____

_____

What are the top three positive life experiences that have shaped the person you are today? How have they changed you?

_____

_____

How does your life before Christ saved you shape the things that are important to you and that you are passionate about doing?

_____

_____

How does the process by which God saved you shape the things that are important to you and that you are passionate about doing?

_____

_____

How does the work God is currently doing in your life shape the things that are important to you and that you are passionate about doing?

_____

_____

Circle 3: Spirit-Gifting

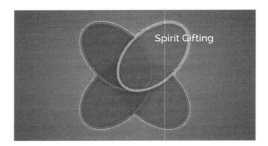

God reclaims worshippers and grants them gifts by His Spirit which are profitable for the building up of the church.

These gifts are mentioned in various places in the Bible, including Romans 12 and 1 Corinthians 12. Look up those passages, and consider whether any of the gifts listed there seem to match your understanding of how God has gifted you.

List the top three gifts that you observe in your life in the space provided below.

_____

_____

Additionally, these gifts can be found by asking a number of internal and external questions:

Internal

- What do you enjoy?

_____

_____

_____

- What would you do even if you would not get paid?

_____

_____

_____

- What areas do you find you most quickly "get in the zone"? Where does work come easily?

  _____

  _____

  _____

- Where are you intrinsically motivated to grow? What areas do you find yourself reading and thinking about most often?

  _____

  _____

  _____

External

- Where are you most fruitful? In what areas do you see clear evidence of God's blessing?

  _____

  _____

  _____

- What areas of ministry are hard or frustrating for you? What areas, even when you truly apply yourself, do you find most challenging?

  _____

  _____

  _____

- Where do people affirm you? What do people say, "Man, you are really good at…"

  _____

  _____

  _____

• What do your spiritual gift inventories say about you?

_____

_____

_____

The gift lists in the Bible provide a helpful place from which to consider your personal gifting. These lists do not include every way that a person may be gifted by the Spirit, but they certainly include some of the more common ways. If you are having trouble discerning your gifting from these lists, you may consider asking your pastor to provide you with a more objective spiritual gift inventory.

Circle 4: Resources

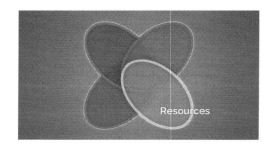

God provides resources to people in different measure. These resources, be they money, tangible gifts, or spare time serve as key ingredients in one's Kingdom investment. Most young leaders do not have ample financial resources, but some do. Those that do should begin to think through the best ways to put them in play for the Kingdom. At minimum, leaders should be faithful givers to their local church and generous givers to tangible needs as they arise.

Another resource is your leadership position itself. This is true whether you are currently serving as a pastor or staff member, leading a small group, or simply making disciples in the local church. Voids in leadership present a viable way for young and developing leaders to get their feet wet in local church ministry. This may mean leveraging a ministry staff position, or it could mean finding an avenue of fruitful service afforded you by your local church. Do not be idle or passive in this process. A healthy local church context is a great Kingdom resource. Find a function, and serve faithfully. Consider the following questions which may help you get in the game:

- Do you have financial resources that you are not investing in Kingdom purposes?

  _____

  _____

  _____

- Are you currently serving in a meaningful leadership role in your local church *that is stretching you to grow and mature?*

  _____

  _____

  _____

- What about your church frustrates you (trust me, it's okay to answer this question)? What can you do personally about the area of frustration? How could you engage to make things better?

  _____

  _____

  _____

Your Fingerprint

A leader's unique fingerprint for effective ministry is found at the intersection of his imago dei, life experience, Spirit gifting, and resources. This combination provides a more robust and holistic picture of the gifting of a leader because it recognizes that everything about you is a perfect gift "coming down from the Father of lights; with Him there is no variation or shadow cast by turning (James 1:17)."

What you do with that fingerprint is up to you. But, do not be deceived—what you do with that fingerprint is a big deal. Consider Jesus' words in Matthew 25:14–30. No, actually consider them. Take a minute to look them up. What do you observe about Jesus' story? How does this inform what you do with your gifting?

_____

_____

_____

Here the entrusting of talents cannot be compared to the message of the gospel; it is clear that the worth of the gospel does not change. Rather, Jesus says that the master entrusts different people with different talents and expects them to be utilized for the sake of his Kingdom. These talents are not meant for safekeeping (as the one talent guy quickly learns)—they are meant to be used to create a profit. In fact, God promises judgment based on how those gifts are used both in this life (more will be given) and in the next (joy). Sadly, these gifts are often neglected. Paul commands Timothy to avoid this trap when he writes, "Do not neglect the gift that is in you; it was given to you through prophecy, with the laying on of hands by the council of elders. (1 Tim 4:14)."

Consider the things that might hinder the utilization of God's good gifts.

Comparison
We wonder why God made us the way he did and led us on the path that he did. Interestingly, in Jesus' story, there is no distinction made between the five talent person and the two talent person. Both were faithful with what they had been given. Comparison follows from a heart of insecurity.

Can the same be said for you? Are you comfortable being who God made you? Is there a person that you admire too much? How are you tempted to compare yourself with others?

_____

_____

_____

Resentment

Resentment rears its ugly head whenever we undermine the gifting of other people. The temptation is to secretly harbor bitterness or anger toward others, rather than being thankful that God created them with good Kingdom abilities.

Is there someone toward whom you harbor anger or resentment? Why is this the case?

_____

_____

_____

Work

Discipleship, and leadership in particular, can mask your gifts. For one, many are deceived into thinking that their gifts are only useful within the church, so they do not put them in play in other contexts (such as work, school, home, etc.). Additionally, many of those working in churches today function and operate outside of their gifting a vast majority of the time. In other words, they spend most of their time doing things outside of the realm of their giftedness.

What about you? Is leadership in the church fanning the flame of your gifts or is it stifling them? What would need to change for you to serve within your gifting more often?

_____

_____

_____

Pride

Humanity's archenemy, pride, confronts disciples at every corner. Gifts are no exception. Ironically, gifts can often become an end in themselves, and leaders can lose sight of the Gift-Giver or the desired outcome of the gift's utilization. Subtly, we can come to believe that God must be quite thankful that He has us serving Him. This hyper-focusing on gifts can ultimately undermine their power by disconnecting them from their life source. Are there things that you are good at that have become idols for you?

Where is pride evident in your life?

_____

_____

_____

Fear

Some disciples fail to use their gifts out of fear. Sure, you want to believe that you are a great leader, teacher, and disciple-maker. But what happens if you actually try to do those things and then find out that you are not great at them (yet)? What happens if others find out that, in spite of your best efforts to hide it, you are pretty average in most every area? These questions create fear and the natural reaction is to do nothing—which is so much easier. Sadly, doing nothing is always worse than messing up. Where is fear currently keeping you on the sidelines?

Where is fear evident in your life? How is it keeping you from fruitful ministry?

_____

_____

_____

Frustration

Finally, disciples often fail to use their gifts out of frustration with themselves or their church. The curse means that all work will require sweat and toil, and the church is no different. As soon as you put your gift in play, get ready—it will be messy. You may find yourself frustrated by your church or fellow leaders, or you may simply grow frustrated at the magnitude of the challenge. You may grow paralyzed with discouragement or despair. However, while you can't do everything, you can, and must, do something.

Where is frustration evident in your life? How is it stifling the utilization of your giftedness?

_____

_____

_____

Gift utilization will test your understanding of the gospel. You will be tempted to give yourself a thumbs-up or thumbs-down based on how well you are doing at ministry. That's why you must beat the gospel into your head regularly. Your identity is fixed and secure. Your sin has been pardoned, and you are clothed in the righteousness of Christ —even if you blow it as a leader. Interestingly, in almost all cases where Scripture discusses the idea of stewardship, it is done in the context of the return of Christ and not in the outcome of a person's accomplishments. Since the time is short, we are told to invest what we have been given with great joy and intentionality now. The goal is to be faithful until the Master returns. With this in mind, service becomes an act of worship.

Week 8: Calling

*"I, therefore, the prisoner in the Lord, urge you to walk
worthy of the calling you have received."*

—*Ephesians 4:1*

"There is nothing more notable or glorious in the church than the ministry of the gospel."[1]

—*John Calvin*

Leaders are produced in the context of disciple-making.

We live in a world where a calling to leadership in the church is thought to be a mystical experience. Some people are called and some aren't. The reality is that every disciple of Jesus is called to be a leader in some fashion.

Most aspiring leaders are going to begin by articulating some type of calling to such a role. Typically, the statements will sound something like, "I just feel like God is calling me to be a leader," or "I don't know…It's just this sense I have that I should do something more for God." Often, once the spiritual veneer is peeled off of these answers, aspiring leaders are left without a clear understanding of what they mean when they say that they are "called" to lead. Some even struggle to articulate what they are actually called to do.

Try your hand at it. How would you define a "call to ministry"? Is there a different call to ministry for a person who is seeking to be employed by the local church and someone who is not? Is there a different call to ministry for those who serve as a pastor and those who serve as a volunteer in youth ministry?

_____

_____

_____

---

1. John Calvin, *Institutes of the Christian Religion*, 2 vol., ed. John T. McNeill (Philadelphia: Westminster Press, 1960), Book 4.3.3.

If you found this process incredibly frustrating—take heart. You are not alone. The nature of God's call on the lives of His people is quite difficult to define. Not only that, but the Scriptures do not contain direct answers to the questions that are often asked about a leadership calling.

What Biblical examples can you provide of people who were called by God? What do we learn from these examples?

_____

_____

_____

The Scriptures simply do not provide readers with a definitive guide for discerning God's call in their lives. However, the Scriptures reveal that all disciples are called to:

- **Intimacy with God:** A leader is called to abide in Christ and find identity, significance, and love from close connection to the Father (Jn 15).

- **A Life of Holiness:** A leader is called to fight for holiness by repenting of known sin and allowing the gospel to propel them to a life of worship (Eph 4:1–3; 1 Pet 1:15; 2:9).

- **Active Mission:** A leader is called to be a minster of reconciliation to a lost world by demonstrating and declaring the gospel message (2 Cor 5:11–21).

- **Disciple-Making:** A leader is called to make disciples of Jesus (Mt 28:18–20).

As a Christian, you can rest assure that you are called to these things. Sadly, these callings are often neglected due to the desire of leaders to figure out the exact contours of their life's vocation. They may say, "Yeah, I know I'm called to those things, but what I want to know is what am I uniquely called to do?"

Before we attempt to answer that question, take a minute to reflect on how you are pursuing the four areas mentioned above:

How are you pursuing intimacy with God?

_____

_____

_____

How are you pursuing holiness?

_____

_____

_____

How are you living on mission?

_____

_____

_____

How are you making disciples?

_____

_____

_____

The reality is that some disciples are consumed with their future calling and neglect present faithfulness. For example, a young college student may feel called to serve as a long-term missionary among an unreached people group in India. This is a worthy goal. However, before she can become a missionary in India, she must live on mission to the people around her currently. If she is not living on mission in her current setting, it is unlikely that she will effectively live on mission in a foreign culture halfway around the world.

Often the question of one's vocational direction is clarified while faithfully undertaking the above tasks. "Walk worthy of the calling you have received" (Eph 4:1) provides ample room for God to clarify other aspects of your life and ministry. There you will find help in discerning your best function in the church and whether you are best suited for vocational ministry in the church or employment in another field while serving in the church.

However, this is not to minimize the importance of the question, "What am I called to do with my life?" This is a valid question, and one that should be asked. Discerning the answer to this question may come in diverse ways.

Vocational vs. Volunteer

Vocational ministry is not the only way to serve God. Certainly, God entrusts leaders to His church and those leaders are to be paid by the church for their labors. However, many will find fruitful and meaningful ways to serve God through vocational employment outside of the local church. Such jobs are often labeled secular employment, though this creates an unnecessary division between secular and vocational work. The reality is that all work is meaningful and those jobs labeled secular may be a valuable means of living a life on mission.

What opportunities might someone who is not employed by a church have in engaging in mission that a local church pastor might lack?

_____

_____

_____

What about you? Do you sense God leading you to vocational ministry? Why or why not?

_____

_____

_____

Momentary vs. Progressive

For some, understanding and taking ownership of one's gifts is instantaneous—a moment of clear and discernable direction from the Lord that is unmistakable, akin to Paul's calling on the Damascus Road (Acts 9). However, for others, it is progressive—the result of a lengthy process of prayer, deliberation, counsel, and often restlessness. Leaders called in this fashion can often doubt the clarity of their call when compared to others who have a more dramatic sense of calling.

What about you? Do you know how God is calling you to invest your life? What is encouraging or frustrating about this process?

_____

_____

_____

Mission vs. Role

All Christians are called to the mission of disciple-making. This must drive and inform how you understand your role in that process. While the ministry role may change over time, the mission never does. For example, a recent college graduate may find her calling to work with children embodied in leading children's ministry in a local church. However, if she marries and has her own children, this same calling may take the form of being a stay-at-home mom while serving in the children's ministry of the local church once a month. The mission of God is like a big bus. In conversion, God puts you on the bus; however, your seat on the bus may change throughout your journey.

In what roles are you currently serving? What are you learning about your role in God's mission?

_____

_____

_____

Work vs. Stewardship

Calling is not a task someone does to earn God's favor. It is a stewardship of God's gifting. Your life cannot be propelled out of a desire to pay God back for His grace. And it can't be a project whereby you prove your worth. The question, "What do I need to do for God?" is the wrong question. Rather, God entrusts men and women with gifts and abilities and uses them to play a role in the accomplishment of His purpose and plan.

How do you feel when you serve? What brings you the most joy and fulfillment?

_____

_____

_____

Internal vs. External

Calling is not simply something that you discover, but rather it is meant to be a process of discovery for both you and the community to which you individually belong (i.e. family and church). Internally, you may begin to sense a passion and gifting toward a particular ministry focus. This type of internal clarity is good and essential, but it is not enough.

Externally, you should also receive counsel from your believing family, friends, church community, and pastors. This balance of internal and external calling is essential to avoid making a decision purely on personal desires. A multifaceted approach to understanding calling should allow you to hold your calling loosely, particularly in the early days. Often, one becomes defensive towards any external counsel or redirection by arguing, "But God called me to do that." Perhaps, He did. Or perhaps, you just think He did, but the reality is that no one around you affirms that calling. In fact, some may believe that you lack the necessary skill set. What would others say you are most gifted in? Consider what these people might say:

- Your spouse, boyfriend or girlfriend, or best friend

_____

_____

_____

- Your parent(s)

_____

_____

_____

- The person you are discipling

  _____

  _____

  _____

- Your pastors

  _____

  _____

  _____

Do you see any common themes? What does this reveal about your calling?

_____

_____

_____

Place vs. People

Disciples are called to places and to people. For example, you may say that you feel called to work with youth, children, or music. On the other hand, you may feel called to a location, such as a country, city, or town (i.e. "I want to serve in a major urban center"). These points of clarity may provide a starting point, but more is needed. Those who feel called to certain types of people are still left to discern where they are going to serve. And those who feel called to a certain place must figure out exactly what they are to do when they get there.

Do you feel called to a place or a people?

_____

_____

_____

Them vs. Me

One of the greatest dangers in understanding one's calling to ministry is to assume that God will work in one person's life the way he did in that of another. Super-imposing another leader's calling on your life can prove deadly. Specifically, this is true for those with a dramatic sense of call or for a very public leadership position. One may be led to believe that since his/her sense of calling did not happen like someone they admire, they are somehow second-class servants. To combat this temptation, leaders must trust that God will work uniquely in all of His children, calling them in unique ways for unique tasks for His glory. There is no one-size-fits-all type of calling.

What do these tensions do to your heart as you seek to discern God's calling in your life? Are they encouraging or discouraging?

_____

_____

_____

Which aspects of the contrasts above do you need to claim as you prayerfully consider your role in ministry?

_____

_____

_____

A word of caution is necessary at this point. Do not underestimate how significantly key life decisions will shape your future options. For example, the choice of a spouse can, and often does, have marked effects on a person's ability to serve God. At times, this may be quite positive. But other times it can derail you. The same is true of financial and educational decisions. Massive debt or unmarketable degrees may hinder your ability to make the choices that you would like to make with your life going forward.

What do you see as the most critical 2 or 3 decisions that you are currently facing? How do your decisions in these matters affect your ability to serve God and His church?

_____

_____

_____

Tools

If calling is much less a one-size-fits-all, instantaneous occurrence and more of an ongoing process, what tools does God provide to assist you in discerning your role in His mission? God provides a number of internal and external means of discernment.

His Spirit

The gift of the Spirit provides an internal means of discernment for a leader. The Spirit, discussed in session 5, serves as a guide, a comforter, and a means of hearing from God. In Acts 16, Paul is led away from His previous plan to a new, unchartered region of Macedonia through the leading of God's Spirit. This same Spirit serves to both guide and redirect today's leaders.

His Word

The Word of God illuminates the path of a leader. Certainly, it is not going to answer the question, "What specific ministry am I called to pursue with my life?" However, a steady diet of the Word of God will be a tool that God uses to sharpen your clarity.

His Church

The church provides two valuable means of discernment. First, it provides a place for you to serve and refine your gifting. Through applying yourself to various tasks in the church, you can sense what areas you should move toward. In addition, the church should provide a rich pool of wise counselors that can speak truth into your life and calling. Like Timothy, the Spirit confirms one's gifting and calling through the affirmation and authority of a church's leaders.

Your Passions

Calling and desire are not mutually exclusive. Often, people think, "If I want to do it, it can't be of God. But if I hate it, then I know that's what God wants me to do." The false dichotomy creates a world where leaders feel they have to squelch or diminish how they are created. The aspiration for leadership, particularly that of pastoral leadership, is commended in the Scriptures as a good and noble desire. Your passions provide a guide to understanding your heart and a means of discerning God's leadership. A good question might be, "What must I do?" or "What naturally flows out of my life?"

Your Rest

You need space, often in quiet reflection, to process the work of God in your life. Active Sabbath practices and the avoidance of mindless time and energy drains are necessary for providing sufficient time to hear from God.

What is God saying to you about your calling as a result of this session?

_____

_____

_____

What did this "call" look like for you?

_____

_____

_____

What would be the outcome of having clarity about your calling?

_____

_____

_____

Do not lose heart if you find it challenging to articulate your calling at this point in your life. Ministry leadership does not function like most other professions. Take a football star. He must begin honing his skills at an early age. If he is not head-and-shoulders faster and stronger than the rest of his peers by age 18, then it is unlikely that he will ever excel as a professional athlete. The same is not true for a disciple-maker, ministry leader, or pastor. It often takes years to develop the discernment and maturity necessary to be positioned to be used by God in great ways. Continue to press forward, using the means of grace given to you by God's Spirit, and trust that your most fruitful days lie in the future.

Week 9: Marriage

"He also said: 'For this reason a man will leave his father and mother and be joined to his wife, and the two will become one flesh. So they are no longer two, but one flesh. Therefore, what God has joined together, man must not separate.'"

—*Matthew 19:5–6*

"This is the secret—that the gospel of Jesus and marriage explain one another. That when God invented marriage, he already had the saving work of Jesus in mind."[1]

—*Tim Keller*

God created marriage as a means of personal transformation.

Marriage can serve as a catalyst for understanding and using your gifts and defining your life calling. Or, if you make poor decisions, it can be a great impediment. It is essential that we discuss this critical area of life—whether or not you are currently married.

Marriage is created by God to be a wonderful gift that serves to bring a man and a woman together for the sake of partnership in God's mission of filling the earth with worshiping image-bearers (Gen 1–2). Not only that, it is meant to provide a picture of the gospel message as it portrays God's love for His church in stunning brilliance.

Unfortunately, what is meant to be a good gift is often a source of great pain. What was meant to fan the flames of mission often serves to smother it. What was meant to be a means of putting the gospel on display actually serves to cloud it.

Before we attempt to think about proactive steps you can take to develop your marital health, let's remember the fruit of our first labs this trimester. If you fail to face up to your own need for transformation, then your marriage will never be healthy. Just like the instructions before a flight, you must first put on your own oxygen mask before you can help others. That is why it is vital that the gospel permeate your life and that intimacy with God is normative so that you can see tangible growth in your marriage.

---

1. Timothy Keller, *The Meaning of Marriage: Facing the Complexities of Commitment with the Wisdom of God* (New York: Dutton, 2011), 47.

> If you are married, engaged, or dating, how is that relationship currently affected by the truths of the gospel?

_____

_____

_____

At this point you should see yourself growing as a disciple of Jesus and you are likely being entrusted with increasing levels of leadership in your church. The context and demands of ministry present some unique challenges to the dating relationships and marriages of leaders, such that, if you are not careful, will hinder your fruitfulness.

Let's consider a few of the reasons why the development of healthy marriages is so difficult for those who serve God and His church. No two relationships are perfectly alike, so some of these factors may affect certain people more than others. Those serving the church and making disciples may see that their relationships (be it dating or marriage) feel the strain of leadership in the church. Why is this?

They get the leftovers. Marriage requires focus and intentionality, something couples have when they are dating. But once they are married and the demands of leadership hit, the active engagement shifts away from marriage and towards work and ministry. Rather than pursuing one another, couples quickly start to pursue church-related tasks and neglect one another in the process.

They get your weariness. Discipleship is taxing, both physically and emotionally. This means that it is difficult for the couple, with an already depleted battery, to fully engage when they are together. It is much easier to seek comfort through passivity or comfort addictions (TV, video games, food, etc.) than do the heart work of growing as a disciple of Jesus together.

They get your second-hand information. While church leaders are on the front lines, often seeing examples of fruitful ministry, their spouses may not be. This is particularly true for those who serve as pastors or ministry leaders. The information that you communicate to about the work God is doing in ministry may be lost in translation and your spouse feel like their dreams are neglected.

They get your passivity. Weariness breeds passivity, which is only heightened by the fact that dating and marriage takes a lot of work. Often men feel like they are more in control in their churches than they are in their homes. They can get things done and see fruit at church but not at home. Thus, they over engage in the areas that they can control and are less engaged in areas where they can't, such as the home.

They get your idols. Remember back in the discussion on idolatry when we discussed leadership idols? Well, this is a prime place they wreak havoc. If a leader is enticed by the idol of pride, his or her spouse will reap the consequences through things like an addiction to social media or a lack of rest.

They get your kids. Most couples have kids early in both their marriages and their ministry careers. The husband heads to work, and often the wife stays at home with the kids. This means that she may feel "stuck" at home with the kids while the husband is out enjoying the thrills of ministry. Or, the husband may resent the way in which parenting hinders his ability to be as flexible with his time as he might otherwise be.

They get your worries and complaints. Since you talk about the things that are on your mind, your spouse is going to get more than a fair share of your worries and complaints. Unfortunately, this will cause your spouse to internalize these issues making her jaded toward people or the church in general. If you are not careful, you will spend way more time venting about those you are discipling than you will celebrating evidences of God's grace.

They get everyone else's attention. And with attention comes expectations. If you are a leader in the church, your spouse will feel like you live in a glass house, with everyone knowing you and what is going on in your family. Anonymity is gone in ministry leadership. This may breed a pressure to meet cultural expectations for a leader in the church, causing resentment from your spouse.

They get lonely. It is hard to be the friend of a church leader and his wife. As you grow as a leader in the church, people, particularly those in your church body, will struggle to treat you like they do everyone else. They will often keep their distance and refrain from being vulnerable. This, coupled with the pressures and demands of ministry, will mean that you may not have many close friends as a married couple. The difference between this situation and the deep friendships she had prior to church leadership may leave you both feeling lonely at times.

They get consistent changes. Change is a constant reality for those who give their lives to making disciples in the church. You will disciple different people over time. You will serve in various ways. Your roles and responsibilities change. Your family changes and grows. Even you change. Ministry alters your personality in numerous ways, making your marriage change regularly as well.

They get your schedule. The pace of life that you set for yourself, or that your ministry tasks set for you, becomes the schedule for your home. Ministry leaders live with the reality that they are always on call, due to the pressing needs of the people they are discipling.

They get your responsibilities. Churches need their leaders, which means that many people are going to be vying for your time and attention. Spouses of disciple-makers quickly realize that they must "share" you with other people in order for you to serve others well.

If you are married, do you see any of these playing out in your family currently?

_____

_____

_____

If you are not married, what do you need to do to prepare for marriage in light of these realities?

_____

_____

_____

Recognizing the struggle is one thing—doing something about it is another. You must give careful consideration to the steps you can take to embrace the gift that marriage is created to be.

Treasure

Gifts are meant to be treasured, and your spouse needs consistent reminders that they are treasured. This requires intentional effort in order to communicate value. For some, this is communicated through time, for some through conversation, for some through gifts, and for some through physical intimacy.

How does your spouse know that you treasure him/her?

_____

_____

_____

If you are married or dating, consider how the following actions might demonstrate that you treasure the other person:

- Leaving a simple note on the bathroom mirror;

- Sending a text message at a random time of the day;

- Planning a special night out or overnight;

- Putting down your work and simply listening.

If you are not married, this does not mean that you do not have ample opportunity to demonstrate love to others. Begin with your close friends or your mentor and focus your efforts on showing them love.

Invest

People use and cultivate the gifts that they value. They invest in them by making sacrifices of time to utilize them to their maximum potential. Marriage requires investment as well. If you are not consistently making sacrifices for your marriage, then you can bet that it will not drift toward health. This means you must develop practices such as a standard date night that serves as an unbreakable time for you to spend time together. For this to work, you must get off the map. Don't take calls, and let the people you are discipling know that you are not available during that time. In addition, spontaneous fun is a must. Find ways to promote joy in your home by doing fun things your spouse enjoys.

Would your calendar and checkbook say that you invest in your marriage, dating relationships, or friendships regularly?

_____

_____

_____

What could you adjust to more strategically invest in these relationships?

_____

_____

_____

Learn

Take time to learn what makes those you love tick. How is God growing or changing them? This will require you to ask questions and give the other person space to answer genuinely. Also, listen for what the person may not be saying that needs to be said. There are two ideal places to ask these types of questions. First, regular date nights provide a quiet and safe time for discussions on the health of your relationship. They serve as regular well checks for your marriage. Second, you should have a time set aside for an annual marriage review, which may best happen on an overnight trip out of town. If you are dating, it is not too early to begin this process. In fact, asking good questions to your boyfriend or girlfriend can establish good patterns for life which can protect you from problems further down the road.

Here are some questions you could ask on a regular basis to assess your marital health.

- How is God growing and changing you?

- What did I do this week that brought you joy?

- Where could I do a better job at affirming you?

- How do you feel about my current schedule?

- Do you feel loved and treasured? If not, what could I do to change that?

- What can I do to help you fulfill your God-given calling in life?

- Where do you see idols in my life that are affecting our relationship?

Here are some good end-of-the-year questions to ask.

- What was the best part of this past year?

- What was the worst part?

- How did you grow in your love for Jesus and His church?

- How did I serve you this year?

- Who are your best friends? Do you have enough time with them?

- What could I adjust in our weekly schedule in order to serve you better?

- What do you think are the greatest needs of our relationship?

- What did we spend money on this year as a family? Were finances a stress for you or a tool that brought you joy?

- How was our sex life? What would you change about our intimacy? (Obviously, only ask this if you are married!)

- What do you suspect will be the greatest trials or challenges of the coming year?

Schedule a date night with your spouse or girlfriend/boyfriend prior to your next meeting with your mentor. Start out by asking this question: "How are we doing in our marriage?" Follow the trail wherever it leads and use the above questions as a guide for the discussion. Be prepared to discuss the fruits of this discussion with your *Aspire* mentor when you meet.

If you are not yet married or dating, consider how your decisions at this point in life are affecting your service to God. Paul argues in 1 Corinthians 7 that singleness frees you to serve God with wholehearted devotion. Is this true of you currently? Are you unnecessarily worried or anxious about finding a spouse? Is this hindering your walk with God? Take some time alone or with a trusted friend to answer these questions this week.

Marriage is a grace-gift of God designed to demonstrate the way in which He loves His church. Deep thought, intentionality, and care is vital in order to maximize the splendor of this wonderful gift.

Week 10: Parenting

"Sons are indeed a heritage from the Lord, children, a reward. Like arrows in the hand of a warrior are the sons born in one's youth. Happy is the man who has filled his quiver with them. Such men will never be put to shame when they speak with their enemies at the city gate."

—*Psalms 127:5–7*

"Give your children big truths they will grow into rather than light explanations they will grow out of."

—*Tedd and Margy Tripp*

Worship begins in the home.

Kids are another good gift from a good God. God built fruitful multiplication into His created design and tasked mankind with the mission of filling the earth with worshiping image-bearers. The primary way that this happens is through discipleship in the home. Even if you are not yet married or have children, it is never too early to start learning.

Parenting is hard work. But this challenge is compounded by your attempts to make disciples through the local church. Stories of the proverbial pastor's kid, who seemingly pursues prodigal living without cause, are abundant. Without diligent labor and careful intentionality, parenting will crumble under the demands of serving God and His church.

That is why this lab is particularly relevant, even if you do not currently have kids. Odds are, you will at some point. And, when you do, it is vital that you have thought through these matters beforehand. Babysitting and/or serving in the children's ministry of the local church can provide one helpful way to begin experiencing the demands of parenting prior to having children.

Warning: This is not simply for the ladies. Most men have little to no experience with children prior to having their own. The local church can provide you with a grace-gift of parenting experience that you would otherwise not have.

There are two opposite dangers that face parents:

- **Passivity**: Certain people may drift toward passivity in the home, particularly with the children. This is most evident in the evenings following a day of engagement in meaningful work, both in one's vocation and in caring for other people in the church. The time between 5–8pm is particularly daunting; it usually involves dinner, play time, baths, and often discipline. A leader may choose to "veg out" during this time rather than engage in the family chaos. Such a person may miss the simple things (like tickle fights) and more important things (like leading in family devotions assisting with discipline).

- **Control**: On the other end of the scale, some parents drift toward hyper-control. "I can't get people to do what I want at work," a parent might say, "So, I will get what I want at home." Many well-meaning parents tend to try to control their homes from valid motives, such as a desire to protect their children from the evils of sin. Yet, if one is not careful, such efforts at control can become authoritarian legalism that may make it hard for a child to rightly understand the love of God. Such a parent may be hypercritical, quick to discipline, and limited in his application of grace. Such parents become bullies at home, driving their kids rather than leading them.

What about you? If you have kids now, place an X on the side of the scale that you more naturally move toward. If you do not have kids currently, where do you think you will fall on this scale?

PASSIVITY⋯⋯⋯⋯⋯⋯⋯⋯⋯⋯⋯⋯⋯⋯⋯⋯⋯⋯⋯⋯⋯⋯⋯⋯IDOLATRY

Neither passivity nor control represents the Biblical picture of parenting. Parenting is much more.

Parenting is Worship

At its core, parenting is an act of demonstrating the worth of God. Parents demonstrate God's character through loving service and patient pursuit of their children, regardless of the circumstance. Parenting as worship requires greater intentionality. It requires that the parents die to themselves daily and apply the good news of the gospel to their parenting strategies.

How does your parenting put the person and work of Jesus on display?

_____

_____

_____

Parenting is Discipleship

Parenting is also an act of discipleship. In fact, children are your God-given, in-house recipients of discipleship. This is why the condition of a man's home serves as a qualification for the office of elder. Thankfully, the same tools (scripture, prayer, relationship, and mission) serve to make disciples in the home as well. In some ways, however, it is more difficult to make disciples in your home. The relationships are built-in, yet they require work to be healthy and fruitful. Scripture is available, yet it requires great intentionality to read the Word together and talk about it often. Prayer is simple, but simple prayers provide a tool for teaching your children about how to pray robust prayers later in life. Mission is ongoing, yet parents must work to demonstrate the value of missionary service to their children.

Think about your home currently. How are you doing in applying the following tools in your home? What are you doing to cultivate each area?

Scripture:

_____

_____

_____

Prayer:

_____

_____

_____

Relationship:

_____

_____

_____

Mission:

_____

_____

_____

Parenting is Sin-Exposing

In the best and worst ways, kids serve as a mirror to expose your sin and idolatry. They are often so much like you in personality and temperament that they allow you to see blind spots toward your own sin. Further, they push you to the limits of your physical and emotional reserve, making it easier for root sin to bubble over to fruit sin.

What do you learn about yourself from looking at your kids?

_____

_____

_____

What fruit sins (week 3) do you see consistently exposed when you are around your kids or around other people's kids?

_____

_____

_____

What root sins (week 3) are revealed by these fruit sins?

_____

_____

_____

Parenting is Historical

Read closely—not hysterical, but historical. Your family history, particularly the model set by your parents, will shape the way in which you engage with your children. The wins and wounds of your birth family influence you in more ways than you often know or affirm.

What did it mean to be a father or mother in your home growing up?

_____

_____

_____

How did your parents go about making disciples in your home? Was it effective?

_____

_____

_____

How are you influenced by these experiences?

_____

_____

_____

Parenting is Establishing Authority

Parenting is all about establishing authority—teaching your children to live under and respond properly to God-ordained authority structures. Rules should be clear and consequences unilaterally given. Children learn obedience through clear and consistent authority that is swift and joyful. Children are natural sinners, so this will not come quickly. But parents must not compromise. They should work to establish authority in their homes and shepherd their children so that they learn to come under the authority of Jesus.

How are rules enforced in your home?

_____

_____

_____

How do you (or would you) define obedience for your children?

_____

_____

_____

Parenting is Protection

Leaders are called to be shepherds, which means they will spend their time both caring for sheep and killing wolves. Baby sheep (kids) of the shepherds are particularly susceptible to wolf attacks. Their parents must protect them from the wolves that will try to prey on them, attempting to manipulate them or earn their friendship. Church leaders will also need to protect their kids from the wounds that come from making hard decisions in leadership and having people lash out in response. Kids also need to be protected from becoming angry at the church. They can easily be led to believe that the church is the enemy—it consumes dad and mom's time, energy, and effort, while distracting from family time. As a result, parents must monitor what they say around their children or to their children.

What steps are you (or would you) take to protect your children from being wounded or jaded to the local church?

_____

_____

_____

Parenting is Service

Parenting requires service—greater service than you may have experienced before. You may be asked to serve long hours, in poor conditions, with little or no tangible reward. It also allows you to teach your children that all of life is service. Church leadership presents an unlimited array of ways that your children can serve in ministry with you—from carrying chairs, to painting walls, to handing out hot donuts, to delivering a meal to a family in need. They can learn to find service opportunities everywhere.

How can you lead your family to love serving God?

_____

_____

_____

Parenting is a Process

Parenting will be a process for both your children and you. You are both changing, and these changes will be hard. There will not only be many days of great joy, but also numerous experiences of pain, frustration, and even hopelessness. The best homes meet this process with high levels of communication. They talk about everything.

What haven't you talked about that you need to?

_____

_____

_____

Parenting is Adjustment

As soon as you feel like you figure things out—your family will change. Some of you who do not have kids, will. Some of you who are thinking about having your first, will have five. Those of you that currently have infants will soon have teenagers. The techniques that once worked will no longer work. This will be intensely frustrating, even to the best of leaders. You should expect frustration and wearisome toil in your home. Remember, the parenting years are short. Your kids will grow up, and you will never be able to recapture those precious days and hours. Godly parents will use the time they are given faithfully and effectively.

Trimester 2: Ministry

How is your family changing and what adjustments do you need to make to prepare for the next life stage?

_____

_____

_____

Family is a beautiful picture of a worshiping community and is a microcosm of the local church. Your worship should start in your home. As we conclude this week's, consider some steps you can take to make your home a place of worship:

- Find a consistent time each day to meet together to read a passage of Scripture and pray.

- Use the same model for Bible reading that you use to make disciples (for example, the seven arrows utilized through *Aspire*).

- Pray for intentional needs each day and ask your children to voice their prayers to God.

- Closely monitor how much time your family spends connected to technology (phone, computer, and TV).

- If your children are teenagers, ask them to read *Aspire* with you (what better mentor for your child than his/her parent).

- If you know a child without a solid family system, ask them to read *Aspire* with you and invest in their discipleship journey.

What additional steps would you need to implement to more effectively make disciples in your home?

_____

_____

_____

Week 11: Time

"Pay careful attention, then, to how you walk—not as unwise people but as wise—making the most of the time, because the days are evil."

—*Ephesians 5:15–16*

"Knowing how to get the right things done—how to be personally effective, leading and managing ourselves well—is indeed biblical, spiritual, and honoring to the Lord. It is not unspiritual to think about the concrete details of how to get things done; rather, this is a significant component of Christian wisdom."[1]

—*Matt Pearman*

Time management is a spiritual discipline that should be done to the glory of God.

There are few mentions in the Scriptures of many of the things that Christians spend the most time talking about today, such as discerning God's will, corporate leadership strategies, or time management. This does not mean that these matters are not essential, only that they were not the focus of the authors of Scripture. Instead, they were seeking to clearly present the gospel and the implications of living in light of those truths. However, the Bible does contain a great deal of simple, practical wisdom—most notably in the book of Proverbs. Paul also includes these wisdom sayings near the end of many of his letters, indicating that they are implications of right gospel understanding and living.

Paul exhorts the church in Ephesus and their leadership to watch their life and their doctrine closely (Eph. 4:16). One chapter later in Ephesians 5:15–16, he writes, "look carefully then how you walk, not as unwise but as wise, making the best use of your time because the days are evil." Working backward through this text will help us in our topic for this week.

First, Paul writes that the days are evil. By this he means that the natural trajectory of our days are steeped in pain, sin, frustration, and failure as a result of the curse. As Jesus

---

1. Matt Pearman, *What's Best Next: How The Gospel Transforms The Way You Get Things Done* (Grand Rapids: Zondervan, 2014), 66.

says, "each day will have enough trouble of its own (Mt 6:34)." And it certainly does. We see evidence of depravity every day in people around us. Additionally, we know that darkness and death loom on the horizon for each of us.

In light of this reality, Paul exhorts the church in Ephesians to "make the best use of your time," or more exactly, to "redeem the time." You can't buy back time. Time is leaking away, and it is critical that we make the best use of the time we have been afforded. While we do not know the number of our days, we know that they are relatively short. Thus, our utilization of those days is a matter of stewardship of one of the most basic gifts we have been given—time.

The application of this principle is that the church "look carefully how you walk, not as unwise, but as wise." To make the best use of our time, we must look at our lives with great care. The moments of life are similar to a walk in the woods. The terrain is bumpy and a misstep is entirely possible. Vigilance is critical.

Proper worship of God should influence how you use your time.

Here are some practical tips for analyzing how you walk in order to make the best use of your time. We will begin working from macro-level to micro-level, or from working "in" your life to working "on" your life. Without a 30,000-foot view of your life and the necessary adjustments at this level, a laundry list of practical changes will have little benefit. You must get above the trees and see your life clearly. Macro-level assessment will help in that task.

Recognize the connection between discipline and worship.
Paul challenges Timothy to "discipline yourself for the purpose of godliness, for while bodily training is of some value, godliness is of value in every way, as it holds promise for the present life and also for the life to come (1 Tim 4:7)." Discipline aids in the production of godliness.

Repent of the sin of sloth.
On the list of acceptable sins in our culture, sloth ranks right up there on the top. Our comfortable Christian subculture combined with an affluent Western society means

that many can live their entire lives passively. The result of a sloth-filled life is poor stewardship and missed opportunities.

Look up the following mentions of sloth in the book of Proverbs and briefly note the characteristics of a slothful person:

6:1–11 _____

10:5 _____

10:26 _____

12:24–27 _____

15:19 _____

19:15, 24 _____

20:4 _____

20:13 _____

21:25–26 _____

22:13 _____

24:30–34 _____

26:13–16 _____

What opportunities might be missed through poor stewardship of time?

_____

_____

Assess your life accurately.

Without intentionality, our lives will drift toward those things that are most urgent, those things that get noticed, or those things that are personally rewarding. How do you currently spend your time? Two practices will help you answer this question well.

Warning: these tools will likely reveal painful truths about your life, so be prepared.

Practice 1

Develop an Excel spreadsheet and break down a week's worth of days in 15-minute increments. For two weeks, jot down the things that you do during each of those 15 minute blocks. You will need to do this multiple times during the day in order to gather accurate information. Consider noting your activities every two hours. At the end of two weeks, take the data you have gathered and create a pie chart that reflects the types of things you spend your time doing. Think through some general categories, such as administration, discipleship appointments, sermon/teaching preparation, work, time with family, pleasure/hobbies, watching TV, playing on the internet, etc.

Take this chart to your next meeting with your mentor and discuss your findings. What does this reveal about you? What do you spend too much time doing? What do you spend too little time doing?

_____

_____

Practice 2

Stephen Covey developed a tool to assess one's life around things that are urgent and that are important.[1] Urgent things are tasks that have to be done right away. Important tasks are those things that need to be done. His four-quadrant chart is represented below, with examples of those things that belong in each category. Using the data you have developed for practice 1, chart the past two weeks by putting a percentage of your time in each quadrant. The goal should be to spend the vast majority of your time living in quadrant 2—meaning that you work on things that are important but not urgent.

---

1.   Stephen Covey, *The 7 Habits of Highly Effective People* (New York: Simon & Schuster, 2013).

Certainly, it is idealistic to assume that you can do this all of the time. There will be things that come up that are urgent, and you will spend some time doing things that are really unimportant. But if you find yourself living in quadrant 1 or quadrant 4 for a large percentage of time, you are in trouble.

Quadrant 1 Urgent/Important	Quadrant 2 Not Urgent/Important
Emergencies, projects that you have put off, unexpected crisis conversations, evangelistic or service opportunities that appear quickly.	Spiritual disciplines, school, work, job tasks, daily family responsibilities, housework, encouragement, service, dating towards marriage, friends for the purpose of mutual edification or evangelism.
Your Percentage:	Your Percentage:
Quadrant 3 **Urgent/Not Important**	**Quadrant 4** **Not Urgent/Not Important**
Needs that you become aware of that are urgent to someone but not to you.	Most mindless pastimes, hobbies, etc.
Your Percentage:	Your Percentage:

What does the chart reveal about you?

_____

_____

Are the things that you put in the "important" category really important?

_____

_____

Plan backwards.

A person should think through a goal for their life and work backwards for that goal in order to determine what is important for this week, this month, or this year. You could be getting a lot done, but not getting the right things done. There is a vast difference between activity and accomplishment.

What would you like your life to look like:

Five years from now: _____

_____

Ten years from now: _____

_____

20 years from now: _____

_____

What would you need to do this year in order to take steps towards those goals?

_____

_____

Is a practice like this antithetical to Jesus' command not to worry about tomorrow? How does the gospel inform these future plans?

_____

_____

Develop Roles to Goals.

Goals are notoriously challenging to define and set meaningfully. Sloppy goals such as "I want to be a better husband," or "I wish I had more time to study," do little to move a person toward life change. Rather, goals should be set clearly and strategically. Let's start by determining the areas in which you need to set goals.

Write down the roles that you currently fulfill (for example father, mother, husband, wife, hobbyist, missionary, etc).

1. _____

2. _____

3. _____

4. _____

5. _____

6. _____

7. _____

Look back through your list. Did you note all of your God-ordained roles, or are some missing? Once you have your list of roles, you are then ready to make goals. A good practice is to move from roles to goals—Meaning, take each of your God-ordained roles and set 2-3 goals in each area. This allows you to have a rifle gun approach to your life as opposed to a machine gun. You can see exactly what you should be doing and target those tasks with specificity. Now, before you attempt to set goals, consider what makes a good goal:

- **Measureable:** How will you know if you have or have not accomplished the goal?

- **Achievable:** Do you have the capacity to reach the goal, or is it too challenging or broad?

- **Dateable:** When are you trying to accomplish the goal?

Example:

> **Bad Goal:** I want to be a better father.

> **Good Goal:** I want to take my daughter on a daddy/daughter date once a month this year.

Here is a good example of the process of moving from roles to goals using the example of the role of missionary.

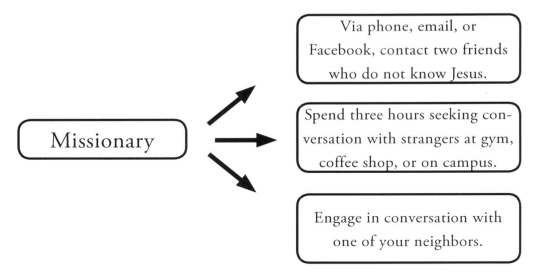

Work through your roles and set appropriate goals. Be prepared to share these with your *Aspire* mentor this week.

Role 1: _____

     Goal 1: _____

     Goal 2: _____

Role 2: _____

     Goal 1: _____

     Goal 2: _____

Role 3: _____

     Goal 1: _____

     Goal 2: _____

Role 4: _____

     Goal 1: _____

     Goal 2: _____

Role 5: _____

    Goal 1: _____

    Goal 2: _____

Role 6: _____

    Goal 1: _____

    Goal 2: _____

Role 7: _____

    Goal 1: _____

    Goal 2: _____

Calendar your goals.

If you set good goals, you should easily be able to put them on your calendar. For example, if you are going to take your daughter on a date night once a month, go ahead and determine when this is going to happen. If you are going to spend 10 hours in sermon preparation each week, when will you work on this? A life well lived happens when we allow our goals to drive our tasks and not the other way around.

Work in Buckets.

No one works well haphazardly. The best approach to actually getting things done is to see your week as a series of buckets and fill each bucket with a goal. The chart below provides a standard list of buckets in four-hour increments. What would you put in each bucket (where does your time with God go, where does work go, where does family go, where do your hobbies go)?

	Monday	Tuesday	Wednesday	Thursday	Friday	Saturday	Sunday
8-noon							

1–5pm							
6–10pm							

Prioritize the buckets.

Which goals are most important for you? Some (such as family time) must get the best buckets. Also, think through how God has wired you as you set these buckets. Do you work best in the mornings or nights? If you think best at night, then put some writing tasks in the night bucket.

Warning: If you are leader in the church, be prepared for a challenging start to your week. Sundays are physically and emotionally draining, so make sure you have something life-giving scheduled on Monday mornings.

Embrace the mornings.

Certainly, everyone does not need to sleep from 10pm to 8am. Most working adults can function and thrive with less sleep. However, it is vital that you choose well how you use those other 2–3 hours. A couple of options are on the table, starting with the evenings (from 10pm–midnight). This may not be the best alternative even though this is the default option for most young people who trained themselves to be night owls during high school and college. It often leads to shortchanging your families in the evenings as they transition to work tasks while their family is still awake. Additionally, once most people have children, they will find that they are not at their best after the challenging string of dinner, bath time, and bed with young children. Finally, many guys will find it challenging to shut their minds off once they get started in the evenings causing them to sleep poorly, and thus be less than their best on the following day.

A better approach for most would be to work to develop a morning ritual that includes time in Scripture reading and prayer, and any discipleship related tasks. Scripture and prayer is the foundation for the day, and thus it is always profitable to remind oneself of the gospel at the outset of the day rather than simply at the end of the day. Also, you can use time before your family awakes to accomplish a host of tasks. This way, even if your mind begins to think about a need, problem, or concern, you have the rest of the day to think on it.

If you were to add 2–3 hours to your primary buckets each day, where would you put them?

_____

_____

What would you put in those additional hours each day?

_____

_____

For example: 5–8am each morning, which would include my personal devotions and prayer, communication with people in the church via email, and end with a family devotion around the breakfast table.

Redeem the gaps.

Every day is filled with gaps—10- to 15-minute segments that develop due to changing contours of the day (someone is late to a meeting, you are early to an appointment, you have to drive from one location to another, etc.). You can redeem those gaps to maximize your time. This could include practices like making phone calls, sending basic emails, or even reading a segment of a book you need to work through.

What tasks best fit in the gaps of your life?

_____

_____

Evaluate the unexpected.

Interruptions come in all forms and fashions. Most often, leaders will find that interruptions come in the form of other people's demands, which they believe urgently demand your attention. The simple reality is that most of the things that other people believe are urgent *are not*. And even if they were, there are more demands than there is time to address those demands. Most can wait. It is up to you to not allow other people's urgent demands or poor life management to force you into habits that will be unhealthy for your family.

Remove time dumps.

The largest interruption in a normal day often comes in the form of technology. The steady stream of text messages, emails, and phone calls never seems to stop—not to mention the distractions that come in the form of social media. Wise individuals are not consistently engaging texts, phone calls, and emails. Rather, you should limit the number of interruptions you allow. To do this, you will need to turn off technology regularly. It is advisable to set strategic times when you will check email rather than having it consistently showing up on your computer monitor. Suggestion: Check and respond to email twice a day—once first thing in the morning and secondly as the last thing you do before you go home in the evenings.

Finish what you start.

Do not allow yourself to consistently leave a task 80 percent finished. If a task is worth starting, it is worth finishing. As much as possible, only start tasks that you can finish, or tackle them in segments that you can finish. For example, writing a sermon will be a larger task than can be accomplished in one bucket. However, you could take one bucket to finish all of your research for a sermon and another to finish outlining your sermon manuscript. The same is true of emails. If you are not careful, they will build up a head of steam and present a seemingly endless task list. One should attempt to read and respond to all essential emails each time one checks his or her inbox. Often the thought is that if you have more time, you will do a better job on the project. Research has shown this to not be the case. Over time, a person will notice diminishing returns on his investment of time.

Collect everything.

Nothing is more frustrating than having to do the same task multiple times. Therefore, if you do something and do it well, save it clearly for use next time. Create a clear filing system so you can quickly find things when you need them. If you are teaching regularly, you would be well-served to create a filing system for research. Create topical folders on your computer that you save and store helpful blogs or research in key areas that you will draw from in the future. Finally, you should develop tools to collect your thoughts by writing them down. Good thoughts come at random times (driving, falling asleep, taking a shower, etc.). If you are not careful, you will forget these thoughts if you do not have systems in place to collect them. Tools like Evernote provide a meaningful way to capture thoughts, ideas, pictures, and reading.

Live a life of learning.

Leaders are learners. There is no exception to this rule. If you desire to lead well, you must actively engage in learning through asking questions and reading often. Find people who are better at life than you are and learn from them. Copy people you admire, both alive and dead.

Embrace community.

Sanctification happens in community, including sanctified time management. Allow your church, your family, and your mentor to assist you in this process. Show them your time charts, your roles to goals, and your calendar, and ask them for input. Set aside a couple of critical people who can hold you accountable to your goals.

What needs to change about your time management in order to more effectively steward the hours that God has given you?

_____

_____

The Gospel and Time

The gospel shapes all areas of life—even time management. No matter how much planning, scheduling, and discipline is present in my life, I will never completely redeem the time. I am a finite creature, limited in what I can accomplish, and further limited by my sin. So it should surprise nobody that I leave to-dos undone each and every day. My joy is not derived from the flawless execution of my goals. My joy each day is derived from the person and work of Jesus Christ on the cross. Only God gets his to-do list done each day. I need the cross of Christ each day. Every day needs to be saved by grace, and God promises sufficient provision for you to work toward living a life that stewards time to the glory of God. May we be people who "number our days carefully so that we may develop wisdom in our hearts (Ps. 90:12)."

Week 12: Rest

"Come to Me, all of you who are weary and burdened, and I will give you rest. All of you, take up My yoke and learn from Me, because I am gentle and humble in heart, and you will find rest for yourselves. For My yoke is easy and My burden is light."

—Matthew 11:28–30

"We too often take credit for what sovereign grace produced."[1]

—Paul Tripp

Rest is an affirmation of the gospel.

There is always one more. One more task. One more person. One more pressing need. If a disciple wants to last, he must learn to find rest within the tornado of "one mores." God did not create us to live under the constant pressure of one more task. He designed creation with built-in rest. Sabbath is an essential part of His created design. God himself rested in the joy of His good creation. His law for the Israelites included the requirement of Sabbath: "You are to labor six days and do all your work, but the seventh day is a Sabbath to the Lord your God (Ex 20:9–10)." Jesus serves as the end of the law, including the Sabbath, yet the need for gospel-informed and gospel-driven rest remains for God's people, the Church.

Fruit Idolatry and Busyness

The opposite is often true in the church, however. Busyness has become a badge of honor. People are prone to celebrate their frantic lives and publicly laud their breakneck pace through social media. They often gripe about their time—"There is never enough time;" "I've got too much to do;" and "Where has all the time gone?" These statements reveal less about the importance of the person than they do about their lack of ability to enjoy God's good gifts. This problem is multiplied by the fact that we live in a culture where the concept of rest is harder than ever to embrace. Globalization and technological advances have made it possible to do more, to do it quicker, and to do it for all to

1. Tripp, *Dangerous*, 153.

see. Prominent leaders seem to accomplish so much, leaving in their wake a stream of aspiring leaders who are struggling to keep up. Unfortunately, the music of busyness has been playing in our heads for so long that we don't even notice it most of the time.

How do you speak about time? What does this reveal about you?

_____

_____

Do you consider yourself to be a busy person? What fuels this busyness?

_____

_____

Root Idolatry of Busyness

Busyness, and the celebration of it, is the result of idolatry deep in your heart. What types of root idols are exposed in your life through an ever-increasing need for "one more"?

_____

_____

To counter this idolatry, a leader must see rest as an affirmation of the gospel.

- **An Affirmation of Jesus:** Rest affirms that Jesus is the one to whom the Sabbath points. We have true rest in Him. He says, "Come to Me, all of you who are weary and burdened, and I will give you rest. All of you, take up My yoke and learn from Me, because I am gentle and humble in heart, and you will find rest for yourselves. (Mt 11:28–29)." One chapter later, Jesus affirms Himself as Lord of the Sabbath. Sabbath rest is found in and through intimacy with Jesus.

- **Affirmation of Sovereignty:** Rest also declares that God is sovereign and does not need your work in order to accomplish his purposes. He is just fine without you. In fact, He is sovereign over your very life and has appointed the length of your days long before you were ever born (Ps 139:13–16; Eccl 3:1–8). He has also ordained His perfect, saving plan for all of human history and will faithfully accomplish that plan. Rest affirms that God is in control, and you are trusting in Him and not in yourself.

- **Affirmation of Dependence:** Rest affirms that you are finite. You can't do everything—nor should you try. You are consistently, fully in need of God's grace to do for you what you cannot do for yourself. Such dependence proclaims to the world your need for the gospel and your lack of self-sufficiency.

- **Affirmation of Success:** Sabbath will reveal your definition of success. If you measure success by your ability to keep up with other recognized leaders, then you will be incapable of rest. If success is measured by work accomplishments, then there will always be a steady stream of projects. If you define success poorly, you will find that more activity does not result in lasting fruit.

- **Affirmation of Identity:** Finally, Sabbath is an affirmation that you trust in your God-given identity. Rather than depending on power or position to affirm you, Sabbath says, "I am a child of God and do not need others to affirm me." You can rest fully satisfied in your labors, knowing that God is fully satisfied in His Son's work in and through you.

Which of these affirmations is most challenging for you?

_____

_____

Rest is challenging to define well. How would you define it?

_____

_____

When do you feel most rested?

_____

_____

Rest is easier to define by its disguises. It can subtly masquerade as a number of sloppy forms of pseudo-rest.

Bodily Rest

Rest must be a rest of the soul as well as the body. Life is often more soul draining than it is physically draining. As a result, a disciple must find tools that replenish the soul. This will often happen through devotional reading that is not part of some teaching or writing project. Silent meditation and prayer will also provide the type of mental refreshment that the heart needs.

How do you allow the Spirit to replenish your soul? What has worked in the past?

_____

_____

Escape

Rest provides recovery, not simply escape. Sadly, rest is often sought by replacing one's labor with a host of trivial or sinful activities (such as video games or pornography). Gospel rest is found by taking joy in the fruit of one's labors. These fruit idols may make you feel better for a period of time, but they only mask the need for rest; they do not really address it.

What do you do to "rest" that can quickly become a source of idolatry? Is there anything inherently sinful about the places you look to find rest (hint: common rest idols for men would be sports, hobbies, video games, or porn)?

_____

_____

Laziness

Rest is active, not passive. As counter-intuitive as it may seem, you need to plan your rest. Down-shifting from the rhythms of life is not easy. You will need a plan in order to do it effectively. If you don't, you will find yourself with spare time and no plan. For example, you may have a free Saturday that could be devoted to refreshing time with your family. However, if you are not intentional, that time could quickly devolve into sitting on the couch or family members pursuing their own individual chores.

What is needed are some go-to activities that serve to replenish your soul. What are these for you? What is an appropriate amount of time to invest in these activities without turning them into idols?

_____

_____

Selfishness

Rest should prompt you to think of others more than yourself. Those who are married or who have children lose the right to an abundance of personal rest time at the expense of their families. Rather, they must work hard to find ways that allow the whole family to find rest together. This will particularly be difficult for men who are more introverted. For them, they may find rest by being isolated from people whereas extroverts may rest with people. Husbands and wives need to work together to find appropriate rhythms for rest that work for one another. A godly wife will serve her husband by finding ways to free up time to foster such rest.

How can you involve your family in your rest? Does this come naturally for you? What conversation do you and your spouse need to have to discuss how you can build patterns of rest into your home?

_____

_____

Work

Rest is not meant to become another form of work; however, it can quickly become a new law. What starts as a good desire to honor God through gospel-driven rest can become a means of justifying oneself before God. Rest becomes another bullet point on the "I hope God likes me" list. Not only that, but one's ways of finding rest can be superimposed on other people and become a standard by which you judge the righteousness of others. To counter this trend, it is advisable to vary your rest so that you do not grow complacent with or dependent on your current version of rest. Additionally, you will be well served to find unplanned and unstructured ways to rest rather than a set "rest time" each day or week.

How can you find rest in 10 minute, unplanned chunks during the day?

_____

_____

Rhythms

Life is seasonal, and not every season demands the same level of exertion (particularly in the church). Certain times, such as holidays or big events, may require an unusually high investment for a short time. During these times, leaders and their families may grow frustrated with unbreakable time patterns. For example, if a family typically has dinner together five nights a week, there may well be an event at the church that requires the leader to miss a couple of family meals that week. This ministry "peak" is often met by an opposing "valley"—a lull in ministry that allows the leader time to rest and recover. Thus, leaders should acknowledge, both to themselves and their families, when the peak seasons are coming and actually embrace the rest of the valley that follows. Otherwise, it is easy for peak seasons to become the norm.

One-size-fits-all

People will find rest in different ways. This has already been mentioned, but it bears mentioning again. A leader must understand how they are built to find rest. Do you rest most effectively around people or away from people? What serves to most effectively recharge your battery? Additionally, you should consider your family life stage, each of which will demand a different form of rest. Rest will be challenging to find when you have young children in the home. Still, you must fight for it.

Name a Christian who is wired like you (introvert vs. extrovert, etc). What can you learn by watching how they rest?

_____

_____

Name a Christian that is doing a similar leadership role as you. What can you learn by watching how they rest?

_____

_____

Idolatry

Worship is the goal of rest. Certainly that sounds strange, but the point is true nonetheless. Rest is not the ultimate end—a love for Jesus is. Rest allows us to know, understand, and worship Him more appropriately—even through our work. In a very real sense, a person does not work in order to rest, but they rest in order to work. Work is the God-ordained output of a well-rested life.

How do you view your work? Do you see it as a God-ordained gift or as a curse?

_____

_____

Complete

Rest will not be complete until that great and glorious day when faith meets sight and the new heavens and new earth are inaugurated. Until that day, rest will always leave you longing for more. Thankfully, we have this promise: "Therefore, a Sabbath rest remains for God's people. For the person who has entered His rest has rested from his own works, just as God did from His. Let us then make every effort to enter that rest, so that no one will fall into the same pattern of disobedience (Heb 4:9–11)."

On the scale below, rate your current sense of rest (with 1 being low and 10 being well-rested)?

$$1 \quad 2 \quad 3 \quad 4 \quad 5 \quad 6 \quad 7 \quad 8 \quad 9 \quad 10$$

What needs to change based on this week's work?

_____

_____

The day awaits when we will rest fully in the presence of our King. Until that day let us labor with the power that the gospel supplies, all the while begging God to hasten the day of His coming.

Trimester 2: Top Ten List

What are the top ten take-aways that you have from this trimester of *Aspire*? How is God bringing transformation in your life?

1. _____

2. _____

3. _____

4. _____

5. _____

6. _____

7. _____

8. _____

9. _____

10. _____

Suggested Reading List

Akin, Danny, Bill Curtis, and Stephen Rummage. *Engaging Exposition*. Nashville: Broadman & Holman, 2011.

Bennett, Arthur, ed. *The Valley of Vision: A Collection of Puritan Prayers and Devotions*. East Peoria, IL: The Banner of Truth Trust, 1975.

Bonheoffer, Dietrich. *The Cost of Discipleship*. New York: Macmillan, 1963.

Carson, D.A. *The Cross and Christian Ministry*. Grand Rapids: Baker, 1993.

Chester, Tim. *You Can Change: God's Transforming Power of Our Sinful Behaviors and Negative Emotions*. Wheaton: Crossway, 2010.

Edwards, Jonathan. *Religious Affections: A Christian's Character Before God*. Vancouver; Regent College Publishing, 1984.

Emlet, Michael R. *Cross Talk: Where Life and Scripture Meet*. Greensboro: New Growth Press, 2009.

Ferguson, Sinclair. *By Grace Alone: How the Grace of God Amazes Me*. Lake Mary, FL: Reformational Trust Publishing, 2010.

Hodges, Brian G. *Christ Formed in You: The Power of the Gospel for Personal Change*. Wapwallopen, Penn: Shepherd Press, 2010.

Keller, Timothy. *Counterfeit Gods*. New York: Dutton, 2009.

Keller, Timothy. *The Meaning of Marriage: Facing the Complexities of Commitment with the Wisdom of God*. New York: Dutton, 2011.

Lane, Timothy S. and Paul David Tripp. *How People Change*. Greensboro: New Growth Press, 2008.

Mahaney, C.J. *Wordiness: Resisting the Seduction of a Fallen World*. Wheaton: Crossway, 2008.

Mahaney, C.J. *Humility: True Greatness*. Multnomah, 2005.

Moore, Russell D. *Tempted and Tried: Temptation and the Triumph of Christ*. Wheaton: Crossway, 2011.

Owen, John. *The Mortification of Sin*. Scotland: Christian Focus Publications, 1996.

Pearman, Matthew. *What's Best Next: How the Gospel Transforms How You Get Things Done*. Grand Rapids: Zondervan, 2014.

Piper, John. *God is the Gospel: Meditation of God's Love as the Gift of Himself*. Wheaton: Crossway, 2005.

Piper, John. *Finally Alive*. Great Britain: Christian Focus Publications, 2009.

Piper, John. *Desiring God*. Sisters, OR: Multnomah, 1996.

Powlison, David. *Seeing with New Eyes: Counseling and the Human Condition Through the Lens of Scripture*. Phillipsburg: P&R, 2003.

Ryle, J.C. *Holiness: Its Nature, Hindrances, Difficulties, and Roots*. Moscow: Charles Nolan Publishers, 2001.

Smallman, Stephen. *The Walk: Steps for New and Renewed Followers of Jesus*. Phillipsburg: P&R, 2009.

Thorn, Joe. *Note to Self: The Discipline of Preaching to Yourself*. Wheaton: Crossway, 2011.

Tripp, Paul David. *Dangerous Calling: Confronting the Unique Challenges of Pastoral Ministry*. Wheaton: Crossway, 2012.

Tripp, Paul David. *Instruments in the Redeemer's Hands: People in Need of Change Helping People in Need of Change*. P & R Publishing, 2002.

Welch. Edward T. *When People Are Big and God is Small: Overcoming Peer Pressure, Codependency, and the Fear of Man*. Phillipsburg: P&R, 1997.

Whitney, Donald S. *Spiritual Disciplines for the Christian Life*. Colorado Springs: NavPress, 1991.

TRIMESTER 3
Mission

Week 1: Mission of God

For the earth will be filled with the knowledge of the Lord's glory, as the waters cover the sea.

—Habakkuk 2:14

"Mission arises primarily out of the nature not of the church but of God himself. The living God of the Bible is a sending God."[1]

—John Stott

You are a missionary.

I know it sounds strange. Most of us were led to believe that missionaries were a special class of people who lived in some country we could barely pronounce and certainly could not locate on a map. We knew that they did risky and God-honoring work in spiritually dark places and that we saw them every so often at a missions banquet at the church or on a prayer card held by a refrigerator magnet.

In some ways this was helpful:

- These people were heroes who made monumental sacrifices in order to declare the good news of the gospel.

- The church had a responsibility to honor, support, and pray for those who were sent to undertake this vital work.

- God was calling out new men and women to leave the comforts of our church in order to live missionary lives in a difficult context among a people in desperate need of the gospel.

Subtly, it became easy to believe that they were the *only* missionaries. They were an elite and honorable class of missionary Christians that a few of us might join one day. In the meantime, the best thing for most of us to do was to honor and pray for our missionaries and go about our task of being Jesus' (mission-less) disciples.

---

1. John Stott, *Christian Mission in the Modern World* (Downers Grove: IVP, 1975), 21.

The Scriptures, on the other hand, tell a different story. It is the story of a missionary God who calls people to Himself and in so doing propels them to live missionary lives. To be a disciple of Jesus, according to the Bible, is to be a missionary. There is simply no such thing as a mission-less Christian.

Sadly, a visit to many evangelical churches reveals an almost palpable lack of missionary zeal among God's people. Why is this so? Why are we, as churches, failing to multiply missionary disciples? And, is there anything that the church can do to reverse this trend?

Yes.

The local church has a responsibility to produce missionary disciples, and this trimester of *Aspire* is designed to assist in this vital task. In the weeks that follow you will be led through a series of labs designed to raise your awareness of God's mission in the world, your responsibility in that mission, and some practical ways that you can live as a missionary disciple daily.

This tool is designed to be a field guide for missionary disciples. Use it to foster your development as a missionary and not merely to download information about missions. Information alone will not produce missionary living. You can't steer a parked car, and neither can you shape a missionary disciple who is not living on mission. Only the hard, often frustrating work of trusting God, loving people, and sharing the gospel will bring about growth in your life. It may feel as awkward as a middle school dance at the outset, but over time, you will grow comfortable with this new, missionary life.

Do you typically think of yourself as a missionary? Why or why not?

_____

_____

The missionary life is birthed from a rich understanding of the gospel. A brief reminder of the gospel foundations is the place to begin this exploration of mission for worshippers of God.

We have seen that our lives are caught up in the great story that God is writing in the world. We see this story all around us, and we know it extends beyond us and somehow encompasses our lives. How we understand this story will shape our life's mission.

Our mission does not begin with our individual life or church, but rather with the mission of God (*missio Dei*). This phrase is used to describe the fundamental reality that God, by His very nature, is always on mission. We must attempt to discover what God is doing in the world long before we can hope to fit our microscopic lives into His grand story.

Think about human history like a giant timeline, extending from God's act of creation until the time when He returns to permanently rule and reign on earth.

Where does your life fit on the timeline below?

◄───►

Creation   New Creation

What effect should this have on your life?

_____

_____

What makes it easy for you to overestimate the significance of your life?

_____

_____

We all have the temptation to think too highly and too often of ourselves. The reality is that our lives are but a small blip on the timeline of cosmic history. We are here today and gone tomorrow—a mere vapor that appears for a moment and is gone (Js 4:14). This could become a discouraging thought, until you pause to consider that your life is a part of the grand story that God is writing in all of human history.

Thankfully, we are not left clamoring in the dark, blindly attempting to discover what God might be up to the in the world. He has told us in the Scriptures and left us over two thousands years of redemptive history as evidence.

Try your hand at it. What is the mission of God? What is God doing in the world?

_____

_____

Created Worshippers

The best way to answer this question is by starting with creation. What was God's mission in creation before sin entered the picture and distorted His good design?

_____

_____

You may find yourself thinking, "There was no mission in creation. Mission didn't happen until God pursued sinful and fallen humanity." However, creation itself necessitates a mission. The Trinitarian God had no lack in His being that necessitated creation which Plantinga reminds us that God was not "doodling one day with a cosmic magic marker, drawing stick men and stick women to idle away a few thousand years of eternity."[1] God was not tired, bored, or lonely when He created.

He created on mission, and His mission was to be known and worshipped by that which He made.

Remember the text we studied in the first trimester of *Aspire*. Read Colossians 1:15–17:

> *He is the image of the invisible God, the firstborn over all creation. For everything was created by Him, in heaven and on earth, the visible and the invisible, whether thrones or dominions or rulers or authorities—all things have been created through Him and for Him. He is before all things, and by Him all things hold together.*

How did God create?

_____

_____

Why did God create? What does this tell us about God?

_____

_____

Creation is for God (Ps 19:1; Is 6:3; Is 43:5; Rom 11:33–36). All things are designed to proclaim the glory, splendor, and majesty of the Godhead. Not only that, but God allowed mankind the privilege of stewarding his good creation, in order to cultivate and

1. Plantinga, *Engaging*, 23.

bring order to the world that He had made. Through this work they would increasingly broaden the horizon of the glory of God. They were also told to multiply, and in doing so to fill the earth with image-bearing worshippers. The picture of creation is of a glorious God longing for His glory to be known among all the earth.

Idolatrous Worshippers

The shalom of the garden was quickly interpreted by the rebellion of Adam and Eve. As George Robinson writes: "The primary effect of the fall is not the presence of sin, but the absence of authentic worship."[1] It was not that worship was absent—but that the worship was misdirected. Adam and Eve chose to glory in His creation rather than finding joy and delight in God alone (Rom 1:23).

Sin is misplaced worship.

As a result of this idolatry, sin entered the world, and God's created world was altered and marred by personal and societal sin. Personally, mankind filled the earth with broken idolaters, incapable of knowing God or rightly worshiping Him (Rom 5:12–21). Societally, mankind developed the created world in ways that harnessed their depravity.

How did sin affect God's mission?

_____

_____

How does sin influence your life's mission?

_____

_____

God's holiness requires a punishment, and His wrath is the proper wage for human sin (Rom 3:23). Had God not acted, mankind would have been handed over forever to a life apart from God in hell. There simply would have been no mission apart from the grace of God.

---

1. George Robinson, "The Gospel and Evangelism" in Bruce Piley Ashford, ed. *Theology and the Practice of Mission: God, the Church, and the Nations* (Nashville: B&H, 2011), 76.

Reclaimed Worshippers

Praise God his mission did not end in the garden. Instead, God graciously continued His mission to fill the earth with worshiping image-bearers. After handing out the consequences for sin, He made a promise that one day a seed would come who would destroy sin and its effects (Gen 3:15), and He made a plan that fallen mankind would be clothed in the blood sacrifice of another (Gen 3:21). Rather than turning his back to His creation, God "turned his face toward it in love. He set out on a long road of redemption to restore the lost as his people and the world as his Kingdom."

From the garden forward, God's mission is to reclaim worshippers.

The small glimmer of hope of Genesis 3:15 progressively breaks through the clouds into full sunlight as Scripture presents the ongoing plan of God to redeem that which sin had broken. The Old Testament tells the story of God's missionary work to gather a people to whom he would once again reveal Himself and entrust His mission (Gen 12:1–3).

This is the story of the mission of God. It is the story of the Bible. While there are many mini-stories in Scripture, each one reveals the path God is taking to reclaim worshippers from every tribe, tongue, and nation. Christopher Wright argues that the central theme of the Bible is this mission. He notes that all of Scripture finds its basis in the mission of God and is often written from a missional context. Paul's letters, for example, are written from the context of a first-century church trying to interpret how to live out the gospel as the mission of God continued to advance.

How does this understanding change how you typically read the Bible?

_____

_____

The true mission of the Scripture crescendos in the person and work of Jesus Christ, the promised seed of the woman, who would right the wrongs of sin by redeeming fallen humanity. Jesus, as God's Son, succeeded where all others had failed. He rightly reflected the image of His father and faithfully fulfilled his mission. This led ultimately to His substitutionary death on the cross.

In His mercy, Jesus fully absorbed the wrath of God on behalf of fallen humanity (1 Pet 3:18; 2 Cor 5:20–21; Heb 9:22). In His grace, He fully clothed image-bearers in

His perfect righteousness (Rom 5:8–11). This great exchange is the means of reclaiming worshippers. Those who trust Christ in repentance and faith are redeemed to do the very thing for which they were created—worship God.

How does knowledge of the person and work of Jesus aid in our understanding of God's mission?

_____

_____

Perfect Worshippers

The reality is that God has fully defeated Satan, sin, and death through the person and work of His Son. As a result, a day is coming when that victory will be consummated, and God will reign among His people and revel in their worship. John's vision in Revelation 21:3–4 pictures this day:

> *Look! God's dwelling is with humanity, and He will live with them. They will be His people, and God Himself will be with them and be their God. He will wipe away every tear from their eyes. Death will no longer exist; grief, crying, and pain will exist no longer, because the previous things have passed away.*

The point is not simply that man will not live under the tyranny of sin, but that man will be freed to forever do what he was created to do—worship God!

How is your mission shaped by the fact that God will one day gather worshippers from every tribe, tongue, and nation to worship Him perfectly?

_____

_____

Sadly, this will not be the story for all people. Those who refuse to bow their knee in the worship of God in this life will receive the due punishment for their sin—a permanent and eternal separation from the only source of love, joy, and peace. Their idolatry will be consummated and the results will be catastrophic.

How should the fate of the lost affect how you view your missionary task?

_____

_____

God is still on mission, because God is a God on mission. It is intrinsic to His very being. The idea sounded strange to me at first. Other characteristics were clear. God is love. God is just. God is on mission? It did not seem to fit with the other marks of God's nature and character. Yet, it is His mission that allows us to see these other aspects of His character. If God were not on mission, we would not know that God is love. If He were not on mission, we would not know that He is Holy. He would still be these things, yet His mission allows these characteristics to be seen by his image-bearers.

God's mission is the foundation for our mission. We are to live on mission, because He lives on mission. This mission is not simply what God does; it is who He is. With each passing day, God is reclaiming worshippers to do what they were intended to do both now and forever. It is to that mission that He calls his disciples. This vital foundation is essential to a right understanding of your missionary task.

Week 2: The Mission of the Church

"But you will receive power when the Holy Spirit has come on you, and you will be My witnesses in Jerusalem, in all Judea and Samaria, and to the ends of the earth."

—*Acts 1:8*

"It is not so much the case that God has a mission for his church in the world, as that God has a church for his mission in the world. Mission was not made for the church; the church was made for mission—God's mission."[1]

—*Christopher J.H. Wright*

The church is the primary focal point of the mission of God.

God's mission spread like kudzu during the first few centuries of its existence. Rodney Stark notes that in 100 AD there were as few as 25,000 Christians in the known world, and yet by 310 AD, a brief two hundred years later, there were as many as 20,000,000 Christians.[2] With the growth of Christianity came the establishment of churches.

This was no accident, but rather the purposeful plan of God who was on mission to reclaim worshippers and unite them under His church. Christopher Wright, in his larger work on the subject of the church's mission, notes that Jesus "commissions his own disciples to go out and replicate themselves by creating communities of obedience among the nations."[3] John Stott notes that "the church lies at the very center of the eternal purpose of God. It is not a divine afterthought. It is not an accident of history."[4]

Is this the way you typically think of the local church? In our day, the church is often viewed as the crazy uncle at a family reunion. Sure, we know that he is supposed to be there, but we just hope that he doesn't do anything to embarrass us.

---

1. Wright, *Mission*, 62.
2. Rodney Stark, *The Rise of Christianity: How the Obscure, Marginal Jesus Movement Became the Dominant Religious Force In the Western World in a Few Centuries* (San Francisco: HarperCollins, 1997), 6–13.
3. Wright, *Mission*, 391.
4. John Stott, *The Living Church* (Downers Grove: IVP, 2007), 19.

> What about you? In what ways have you or those that you know undermined the importance of the church in God's mission?

_____

_____

Paul speaks of the church in vastly different ways than you might read on the modern blogosphere—referring to it as the very Body of Christ, his beautiful and spotless bride, the robust pillar and buttress of truth, and the outworking of the manifold wisdom of God. Paul could speak this way because he saw the church in its proper place in God's mission.

The church is the picture of the mission of God.

God's mission is to reclaim worshippers. Worship is a communal act done by a people who are called by God and united to Him through adoption. God's Kingdom finds expression in the local church—no one church is the Kingdom, but the church is a representation of the Kingdom and needs to work together with other churches.

Note the communal language in 1 Peter 2:9–10:

> _But you are a chosen race, a royal priesthood, a holy nation, a people for His possession, so that you may proclaim the praises of the One who called you out of darkness into His marvelous light. Once you were not a people, but now you are God's people; you had not received mercy, but now you have received mercy._

How does Peter connect the church and worship?

_____

_____

In the church we see the communal nature of God's mission. The universal church is comprised of God's people at all times and in all places, while the local church is made up of those who have been saved by God and have committed themselves to one another at a particular time and place.

What does the local church provide that the universal church does not provide? Why is the local church vital for Christian growth?

_____

_____

The church is the evidence of the mission of God.

The church demonstrates *what* God is doing in the world, and it also demonstrates *that* God is continuing to fulfill that mission in our day. The word church is only used twice in the Gospels, but it is used extensively after God sent the Holy Spirit at Pentecost.

What might this indicate about the nature of the church?

_____

_____

At a minimum, it demonstrates that the church is the tangible manifestation of the work of God's Spirit to gather a people to Himself. Where God is at work, a church is soon to follow. And not only a church, but a church made up of an increasingly diverse group of people, which demonstrates God's desire to save people at the very ends of the earth.

Think for a moment about the fact that your church is a tangible expression of God's mission to reclaim worshippers. Every true believer is there because God sought them out and opened their eyes to the glorious gospel of Jesus Christ through His grace. The existence of the church reveals that "God is still at work!" to His people every time they gather.

How should the church prompt you to worship?

_____

_____

How should the fact that God uses you as a conduit for His mission prompt you to worship?

_____

_____

The church is the proper vehicle for the mission of God.

The church is not a knee-jerk reaction by God; it is not simply a sociological phenomenon. Rather, it is a concrete, visible demonstration of God's mission to the world. God gives His mission to the church, not simply to individual Christians (Mt 28:18–20; Acts 1:8). Bartholomew and Goheen describe the church as "the continuing mission of the exalted Christ by the agency of his Spirit to give salvation to the church and through the church to the whole world."[1] God implants His mission in the church and gives it the glorious task of living it out.

Mission is the expected outcome of a worship-fueled local church.

It is not simply something:

- That only the really healthy churches do;
- That only certain people in the church do;
- That individual Christians do in isolation from the church;
- That the church outsources to trained missionary professionals;
- That the church does alongside a host of other meaningful ministries (i.e. youth, kids, college, seniors, oh and by the way, missions).

Mission is at the center of the life of God's people. It is something that the church must do by nature of its being and not some secondary activity that relatively few people within the church may give themselves to.

How have you seen the models of mission mentioned above in the life of the local church?

_____

_____

The lack of mission in most churches has led to a modern resurgence of the "missional church." Missional is simply the adjectival form of the word missionary and is used to

---

1. Goheen and Bartholomew, _Drama_, 172.

describe the purpose of the church. Lesslie Newbigin and David Bosch served as prophetic voices to remind the Western church of its missionary calling in an increasingly secular age.[1] Darrell Guder's edited volume, *Missional Church: A Vision for the Sending of the Church in North America,* served as a clarion call to the church to reclaim its missional center.[2] Goheen notes "At its best, 'missional' describes not a specific activity of the church but the very essence and identity of the church as it takes up its role in God's story."[3] He says the missional church stands in stark contrast to other common ways of understanding the church:[4]

- The church as a mall or food court designed to provides good and services to religious consumers;

- The church as a community center designed to meet the social needs of its members;

- The church as a corporation designed to run a religious business;

- The church as a theater designed to produce a religious performance;

- The church as a classroom designed to teach and train Christians;

- The church as a hospital or spa designed to provide healing, rest, and rejuvenation;

- The church as a motivational seminar designed to provide tips on how best to live life;

- The church as a social-service office designed to care for the needy and broken;

---

1. For a more thorough treatment of the need for missional ecclesiology in the North American context see David J. Bosch, *Transforming Mission: Paradigm Shifts in Theology of Mission* (Maryknoll, NY: Orbis,1991); Lesslie Newbigin, *The Gospel in a Pluralistic Society* (Grand Rapids: Eerdmans, 1989); Lesslie Newbigin, *The Open Secret: An Introduction to the Theology of Mission* (Grand Rapids: Eerdmans, 1978); Lesslie Newbigin, *Foolishness to the Greeks: The Gospel and Western Culture* (Grand Rapids: Eerdmans, 1986).
2. Darrell Guder, ed., *Missional Church: A Vision for the Sending of the Church in North America* (Grand Rapids: Eerdmans, 1998), 46–60.
3. Goheen, *Light to the Nations*, 4.
4. Ibid., 15–16.

- The church as a campaign headquarters or social advocacy group designed to foster a certain political or philosophical agenda.

Which of these images of the church have you seen in the past (Be careful—this is not the place for church bashing. Rather, ask yourself what that view of the church does to the mission of the church)?

_____

_____

Are the aforementioned models "bad" or just not "central"?

_____

_____

In contrast, healthy missional church has:

- A Derived Mission that understands its missions to be the same as the mission of God, namely to reclaim worshippers. A church does not need to manufacture an arbitrary mission statement but simply see itself as living in light of God's mission.

- A Worshiping Mission that flows out of a deep understanding of the reality of human sin and a supreme joy at the beauty of the redemption that is offered through Christ. As John Piper famously notes:

  Mission is not the ultimate goal of the church. Worship is. Missions exists because worship doesn't. Worship…is the fuel and goal of missions. It's the goal of missions because in missions we simply aim to bring the nations into the white-hot enjoyment of God's glory…But worship is also the fuel of missions…You can't commend what you don't cherish…Missions begins and ends in worship.[1]

- A Gospel Mission that commends the person and work of Jesus as the only hope for a desperately idolatrous world.

---

1. Piper, *Nations,* 35–36.

- A Central Mission that sees missions as essential to the life of the church. Missions is the catalyst for all of its ministries and not simply a secondary addition to an already overflowing church calendar.

- A Holistic Mission that is directed towards the spiritual, physical, economic, and environmental factors that have been effected by the fall.

- A Disciple-Making Mission that evaluates success based on lasting and fruitful disciple-making and not simply professions of conversion.

- A Submissive Mission that rightly understands that God is the architect of the church, and that any fruit is a derivative of His mercy, grace, and provision; not human ingenuity.

- An Organic Mission that grows naturally out of the life and health of the body, not one that is derived from programmatic methods.

- A Whole-Earth Mission that seeks to bring the gospel to every tribe, tongue, and nation by leveraging the vast resources available to the modern church, so the worship of God will fill the earth (Mt 28:16–20; Mk 16:9–20; Lk 24:44–49; cf. Jn 20:19–23; Acts 1:8).

- A Marginalized Mission that propels the church to the fringes of society to embrace society's outcasts and abandoned with the love given through Christ.

- A Church Planting Mission that sees the establishment of the local church as the primary means of reaching new locations with the gospel (Rom 15).

How would you know if this type of mission were happening in your church?

_____

_____

What are some potential dangers for "missional churches"? How might they be tempted to compromise?

_____

_____

Trimester 3: Mission

Is there such a thing as a "non-missional church"? What might a lack of mission say about a church?

_____

_____

Throughout church history, various marks have been used to define a true church. Consider the following marks and how they might either serve to enhance or suppress the mission of the church.

Mark of the Church	How might this mark serve to foster the mission of the church?	How could this mark detract from the mission of the church?
Authoritative Doctrine		
Expository Preaching		
Administration of Baptism and the Lord's Supper		
Regenerate Church membership		
Church Discipline		
Unity		
Holiness		
Godly Leadership		

These factors are not arbitrary marks for a church; the are missionary fuels. When they are utilized effectively, they fan the flame of the mission of God through His people. Are there any mission-fuels that you might add to the above list?

_____

_____

Based on your reading and sessions, what is the mission of the church?

_____

_____

You have a role to play. The institution of the church is insufficient to produce a missionary people. God's people must see their own personal responsibility in living on mission and, in turn, lead the church to embrace its missionary calling.

Week 3: The Mission of the Disciple

"As the Father has sent Me, I also send you."

—John 20:21

"When people are saved by God through faith in Christ they are not only being saved from their sins, they are saved in order to resume the tasks mandated at creation, the task of caring for and cultivating a world that honors God and reflects his character and glory."[1]

—James Davidson Hunter

We must learn to take personal responsibility for living all of life on mission.

Short-term missions are a common practice among most evangelical churches. They are designed to mobilize the church to take the gospel to the nations.

Have you ever been on a mission trip? What was it like? What did your trip teach you (positively or negatively) about missions? If you are planning on participating in your first mission trip soon, what has this caused you to think about the missionary task?

This doesn't always happen, though. At times the trips can lull us into a slumber by causing us to assume that missions are simply something that we do at certain times and in certain places. The beauty of these trips, however, is that they serve to remind those who participate of the *personal responsibility* that they have to be about the mission of God.

God has entrusted His people with a great treasure in the gospel. Jesus encourages and exhorts His followers that "you did not choose Me, but I chose you. I appointed you that you should go out and produce fruit and that your fruit should remain (Jn 15:16)." When Jesus called His disciples, He called them to mission. He did not invite them simply to learn about Him, but rather to learn from His teaching and His ways. He wanted them to live on mission and to invite others into the Kingdom of God. Jesus commissioned the sent ones (apostles) who were tasked with taking God's message to the world.

---

1. James Davidson Hunter, *To Change the World: The Irony, Tragedy and Possibility of Christianity in the Late Modern World* (Oxford: Oxford University Press, 2010), 236.

Trimester 3: Mission

Fruit bearing through missional living is not an optional add-on to an otherwise self-sufficient religious life. Instead, it is the expected outcome of all disciples.

This becomes the repeated refrain in the Scriptures—God saves and He sends. Read Paul's words in 2 Corinthians 5:17–21:

> *Therefore, if anyone is in Christ, he is a new creation; old things have passed away, and look, new things have come. Everything is from God, who reconciled us to Himself through Christ and gave us the ministry of reconciliation: That is, in Christ, God was reconciling the world to Himself, not counting their trespasses against them, and He has committed the message of reconciliation to us. Therefore, we are ambassadors for Christ, certain that God is appealing through us. We plead on Christ's behalf, "Be reconciled to God." He made the One who did not know sin to be sin for us, so that we might become the righteousness of God in Him.*

What do you observe about the mission of a disciple from this passage?

_____

_____

It is all too easy and common to pawn the responsibility for missions off on someone else: It is the pastor's job, the skilled missionary's job, or someone else's job. However, as Andreas Köstenberger and Peter O'Brien note, participation in this mission is "not optional but mandatory."[1]

Do you feel the weight of your missionary responsibility? On the scale below indicate how intentional you are in living every day on mission (with 1 indicating that mission is largely absent from your life and 10 indicating that you consistently live a missionary life).

1   2   3   4   5   6   7   8   9   10

What evidence would you give for the rating you selected?

_____

_____

1. Andreas J. Köstenberger and Peter T. O'Brien, *Salvation to the Ends of the Earth: A Biblical Theology of Mission* (Downers Grove: Intervarsity, 2001), 19.

If you notice that your missionary fervor is inadequate, consider a number of fuels that serve to fan the fire of mission in your life.

Personal responsibility is fueled by proper understanding of the gospel.

This was not any old message, but the *euangelion* (the good news) that the Messiah had come in the person of Christ, and that those who trusted in His person and work could worship Him rightly. The life of a reclaimed worshipper is one of mission. You simply have to live on mission if you rightly understand the gospel.

Mission is a fruit of worship: No worship—no mission. Those who rightly understand their desperate need for the gospel, and the grace that was given to them in Christ, will live on mission. The paltry condition of missions among many evangelical churches is often symptomatic of an impoverished view of the grace of God. As Matt Chandler writes, "the reality is that all God has to do is reveal himself to you, and you'll gladly join the mission in service to his kingdom."[1] The gospel is the only thing capable of sustaining a life on mission.

Imagine, for example, that you are a parent of an elementary school child who wins first prize at the annual school talent show. As a parent, no one is going to have to tell you to share this news. The nature of the good news will simply ooze out of your life. "Did you hear what my daughter did?" will be the common refrain. Not only that, but you will find yourself saying, "Sweetie, why don't you show our friends that dance you did in order to win first prize." You will naturally want to declare and demonstrate the good news.

The beauty of the good news of the gospel should cause other things to pale in comparison. Your child's performance, the victory of your favorite sports team, or the surprising ending of that classic TV show simply do not compare.

Why is it that we often struggle to live the life of a missionary?

_____

_____

_____

1. Matt Chandler and Jared Wilson, *The Explicit Gospel* (Wheaton: Crossway, 2012), 31.

Think about your own life. How would you rate your daily missional efforts on the scale below (with 1 being non-existent and 10 being outstanding)?

1   2   3   4   5   6   7   8   9   10

Are there times or seasons where your worship intensifies and you notice an increase in missionary fruitfulness as well? Do you notice a precipitous drop off in fruitfulness when your worship of God is lacking?

_____

_____

Personal responsibility is fueled by a right understanding of what it means to be the church.

Mission is essential to what it means to be a worshipper of Jesus and to what it means to be a member of the local church.

On one hand, the church is a gathering by its very nature (the church gathered). The church is a group of people (not an isolated individual) who are united to one another and gather together regularly. In these gatherings they sing songs of worship, pray prayers of longing and hope, sit under the teaching of the Word, observe baptism and the Lord's Supper, submit to Godly leadership, and practice the dozens of "one another" commands that God gave His church.

The gathered church certainly has a missionary thrust. People may be drawn to repentance and faith in the gospel through the fellowship of the saints, or may be humbled under the teaching of the Word. The gathered church is a powerful missionary front-door for many. From this gathered church comes a wide range of "top-down" mission projects that the church and its leaders deem to be wise investments of the church's time, effort, and energy. This might mean sponsoring an after-school club, serving in a rescue mission, partnering with an unreached people group around the world, or a host of other noble projects.

How can the gathering of the church be appealing for a non-Christian?

_____

_____

How might the gathering of the church hinder the work of missions?

_____

_____

The church also lives on mission through the scattering of its people (the church scattered). Here, the members of the Body of Christ fill their neighborhoods, schools, workplaces, restaurants, and businesses with missional presence.[1] This need not be a special project put forward by the church. It may come in the form of a grassroots mission fueled by the passions of God's people.

All of life is a mission trip. You are always on mission: every day—everywhere. Missions are neither some arbitrary tag-on to an otherwise busy schedule nor is it a religious assignment designed to appease a guilty conscience. *Missions are the whole life response of reclaimed worshippers to the glory of God.*

How does the scattered church serve as an effective missionary tool?

_____

_____

Personal responsibility is fueled by a right understanding of the example of Jesus.

Jesus' life provides the prototype for missionary living. Jesus prays that His disciples will be sent in a similar fashion as He was sent in the incarnation. The disciples mission would clearly be different than the mission of the very Son of God (for example, they would not die for the sins of God's people) and yet it should be patterned after His mission.

Jesus lived on mission by making His dwelling among fallen humanity in order to seek and save the lost (Lk 15; Jn 1:1, 14). His life was lived on mission to the poor, broken, wounded, and wayward. In fact, it was these people that were seemingly the most

---

1. Michael Goheen, "The Missional Church: Eccelsiological Discussion in the gospel and Our Culture Network in North America,' in *Missiology 30, 4* (2002), 479–490.

comfortable around Jesus. The religious leaders opposed His mission from the outset and condemned Him for His association with these outcasts.

Look up the following passages of Scripture and note what they demonstrate about Jesus' mission.

Matthew 4:17–22 _____

_____

Matthew 8:1–4 _____

_____

Matthew 9:1–8 _____

_____

Matthew 9:35–38 _____

_____

Matthew 11:1–19 _____

_____

Matthew 13:47–52 _____

_____

Matthew 18:10–14 _____

_____

Matthew 19:16–30 _____

_____

Mark 4:1–20 _____

_____

Mark 5:1–20 _____

_____

Mark 10:13–16 _____
_____

Luke 6:12–16 _____
_____

Luke 10:25–37 _____
_____

Luke 12:49–53 _____
_____

Luke 13:22–30 _____
_____

How is your mission like the mission of Jesus?
_____
_____

How is your mission different than the mission of Jesus?
_____
_____

Mission is a response to love for God and love for all people. The plight of those apart from the grace of God should compel us towards mission, even if the people are unlike us. We will live with a relentless passion to give all people repeated opportunities to see, hear, and respond to the good news of Christ. If we truly love others, it will overflow into a life of mission.

For our mission to model that of Jesus, we must also pursue those on the margins of society. This includes those who are crushed under the weight of poverty and oppression as well as those whose sinful choices have led to a host of disastrous consequences. The Kingdom is open and available to these people as well.

What types of people has the church most often abandoned? How is the gospel good news for these people as well?

_____

_____

How would you rate your passion and love for those without Christ?

         1   2   3   4   5   6   7   8   9   10

What types of people are most challenging for you to love?

_____

_____

Personal responsibility is fueled by the power of the Holy Spirit.

Worshippers are empowered by the very Spirit of God to live a life on mission. Jesus, prior to His post-resurrection ascension, told His followers to wait. Rather than embark on the mission, they were to wait for the coming of the Spirit of God who would give them the power to live a life of mission. Their mission would be impotent apart from the power of the Holy Spirit (Lk 24:49). With the Spirit, however, the first followers of Jesus were powered to live a life of mission that would extend to the very ends of the earth.

How does God's Spirit power mission? How do you avail yourself to the power of the Spirit on a daily basis?

_____

_____

While God has called all disciples to live on mission, He has not called all disciples to an identical mission. Rather, He has hard-wired His image-bearers for strategic and multi-faceted mission in a complex world. This should give you great comfort. You have been given gifts by God for use in His mission (1 Cor 12–14; Rom 12:3–8). This means that your mission does not have to look like your best friend's mission.

For example, in *Just Walk Across the Room*, Bill Hybels outlines a number of different evangelistic styles:

- **Confrontational:** calling out the idolatry and disobedience of people or societal forms of rebellion from God;

- **Intellectual:** defending the truth claims of the gospel through clear, compelling, and logical arguments;

- **Interpersonal:** developing lasting and long-term friendships with non-believers and finding ongoing opportunities to speak of the gospel;

- **Invitational:** boldly and often publically inviting people to turn from their sins and place their faith in Jesus;

- **Serving:** giving of yourself in humble service to those who are far from God and earning a right to be heard;

- **Testimony:** sharing your life journey and conversion story in such a way that it connects with the life stories of others.[1]

Which of these styles best represents how you are wired to live on mission?

_____

_____

Does this style have a down-side? Are there things that you need to be aware of in light of your default style?

_____

_____

Personal responsibility is fueled by a humble submission to the King.

Finally, missionary living requires humble submission. This is the foundation of the great commission. Jesus, as King, says that He has "all authority on heaven and on earth" to command His followers to live a life of mission. The language of sentness in the

---

1. Bill Hybels, *Just Walk Across the Room* (Grand Rapids: Zondervan, 2006), 85–86.

Scriptures, which is used over sixty times in the book of John alone, refers to something that is thrust out. This is not an optional extra for certain high-capacity Christians but rather the expected response of worshippers. This also means that to fail to live a life of mission is sin against a holy God.

Week 4: The Nations

May God be gracious to us and bless us; look on us with favor so that Your way may be known on earth, Your salvation among all nations.

Let the peoples praise You, God; let all the peoples praise You. Let the nations rejoice and shout for joy, for You judge the peoples with fairness and lead the nations on earth. Let the peoples praise You, God, let all the peoples praise You. The earth has produced its harvest; God, our God, blesses us. God will bless us, and all the ends of the earth will fear Him.

—Psalm 67:1–7

"Worship, therefore, is the fuel and goal in missions. It's the goal of missions because in missions we simply aim to bring the nations into the white-hot enjoyment of God's glory."[1]

—John Piper

God is always at work gathering a people for His glory.

The glorious reality of the mission of God is that you can be assured that wherever you are working in the world, God is also at work. He is passionate about gathering people from every tribe, tongue, and nation to worship around His throne. For example, consider the Psalmist's focus on the nations:

May God be gracious to us and bless us; look on us with favor so that Your way may be known on earth, Your salvation among all nations. Let the peoples praise You, God; let all the peoples praise You. Let the nations rejoice and shout for joy, for You judge the peoples with fairness and lead the nations on earth. Let the peoples praise You, God, let all the peoples praise You. The earth has produced its harvest; God, our God, blesses us. God will bless us, and all the ends of the earth will fear Him (Ps 67:1–7)!

---

1. Piper, *Nations*, 11.

Jesus' most famous commission to His disciples includes a focus on making disciples of all nations:

> *Then Jesus came near and said to them, "All authority has been given to Me in heaven and on earth. Go, therefore, and make disciples of all nations, baptizing them in the name of the Father and of the Son and of the Holy Spirit, teaching them to observe everything I have commanded you. And remember, I am with you always, to the end of the age." (Mt 28:18–20)*

John's end times vision prophecies of a coming gathering of the nations:

> *After this I looked, and there was a vast multitude from every nation, tribe, people, and language, which no one could number, standing before the throne and before the Lamb. They were robed in white with palm branches in their hands (Rev 7:9).*

The modern notion of geopolitical nation-states is not in view here, however. Rather God is stating, through the Scripture, that His mission is to reclaim from every people group on the earth. Such groups often share a common heritage, language, and culture. From these people God is fulfilling His mission in creation by filling the earth with image-bearing worshippers. His covenant with Abram in Genesis 12 demonstrated that His mission to reclaim worshippers, even after the fall, would extend to include the nations.

In our day, it is clear that God is redeeming the nations. Consider the following:

- In 1970 there were approximately 3 million Christians in China, and by 2010 that number had ballooned to over 130 million.[1]

- Christians in Indonesia numbered a little over one million in 1970, and today that number is over 11 million.[2]

---

1. http://www.christiantoday.com/article/church.in.china.experiencing.tremendous.growth/26420.htm
2. http://www.operationworld.org/

- The Jesus Film has been translated into approximately 1,000 languages, with 200 million people indicating that they have trusted Christ as a result of watching the film.[1]

- Christians were not allowed to live in Nepal in 1960, and today there is a church in every one of the 75 districts of the country, with over 500,000 believers.[2]

- As recently as 1900 there were no Protestant churches in Korea, and today that country is 30% Christian—with over 7,000 churches in Seoul alone. The rapid growth of the church between 1960 and 1980 has seen the Christian population swell from 623,000 in 1960 to 6,489,000 by 1985—a ten-fold increase.[3]

- Similar reports are found in China, where conservative estimates indicate at least 40 million Christians. This number has grown from 1 million on the eve of the communist victory in 1949.[4] *First Things* recently reported:

Chinese Christians are now sending missionaries of their own. They're avid proselytizers within their own borders, spreading the Word across provinces. Many feel a special calling to bring the Word back to the Middle East; others become unintentional missionaries as their work carries them to the West and beyond. Christianity has become Chinese. Now, its converts are paying it forward.[5]

God is at work among the nations, and yet there is still much work to be done. You may find yourself thinking, "Sure, but there are lost people in my neighborhood or school. Why is it so important to think about the nations?"

The short answer is this: "Because the nations are that important to God." For most of us, the lost in our neighborhoods and communities have ample access to the message

1. http://www.jesusfilm.org/
2. http://www.operationworld.org/
3. Joon-Sik Park, "Korean Protestant Christianity: A Missiological Reflection," *International Bulletin of Missionary Researh 36,* no. 2 (April 2012): 62.
4. Tony Lambert, "As for Me and My House: The House-Church Movement Survived Persecution and Created a Surge of Christian Growth Across China." *Christian History and Biography 98* (Spring 2008): 19–23.
5. Jillian Kay Melchoir, "China's New Christians," *First Things,* 236 (October 2013): 25.

of the gospel. Many around the world have little or no access to the gospel message, however. Among the Nations, people groups are typically classified using one of the following labels:[1]

- **Unreached:** A people group without an adequate number of indigenous Christians to evangelize this group. Unreached people groups are often statistically defined as those with less that two percent evangelical believers.[2] In their book, *Introducing World Missions*, Moreau, Corwin, and McGee write that unreached people groups are those that "currently have no access to the gospel. They are 'hidden' not in the sense that they are invisible, but in the sense that there is no way, given current conditions, that they can hear the gospel in their own language in a way that makes sense to them."[3]

- **Unengaged:** A people group with no known believers or church planting work. The International Mission Board of the Southern Baptist Convention defines such groups as those where "there is no church planting strategy consistent with Evangelical faith and practice under way. A people group is not engaged when it has been merely adopted, is the object of focused prayer, or is part of an advocacy strategy."[4]

They further clarify the state of the unreached and unengaged people groups.[5] On their website they list four groups of people as either unreached or unengaged:

- **Status 0:** People with no known Christians or churches and without access to any gospel resources (print, technology, video);

- **Status 1:** Less than two percent evangelical, no known church planting work in the last two years, and limited access to gospel resources;

---

1. Find the Joshua Project online at www.joshuaproject.net.
2. Global Reseawrch, "Research Data," Internatinoal Mission Board, http://public.imb.org/ globalresearch/Pages/default/aspx (accessed April 12, 2014).
3. A. Scott Moreau, Gary R. Corwin, and Gary B. McGee, *Introducing World Missions: A Biblical, Historical, and Practical Survey* (Grand Rapids: Baker, 2004), 13.
4. Global Reseawrch, "Research Data," Internatinoal Mission Board, http://public.imb.org/ globalresearch/Pages/default/aspx (accessed April 12, 2014).
5. This information can be found online at http://public.imb.org/

- **Status 2:** Less than two percent evangelical but some church planting activity in the last two years;

- **Status 3:** Less than two percent evangelical with active church planting work in the last two years.

In 2014 they listed the following data on people and people groups using the above classifications:

	Status 0	Status 1	Status 2	Status 3
People Groups	490 (4.4% of people groups in the world)	4010 (35.7%)	1720 (15.3%)	323 (2.9%)
Population	10,797,875 (0.2% of the world's population	811,184,275 (11.6%)	1,909,746,000 (27.4%)	1,234,772,700 (17.7%)

The following conclusion can be made using the numbers above:

- There are 6,543 people groups that are unreached as of 2014;

- This represents 3,966,500,850 people who will likely live and die with little or no access to the good news of the gospel.

How do these numbers make you feel? What does this reveal about your heart?

_____

_____

The vast lostness of the world, coupled with the lack of access that many around the world have to the gospel, demands that missionary disciples engage in the task of getting the gospel message to the nations.

How can you intentionally engage the nations with the gospel right where God has placed you?

_____

_____

Move

The first answer is that you can go. It is all too common to hear people excuse themselves out of going to the nations. Certainly this task is not for everyone. But it is a task for more than are currently going.

Mission leaders attest to the fact that most North American church planters start churches within 100 miles of their biological parents. Additionally, among international missionaries, the ratio of women vastly outnumbers men on the mission field. The shortage of men willing to take the gospel to the nations is something for which the North American church will have to give an account.

What about you? Rather than asking why you should go, ask why you should stay. What would be the top three reasons for staying in your current context rather than replanting your life among the nations?

_____

_____

Travel

If you stay, you can go temporarily via short-term mission trips. These trips provide a way to connect you with the nations and to give you a taste of what God is doing around the world. Certainly, these trips can be little more than Christian tourism; however, they can also be vital conduits for God's grace to be displayed in your life and in the lives of those you go to serve.

The best way of planning a short-term trip is through relationships in your local church. These relationships provide a context for long-term connection to missionaries rather than sporadic excursions to unknown people. Additionally, they provide a relational context for meaningful work when you arrive.

Does your church have a partnership with another country for strategic mission?

_____

_____

If so, when is the next trip and what would it take for you to go?

_____

_____

Pray

If you stay, you can pray. Pray that God would glorify Himself by drawing the nations to Himself. This will require intentionality on your part. A valuable tool to aid in your prayers is provided on the website of the International Mission Board of the Southern Baptist Convention. Here you can find information on people groups and prayer needs.

Look over the list and write down one specific nation or people group to which the Spirit directs your attention.

_____

_____

What is it about this people group that makes it compelling to you?

_____

_____

Another method for intentionally praying for the nations is to pray for a location where someone you know is serving. If your church has a missionary stationed internationally, this would be a great place to start. If not, consider your other relational networks and see if there are any connections to the nations.

Who immediately comes to mind?

_____

_____

How could you pray intentionally for them?

_____

_____

Give

North American Christians live in a time of abundant provision. While not everyone is wealthy, there are resources at our disposal unlike any other time in redemptive history. Like the Corinthians, we must give with a generous heart as a worshipful response to the grace of God. This giving could take the form of financial giving through your local church. Most churches, particularly among the SBC, give a standard percentage of the church's tithe to the Cooperative Program which goes to fund mission work around the world. Other churches and denominations have various funding streams which serve to mobilize money to the nations. What percentage of your church's giving goes to support the work of international missions? (_____) If you don't know the answer to this question, take the time this week to ask one of your pastors for this number.

How does this encourage your giving to your church?

_____

_____

Or, you can give financial support directly to missionaries or church planters. Perhaps you know a strategic missionary that you would like to support directly. You could give towards the missionary's needs even if its a small amount of money. Warning: Do not neglect to give to your own church as you redirect money to international missionaries. It should be a both/and and not an either/or. To channel money away from your church for the sake of the nations would show distrust for the leadership of the church and potentially hamper its overall mission. If you are not pleased with the way your church gives to support the work of missions among the nations, one of the best things you can do is set up a meeting with your pastor and discuss how you can help raise awareness of the need for international missions support.

A final way that you could give would be by meeting a tangible, physical need. What could you send a missionary or church planter that would bring encouragement?

_____

_____

Engage

Finally, God in His kindness, has seen fit to send the nations to us. Many of you who are using *Aspire* live in the midst of the nations. They work alongside of you, go to school with you or your children, or are moving into your neighborhoods and apartment complexes. This provides you with a natural context to make disciples of the nations. Perhaps, through your active engagement in mission, God will bring salvation to these people, who in turn, can take the gospel back to their nation by sharing the gospel with their family and friends.

Think about the people in your life currently. Where do you see the nations represented? Who are three international people in your life who do not know Jesus?

1. _____

2. _____

3. _____

Whatever you do, you must do something. God is reclaiming worshippers from among all peoples and it is insufficient for the church to sit on the sidelines. As God sparks our hearts for mission among the nations, we will likewise see our hearts expand for mission in our own backyard.

Week 5: Your Culture

"Do not be conformed to this age, but be transformed by the renewing of your mind, so that you may discern what is the good, pleasing, and perfect will of God."

—*Romans 12:2*

"But Christian action, done as in the sight of God, for His sake, acknowledging that He alone is final judge, and that the Kingdom must be His gift—such action is a kind of prayer offered to God that He may hasten His Kingdom."[1]

—*Lessslie Newbigin*

God places missions at our doorstep everyday.

I remember my first large-scale mission project. I had participated in a number of week-long trips as a teenager. But, when I graduated from Furman I moved to the inner-city of Toronto, Canada. Talk about a change in culture! That summer, I lived in the choir room of a Pentecostal church and served the inner-city poor of Toronto through social ministries and street evangelism. Looking back, there is much that I would change about that experience. But I'll never forget certain moments. Like the last day I had in the city. I met Abraham my very first day in the downtown homeless park. I clumsily stumbled over him as he sat behind a tree drinking the rubbing alcohol he had purchased from the adjacent Dollar Store. Over the next 10 weeks, I built a friendship with Abraham and learned his story—his estranged marriage, his young children, and his path to full-blown addiction. We spent the summer talking (when he was sober enough to do so) about life and God. On the final day, I boarded the bus to leave town while Abraham stood in the park, waving goodbye. I still have that picture in my office to remind me that missions has *a face* and *a place*.

We can quote stats all day. For example, there are an estimated 259 million people in the US without saving faith in Jesus Christ. David Olsen reports that the percentage of people attending a Christian church in the US is declining rapidly (20.6 percent

---

1. Lesslie Newbigin, *Signs amid the Rubble: The Purposes of God in Human History* (Grand Rapids: Eerdmans, 2003), 51.

in church in 1990, 17.3 percent in 2005, and a prediction of 14.7 percent by 2020).[1] There were roughly the same number of people attending a Christian church on any given Sunday in 1990 as there were in 2005. However, the national population has grown by over 91 million people. While the number of mega-churches has drastically increased (10 in 1970, 835 in 2003 and over 1300 in 2007), it seems that there are fewer and fewer people meaningfully connected to God's church.

Those figures are sadly insignificant for most of us. We must have a face to go with the numbers.

It's one thing to talk about living a life of mission in the abstract, it is another to put missions on the map and begin the hard work that missionary living requires.

Try your hand at it. Describe the *place* and *face* of missions for you. What comes to mind when you think about missions?

_____

_____

Let's start with the place of mission. Is mission simply something that happens "over there" with "those people"? Most of us are aware that this is not true. Every place in the world presents a unique sent of contextual challenges for effective missionaries. Even at the surface level, it is clear that missions does not happen in a vacuum.

Culture

Mission is bound up in culture, and that culture shapes the way in which you can and should undertake missions. The word culture is used to describe the sum total of the beliefs, values, influences, and way of life of a certain people group, nation, or city.

How would you define the culture of North America?

_____

_____

----

1. Dave Olson, *The American Church Research Project* online at: www.theamericanchurch.org.

What different types of cultures make up the culture of North America?

_____

_____

The fruit of culture is seen in:

- The things people watch;

- The stories they tell;

- The values they profess;

- The philosophical basis for their decisions;

- The voices that speak into their lives;

- The things they fear.

The face of missions in North America has changed drastically. At one point, homogenous cultures were the norm in North America. Most people in the same geographical region looked, talked, and thought alike. For many those thought patterns were informed by a Judeo-Christian worldview.

Not anymore.

As the world continues to change, some macro-level cultural changes will shape the mission to which you are choosing to give your life. Those factors include:

- **A globalized society:** Culture is rapidly diversifying and with that comes the reality that various truth claims and ideologies and now living, shopping, and working as neighbors;

- **A pluralization of truth:** Authoritative truth that applies for all people at all times is dismissed;

- **A marginalization of Christianity:** The west has been "dechristianized," according to David Bosch.[1] The Christian worldview and its societal implications is increasingly the minority position;

---

1. Bosch, *Transforming*, 3.

- **A secularized marketplace:** People can believe whatever they want to believe in private, but this faith must not be imported into the public domain, where empirical science is thought to reign supreme;

- **A shrinking middle-class:** People are either wealthy or impoverished, and there is increasingly no middle ground. This means that the societal implications of poverty (crime, drug addition, genocide, sex trafficking, and the like) are all-too-common realities in a world of oppression;

- **A technologically integrated world:** All people are influenced by a common cultural ethos by means of technological advances. [1]

How do these trends shape missionary living?

_____

_____

Do these trends shape the church gathered and/or the church scattered? How so?

_____

_____

Are these trends obstacles or catalysts for missions?

_____

_____

This is surely not the first time that God's people have found themselves as a minority people. The exile, while a form of judgment from God, informs the way in which God's people are to live in a culture antithetical to the worship of God. Jeremiah says:

> *Build houses and live in them. Plant gardens and eat their produce. Take wives and have sons and daughters. Take wives for your sons and give your daughters to men in marriage so that they may bear sons and daughters. Multiply there; do not decrease. Seek the welfare of the city I have deported you to. Pray to the Lord on its behalf, for when it has prosperity, you will prosper (Jer 29:5–7).*

---

1. Michael W. Goheen and Craig G. Bartholomew, *Living at the Crossroads: An Introduction to Christian Worldview* (Grand Rapids: Baker Acdemic, 2008), 103–06.

The language here is intriguing. God does not tell them to fight but rather to settle down and live decent, trustworthy lives among a foreign people. They are even to continue the work of creation by tending the earth and being fruitful in childbearing. In so doing, the city would prosper and the mission of God would be seen.

It is possible to engage culture from the fringes. If the church in North America is going to thrive in the twenty-first century it is going to have to learn how to do this. A number of God-given tools allow for the mission of God to engage culture from the fringes.

Scripture

An authoritative Bible is the greatest tool for mission that is viable in any culture. The challenges are endless, and thus we must consistently labor over the Word of God and seek to discern how to engage God's world. The message of the gospel does not change—regardless of the culture to which it is applied.

Missions happens as God's Kingdom intersects human culture by means of His Word. The authority of the Word means that we possess a resource with supra-cultural validity. Scripture is not bound to a particular time, place, or culture; it is the basis by which all cultures will be judged.

How does an authoritative Bible serve to critique all cultures and help you live on mission?

_____

_____

Contextualization

The influence of culture requires that the gospel be uniquely and skillfully applied to the context in which God has placed us. This process of thoughtful and skillful contextualization is one of the greatest challenges of missionary living in the postmodern world. There is simply no "one-size-fits-all" way to live on mission.

Mission is shaped by culture from the very outset. In fact, three cultures collide every time the gospel is presented: the culture of the Bible, the culture of the one sharing the message, and the culture of the one hearing the message. The intersection of these cultures poses the great missional challenge of our day.

Write your own definition of contextualization:

_____

_____

Tim Keller uses the following definition in his book *Center Church*. Contextualization is "giving people the Bible's answers, which they may not all want to hear, to questions about life that people in their particular time and place are asking, in language and forms they can comprehend, and through appeals and arguments with force they can feel, even if they reject them."[1]

What do you observe about this definition? What do you like? What would you change?

_____

_____

Think about the culture in which you currently live. What evidence of the impact of culture do you observe?

_____

_____

Missionaries must begin by prayerfully and thoughtfully considering how the gospel will uniquely engage that culture. The focus of a missionary disciple must always be to obey God and remain faithful to His call by joining Him where He is working in the world. Prayer places the missionary in a visionary posture—seeking, asking, and expecting guidance from the Lord for how best to enter the culture. Much like Paul, missionaries must have the unique ability to be led by the Holy Spirit into new ventures. Since the Bible does not give a magical formula for the implementation of contextualization, prayer is a means of receiving insight about things the Scriptures do not directly address. As you think about your culture, ask yourself the following questions:

1. Keller, *Center,* 89.

What aspects of the culture should I accept and embrace (for example, ethnic diversity is a beautiful picture of the reality that God is saving and uniting people from every tribe, tongue, and nation)?

_____

_____

What aspects of culture should I reject (for example, technological advances make it increasingly possible for heinous sexual sins that take advantage of the wounded, broken, and needy)?

_____

_____

What aspects of culture should I challenge (for example, the seemingly universal drive for more: more money, more possessions, more freedoms, and more stuff drive the modern world)?

_____

_____

What aspects of culture should I work to change (for example, childhood illiteracy is a factor that serves as a forerunner to a host of unhealthy adult behaviors)? A disciple could apply himself to working to bring about change in this area in the city.

_____

_____

You cannot escape culture, so you must learn to engage it with gospel intentionality. This requires an awareness, not simply of the culture at large, but of your particular culture specifically. All cultures are different, as evidenced by the conflicting cultural norms that exist among varying subcultures. So, you can't just learn to engage culture in general, but you must engage the culture in which God has placed you—your own circle of accountability found in the city in which you live.

Week 6: Your City

"Then the Lord said to Paul in a night vision, 'Don't be afraid, but keep on speaking and don't be silent. For I am with you, and no one will lay a hand on you to hurt you, because I have many people in this city.' And he stayed there a year and six months, teaching the word of God among them."

—*Acts 18:9–11*

"As God's people, we are a 'good news' community that erects signs of God's present-and-yet coming kingdom n our communal life, in our callings in the public life of culture, cross the whole spectrum of our family and individual lives."[1]

—*Michael Goheen and Craig Bartholomew*

A city is a geographical location of great population density and diversity.

Culture comes to life in real cities, towns, and villages made up of people in need of the gospel. In these cities, churches are planted in an effort to bring the gospel to bear on the people who call that geography home. We see this in the Pauline epistles as he writes to churches such as the one in Corinth (1 Cor 1:2), Galatia (Gal 1:2), and Thessalonica (1 Thess1:1). Each of these churches presented a unique context for the gospel. Additionally, the movement of the gospel in the New Testament flowed through major hubs of culture. In these cities, cultures take overt shape. By targeting locations of influence, such as cities, missionaries can strategically share the gospel and plant churches in areas of great cultural traffic, knowledge transference, and world authority. Cities provide a fertile soil for the gospel message because of:

- **The Need:** There are simply more people per square mile in a city as opposed to a rural or suburban area. Thus, there is a great need for missionaries in these locations.

---

1. Goheen and Bartholomew, *Crossroads,* 61.

- **The Receptivity:** Diversity means that there are a host of people looking for answers that make sense of their lives and stories. As a result, one is certain to find some who are fertile soil for the gospel message in urban centers.

- **The Influence:** Modern sociologists and missiologist argue that the best place for cultural influence are strategic cities. Here, people learn, think, write, publish, act, sing, and legislate. As they do, they shape the culture in the surrounding region, and with the influence of technology, these cites may in fact shape the entire world.

What do you like or dislike about life in a city? Do you prefer an urban or rural setting? How does this shape the way you engage in mission?

_____

_____

Describe the context in which you currently live? What defines it?

_____

_____

God wants us to influence the cities where we live.

Whether it is a major urban center or a mill town, the issue is how do you, as a missionary disciple, go about influencing that region. Thankfully, in God's wisdom he decentralized the church, scattering it through the domains of work, art, business, recreation, education, and the like. There, God's church enters the web of social relationships and develops the cultural capital to speak about the gospel. The exiles of Jeremiah's day were instructed to do just that—to settle down, live in the city, and seek its welfare (Jer 29:4–7). In so doing, they would be a distinctive influence in a specific geography.

This is your mission too. God wants you to live and love a place in such a way that the presence of Christ is a felt reality in that place. Caution: Don't get overwhelmed by the sheer size of the city. Sure, there are a ton of people, and you can't do everything; But you can do something. Start small and allow God to bring fruit from your seemingly meager efforts.

Project 1

On page 317 you will find a survey that you can use to gather data about your city. Think of this as military intelligence prior to a battle. You are gathering data that will be used in strategic mission in the future, by you and your church. This week, take 10 copies of this survey and use it to initiate conversation with strangers in your circle. This will work best if you diversify the types of people you ask. Try to find a professional businessman, a local shop owner, a mother, a homeless man, a first responder, and perhaps even a local religious leader.

Once you are done, sit down with your surveys and compile your notes. Based on this data, what shape does the good news of the gospel take for these people? How would you contextualize the message of the gospel to connect with this circle? What fears or hurts do you see in the people you interviewed?

_____

_____

_____

_____

Project 2

Next, take the personal survey on page page 318 and use it to gather your own observations about the city. If you are in a new location serving as a missionary this will be a useful tool for you to begin to assess nature of your new work. If, however, you are living in your hometown, such a project will hopefully give you fresh eyes to notice needs and be broken by the overwhelming reality of a people apart from God.

Project 3

Spend some time with someone who knows the city well. This could be a city leader or simply someone who has lived in the city for a long time. Ask them to come and share about the history of the city. If you are serving as a missionary with a church plant, ask the pastors of the church to help you set up a meeting with such a person.

Based on the history of the city, what new insights do you have about how best to engage it with the gospel?

_____

_____

God wants us to influence our spheres of influence in the city.

You have a circle of accountability for missionary living. Paul tells us that God is sovereign over the specific timing and location of our lives. As a result we can be assured that He has placed us in our unique location for His grand purposes (Acts 17:26–27). This circle should be defined as the place where you spend the vast majority of your time. Ideally, it is a place in which you live, work, play, and gather with a church. This circle in a much larger city is the place to start living like a missionary (consider a 2–3 mile radius as the place to start). You are now well on your way to living as an intentional missionary in your context. To do this you will need to live as a missionary in the following areas:

Home

Your home is one of the richest resources God has given you for engaging with people who need God. We do not have to look far to find someone: they are our neighbors. The increasing diversity of the landscape of North America means that the nations are living within walking distance of us. It requires intentionality on your part to engage them with the gospel, however.

Take some time to map your neighborhood. Learn their names and try to discover their spiritual condition. Use the following chart to help with this:

An adjacent home	The people directly across from you	An adjacent home
The people who live to your left	YOUR HOUSE	The people who live to your right

Work

Work is not a consequence of the fall, but rather is a means by which God's glory can be spread to the end of the earth. Granted, work is going to be hard as a result of the fall, but it is necessary. You have to work, so why not be intentional about viewing your work as a missionary venture. Missionary work involves:

- **Doing what you do well.** You will lose the right to be heard if you have a slack work ethic. However humble, gracious, and solid work, on the other hand, will produce an exemplary life that wins favor with outsiders. Not only that, but your work is a tool for displaying the glory of God by bringing beauty and order from the things that He has made.

- **Doing what you do joyfully.** Rather than begrudging work that is steeped in frustration, missionary disciples make it a point to do their work as unto the Lord. In this way, God is honored and those around you are encouraged.

- **Doing what you do strategically.** Your decisions about your vocation must not be haphazard. Instead, think through how to leverage your unique gifts and talents in a way that provides maximum opportunity for missional witness—even your vocation.

Describe your current job: How is it a tool for missionary opportunities? What would need to change in order for you to leverage your job as a missionary?

_____

_____

_____

_____

School

Most city-dwellers will either be in school or have children who attend school. This may be formal education, or it might be informal classes built around hobbies or pastimes (such as a scrapbook class or photography workshop). These classes provide an immediate inroad to relationships. Even if you are not currently enrolled in formal schooling, it may be wise to take a course or two at a local school simply for the relationships that it might produce. Additionally, the need for mentors for school-age children without stable homes is always a viable way of engaging school systems with the gospel.

Recreation

Christian have fun too (at least some of them do). Leverage the things that you enjoy for gospel purposes. You could simply find ways to strike up conversations with nonbelievers while doing something you enjoy, such as working out at the gym. Or you could invite a non-believing friend to participate in a new activity with you, such as teaching someone how to fly fish or hunt.

If you have five hours of unplanned time, how do you fill it? How could this serve as a catalyst for mission?

_____

_____

Arts

The arts are a final inroad to mission in a city context. Be it a street festival or a formal show, arts provide a means of demonstrating the skill and creativity of God's image bearers. Sadly, this portion of society is often thought to be off-limits for Christians. Many simply do not know how to engage the arts with the gospel. But, for some of you, God has wired you with a unique giftedness that makes this a prime mission field.

What arts do you enjoy? How could you leverage that passion to build relationships with non-believers?

_____

_____

These five areas demonstrate that it is not enough to know and love a city. Missionaries must take their knowledge of themselves and their city and apply it to specific and intentional missional practices, and in so doing, they live life on mission.

City Survey

What do you like most about this city?

_____

What do you like least about this city?

_____

What brought you here?

_____

What would you like to change about this city if you could?

_____

What type of work do you do?

_____

What do you do for fun?

_____

Who are the influential people in this city?

_____

What do people who live in this city value?

_____

What are the greatest needs of this city?

_____

What is the perception of the churches in this city?

_____

Personal Survey

What is unique about this city?

_____

Where do people hang out?

_____

What is beautiful about this city?

_____

What are the primary occupations in the city?

_____

Where do people shop?

_____

What do people seem to value?

_____

What are people reading, watching, or talking about?

_____

What physical or spiritual needs do you observe?

_____

Do you notice any natural boundary markers that serve to divide people (for example a street that divides the Hispanic population from the Anglo-population)?

_____

What is God already doing in the city? What are the churches already doing in the city?

_____

Week 7: Pray

"The Lord is not slow in keeping his promise, as some understand slowness. He is patient with you, not wanting anyone to perish, but everyone to come to repentance."

—*2 Peter 3:9*

"Prayer is as mighty as God, because He has committed Himself to answer it. God pity us that in this noblest of all employments for the tongue and for the spirit, we stammer so. If God does not illuminate us in the closest, we walk in darkness. At the judgment seat the most embarrassing thing the believer will face will be the smallness of his praying."[1]

—*Leonard Ravenhill*

Prayer is the foundation for a worshiping missionary.

Missionary intentionality will require your very life. The size and scope of the mission should drive you to a deep awareness of your inability and insignificance and your dependence upon God for the production of any lasting fruit (1 Cor 3:5–9). As a result, fervent prayer should mark the life of a worshiping missionary who understands that he or she is dependent on the Spirit.

Prayer served as the foundation for the church at Pentecost, and it has been a chief mark of its effectiveness ever since (Acts 2; 1 Thess 5:25; Rom. 15:31–32). Prayer affirms that God is sovereign over salvation and, while we may scatter seed through a life of mission, only God can send the growth. Without God's power to raise the dead to life, no amount of human ingenuity will result in fruitfulness. As a result, a missionary will forever be in a dependent posture. If you are doing missions correctly, you should never come to a place where you think: "I've got this."

Rather, you should live with a growing awareness of how much you need God to work in your ministry. Prayer is an affirmation of such dependence. I am certain that you have been praying prior to this point in the study—at least I hope so! Here are some motives of a praying missionary disciple.

---

1. Leonard Ravenhill, *Why Revival Taries* (Minneapolis: Bethany House, 1987), 151.

Motives

- **We pray because God grants salvation by grace through faith (Eph 2:8–9).** Only God can save which means that you should pray that He would do what only He can do. Disciples pray that God would remove the scales from the eyes of the lost and soften the soil of their hearts to the truth claims of the gospel (Lk 4:1–20).

- **We pray because the plight of human sin and depravity is so great that only God can heal and bind up the broken (Mk 9:29).** There is no self-help method for depravity, nor can skillful missionaries "fix" the problems that people's sinful choices have caused for them. Disciples pray that God would mend the physical suffering of broken people, while revealing their deep need for the spiritual healing that can only come from the gospel.

- **We pray because God is capable of guiding our steps in order to position us for missionary encounters.** Not only has he placed you in the unique context in which He wants you to serve, but He also orders your choices so that you are in position for missionary encounters. Therefore, disciples pray that God would guide even the minor decisions of their day so that divine encounters may occur.

- **We pray because God is willing to convict us of a lack of missionary fervor and once again break your heart for the needs of the lost world.** Disciples pray that God would consistently crush them under the desperate fate of the lost and move them to action.

- **We pray because living on mission is a minefield of spiritual warfare, and missionaries need to be ready for battle (Eph 6).** Therefore, they pray that God would clothe them in His armor so that they can withstand the onslaught of life in the battle.

- **We pray because the work is too great for any singular missionary or church.** The harvest is so vast, and the needs so great, that Jesus challenges His disciples to pray that God would raise up more laborers for His harvest fields.

- **We pray because God is the only one capable of building the church.** The early church saw this growth, and Luke affirmed, "God added to their number those who were being saved (Acts 2:47)." This was a work of God alone. He is the one who saves by doing the "heavy-lifting" of your missionary labors. Disciples pray that God would grow His church through the conversion of the lost and the sanctification of the saved.

Does your current prayer life reflect these motives? What about your life fuels or quenches a passion for prayer?

_____

_____

God's control over the work of evangelism need not render a missionary disciple passive. Instead, the reality that God is calling a people to Himself through His grace in Christ should prompt confidence, boldness, and increased dependence on the part of the missionary disciple.

Prayer is a disciplined act. If you are not careful, you will feel the mounting pressure of the missionary needs of your city and run headlong into your missionary efforts without spending time with God. Here are some methods for developing a disciplined prayer life.

Methods

- **Journal your prayers:** Not only will this keep you focused during your times of prayer, but it will serve as a helpful reminder of God's grace through your missionary efforts. If you do not already have a prayer journal, make plans to get one today and use it alongside of your *Aspire* guide. Make notes of missionary contacts, how you see God at work, and answers to prayer along the way.

- **Put a face to your prayers:** As you begin to meet people in the city, pray for them by name. For example, rather than praying an abstract prayer that God would save the lost, pray specifically that God would grant salvation to Steve, the young barista at the coffee shop you have begun to frequent. A missionary disciple should be able to list the names of at least five non-believers for whom he is praying regularly. Take 10 minutes to list the names that come to your mind. One effective method would be to think through the domains we listed in the previous section and list two non-believers that you know in each of these areas:

HOME

1. _____

2. _____

WORK

1. _____

2. _____

SCHOOL

1. _____

2. _____

RECREATION

1. _____

2. _____

ARTS

1. _____

2. _____

- **Pray as you walk:** Walking in prayer allows you to raise your spiritual antennae to the needs of the world. For example, as you walk and pray that God will free people from the shackles of slavery to money, you are able to look around and pray for specific business owners directly. This can also be a profitable way to continue to make yourself aware of the needs of your city and position yourself for divine encounters. Warning: Don't hover outside on the street corner and attract attention to yourself. You will look strange and people will be scared.

- **Pray strategically:** Your prayer list will grow exponentially because there is no shortage of things for which to pray. As a result, it is important that you plan for prayer. One method might be to select a certain topic to pray about each day. For example you may pray for co-workers on Monday, classmates on Tuesday, former high school friends on Wednesday, and so on. Or, you may pray alphabetically for the lost. Take those whose names begin with A–C and pray for them each Monday, those whose names start with D–F and pray for them on Tuesday, and so on. Think about a prayer-plan now and be prepared to share it with your mentor the next time you meet. Here is one example:

Sunday	Monday	Tuesday	Wednesday	Thursday	Friday	Saturday
THANKFULNESS	SALVATION	MISSION	COMMUNITY	NEEDS	LEADERSHIP	GATHERING
Thank God for the joy of salvation and the hope of the gospel.	Pray specifically for those you know who are far from God and/or the local church.	Pray for the mission partners of your local church—both local and those around the world.	Pray for the relationships of the members of your local church—that God would grow your love for one another in Christ.	Pray for the specific needs of those in your church (health, job loss, etc.).	Pray for the leadership of your home, church, and country.	Pray for the upcoming gathering of your church.

- **Pray the Scriptures:** Often times we find ourselves paralyzed by our inability to pray well. There is seemingly so much to pray for and it is challenging to put words to the thoughts and desires of our hearts. Thankfully we are given the gift of God's Spirit who can bring our frail and broken Words before the throne of

God. In addition, we are given the Scriptures, which provide a record of some of the prayers of God's people through the ages as well as specific instructions from God on what we should pray for. For example, we can use the Bible to pray that:

1. God would give us a deep burden for those apart from the love of Christ (Lk 18:41–42);

2. God would give us a heart of compassion for the poor and the marginalized (Js 1:27);

3. God would bring light into the darkness of our world (Mt 5:14–16);

4. God would draw people to Himself by revealing the beauty of Christ (Jn 6:44);

5. People far from God would be saved by grace through repentance and faith (Eph 2:8–9; 1 Jn 1:9–10);

6. God would give His church a good reputation with unbelievers (1 Thess 4:12);

7. God would crush pride and bring about servant-like humility (Js 4:10; 1 Pet 5:6);

8. God would season our words with truth and grace (Col 4:5–6);

9. God's people would be doers of the Word and not simply hearers (Js 1:22);

10. God would raise up disciples who could make other disciples (2 Tim 2:2);

11. All people, especially the leaders of the church, would rightly handle God's Holy Word (2 Tim 2:15; 3:16);

12. God would unify His church (Eph 4);

13. God would build and protect healthy marriages among His church (Eph 5);

14. Satan would be restrained and the church protected (Mt 13:19; 2 Cor 4:4).

- **Post your prayers:** Write missionary Scripture verses, gospel quotes, or personal prayers on index cards, then, post them in specific locations that you will see every day, like your bathroom mirror, refrigerator, or dash board. Spend some time now making five cards and posting them in strategic locations.

- **Redeem your gaps:** Every day is filled with gaps—15 minute chunks of time when you have nothing to do. Perhaps it is before an appointment, during a break at work, sitting in a drive-through line, or waiting in traffic. These gaps are God-ordained times for prayer. Sadly, we are often guilty of filling them with social media visits. Use these gaps for intentional prayer each day.

- **Mobilize others to pray:** Think about other believers who are known for effective prayer. Even if they live in another city, they can be mobilized to pray. Paul was consistently encouraging his church to pray for His work of missions (Rom 12:12; Col 4:2). Target three prayer-warriors in your life, and ask them to pray for three of the names on your list.

Prayer is perhaps the most wasted resources in the average missionaries life. We are all quick to run after tools and methods that we hope will produce effective evangelistic results. All the while, our prayer lives remain dormant. These misplaced priorities reflect a misunderstanding about the nature of God's work in the world, which is in desperate need of correction.

You are a missionary disciple who is growing in your understanding of the gospel and its implications for all of life. Therefore, you are rightly positioned to understand that the place to begin living as a missionary is not with another form of religious performance, but with prayer.

Week 8: Invest

"Now the end of all things is near; therefore, be serious and disciplined for prayer. Above all, maintain an intense love for each other, since love covers a multitude of sins. Be hospitable to one another without complaining. Based on the gift each one has received, use it to serve others, as good managers of the varied grace of God. If anyone speaks, it should be as one who speaks God's words; if anyone serves, it should be from the strength God provides, so that God may be glorified through Jesus Christ in everything. To Him belong the glory and the power forever and ever. Amen."

—1 Peter 4:7–11

"Most people in the West need to be welcomed into community long enough for them to hear multiple expressions of the gospel—both formal and informal—from individuals and teachers."[1]

—Tim Keller

God wants us to develop relationships with the gospel in mind.

We've all seen it done—a gospel tract left on a urinal, as a tip, or passed between strangers in a crowded inner city. This type of missionary drive-by may work on occasion. Certainly, God can use all types of gospel methods to bring about salvation. However, the most effective missionary strategy by far results from the conduit of genuine relationships.

When God invaded human history, He did so in the person of Christ. He sent His Son to dwell among people as the exact representation of the image of God. Jesus was known, and often criticized, for His relationships with the lost (Mt 20:20-–34; 23:1–39; Mk 10:21; Lk 15:1–3; 19:1–10; Jn 4:5–42). Mark tells us that Jesus was known as a friend of tax collectors and sinners, and He made them His disciples in the context of table fellowship, shared travel, hard work, informal stories, and challenging missions.

Relationships will be vital to your developing mission as well. Now that you have a solid understanding of God's mission and your culture, and have begun to pray

---

1. Keller, *Center*, 281.

intentionally for God to work among a people, you are now positioned to develop four critical relationships. John Stott writes that "we are not just to receive the stranger when he comes to us, but actually to inquire after, and look carefully for, strangers, to pursue them and search them out everywhere, lest perchance somewhere they may sit—in the streets or live without a roof over their heads."[1] These "strangers" are everywhere—all we have to do it take the time invest in these relationships.

Relationships with non-Christians

Non-Christians are everywhere, particularly in a major urban city. So it is not hard to find those in need of the salvation offered through Christ. Consider people that you meet in the following contexts:

- People who work with you or go to your school;

- People that you seem to cross paths with daily;

- People who work in shops that you frequent;

- People who serve you food or coffee regularly;

- People who live nearby;

- People who enjoy the same hobbies;

- People who are open to conversation.

This is your mission field. Locating non-Christians is not hard—making them your friend is a massive challenge, however. How does it happen? You must make an intentional and meaningful investment of your time and energy for meaningful relationships to develop.

Think about your best friends growing up. What did you do in order to be a good friend?

_____

_____

---

1. John Stott, *Romans: God's Good News for the World* (Downers Grove, IL: IVP, 1995), 337.

Who is the last person in your life (Christian or non-Christian) that moved from being a total stranger to being a good friend? How did this process happen?

_____

_____

Sadly, most adults forget how to make friends. They either maintain the ones they had when they were young, maintain a vast array of forced or surface-level friendships, or do not try to develop new friendships. Few adults know how to initiate a friendship with anyone, much less with someone who shares a drastically different worldview then they do. How do these types of friendships happen?

Exude Joy

Be the type of person that others would want to befriend. Make the gospel appealing through your joyful presence around the lost. This is not hypocritical happiness, but true joy that results from a right understanding of the gospel. In a world that lacks joy, you become a prime inroad to the gospel simply by living a joyful life. Make it your mission to brighten the room and the spirits of those that you meet.

Take a moment to consider other's impressions of you. What five words do you think most people would use to describe you? What first impression do you think you convey to strangers?

_____

_____

Ask Questions

Find out about people through simple, non-invasive questions. What do you do for a living? How long have you been in the city? What are you reading? Where might I go to get a good cheeseburger? Good questions—even those for which you already know the answer will open the door for conversation, and conversation serves as the oil on which relationships run.

What are three go-to questions you could ask any stranger in your city in order to get a conversation going? It would be wise to have a few of these ready when a missionary opportunity presents itself.

_____

_____

_____

Listen

As people answer questions, listen well. Learn their names, pieces of their stories, things they enjoy, or perhaps even wounds in their lives. This means that we must not treat people as tally marks in our evangelism scorebook. We must be fully present in the conversation, listening intently, and in so doing communicate genuine care and respect. A vibrant prayer life, including collecting these prayers in a journal, is a great tool in order to burn these facts into your mind.

Slow Down

The rapid pace of the modern world tends to thrust people into their days with a figurative "do not disturb" sign around their necks. People know if you are simply rushing into and out of conversation or if you genuinely care about their stories. Many strangers, who might need for someone to listen to them, are not likely to talk to someone who is seemingly in a hurry or tied to their computers, iPads, or cell phones. It is wise to consider how you can create missionary margin in your life—the space between your daily activities that allows you to have a meaningful conversation or meet a tangible need of those that you encounter. Without intentionality, you will be prone to miss God-ordained opportunities.

Do you live hurried life? How might you create missionary margin in your schedule? It may be wise for you to remind yourself of the time-management tools that we developed in 2.11 of _Aspire_.

_____

_____

Tell Stories

Stories are the currency of relationship. Following the death of a loved one, what do people do? They tell stories. These narratives connect humanity and are often one of the first signs of a developing friendship. Be prepared to share some personal stories from your life that connect with the flow of the conversation, and pray that the other person trusts you enough to begin to open up as well. Be careful that you do not over talk, however. Share enough about yourself to get the conversation moving, but be sure you create time and space for the other person to share as well. Be encouraged—most people want relationships so much that they will be quick to tell stories if it seems that someone genuinely wants to listen.

Remember and Ask

Asking good questions moves the conversation, and the relationship, forward. The story that the person has shared may prompt natural questions. Or you may bring up something that they have shared with you and ask them about it the next time you are together. For example, if a person has shared with you that they are at the coffee shop during the workday because they are looking for a new job, you can ask them how the job hunt is going. Avoid yes or no questions at this point, such as, "So, have you found a job yet?" These questions tend to stifle the conversation rather than push it forward. Good questions, particularly those that reflect that you remember an issue, says, "I am listening to you and care about you."

Think about three people that do not know Jesus with whom you are currently building a relationship. What is an example of a major life issue facing that person or their family? What question could you ask them that would demonstrate care and concern?

Person 1 _____

   Life Situation: _____

   Question: _____

Trimester 3: Mission

Person 2 _____

    Life Situation: _____

    Question: _____

Person 3 _____

    Life Situation: _____

    Question: _____

Take a minute to follow up with these questions, while God has them on your mind. You could call them, send them a text message or an email, or drop by where they live or work. Ask them about their life situation and see what doors God opens.

- **Spend time on their turf:** Frequent places where your new friends hangout and spend as much time there as you can. Non-Christians are not likely to come to your turf first, so establish yourself on their turf, and become a regular there. We will think more about these places in a minute, but it is worth noting here that the only way that you can develop relationships with non-believers is to be around them. This could mean working out at a local gym, frequenting the same restaurant, or going on an evening walk through your neighborhood.

- **Show hospitality:** The first act of true friendship is often a shared meal (Mt 25:31–46; Lk14:12–14; Rom 12:13; Heb 13:2; 1 Pet 4:9). As soon as possible, invite them to share a meal with you. Ideally, you should open your apartment or home and invite them over for a home-cooked meal. Authentic hospitality welcomes outsiders into your life and demonstrates love. It also presents a host of ways for you to share about your life experience as people observe your family pictures, books on the coffee table, cards on the refrigerator, and the like. Go ahead and plan something now. Who is a non-believer in your relational network that you could invite over to dinner in the next week or two? Get it on the calendar now.

- **Mention Jesus:** Find an appropriate inroad in the conversation to mention that you are a follower of Jesus. Do not simply say that you go to church or that you are a Christian. These labels have such a negative stereotype in the minds of most that they hinder your gospel witness from the outset. Affirm your faith, hope, and love for Jesus in the normal dynamics of an informal conversation between friends.

- **Live Well:** A disembodied gospel message is of little worth. Once a person knows that you are a follower of Jesus, he/she can begin to watch your life and think "Oh, so this is what it looks like if I were to become a Christian." You have now placed yourself in the spotlight by entering into a relationship with a non-Christian. They will now begin to watch the way you talk, react to stress and suffering, love your spouse, or strive for excellence in your work. You are now positioned by God to be a gospel light for those around to see.

Who are five people in your city with whom you are currently trying to develop a friendship using the above strategies. Beside their names write an appropriate next step from the list above that you could take in order to foster the growth of the relationship.

1. _____

2. _____

3. _____

4. _____

5. _____

Relationships with the Marginalized

Worshiping missionaries should invest in the marginalized as well. Certainly these may be overlapping categories, but it seems that God was especially concerned about the marginalized: the widows, orphans, wounded, broken, and outcasts (Js 1:27). These marginalized portions of society provide ample opportunity for missional intentionality. You will have to cross barriers of comfort in order to meet the marginalized on their turf. But if you do, their desperate physical needs and isolation will lead to quick friendships.

Who are the widows and orphans in your city? Most often this answer will come by considering the people that are typically thought of as "other" by the dominant group in your culture. This may be someone of another ethnicity (i.e. the Hispanic community in a suburban Anglo context), of another socio-economic strata (i.e. the wealthy couples that live around the country club), or people from another religion or lifestyle (i.e. the Muslim or homosexual community).

The church, particularly in North America, now finds itself on the fringes of society and culturally distant from those they are called to reach with the gospel. These groups may be generally labeled as follows:

- **The True Church:** People who have genuinely repented of their sins and placed their faith in Jesus Christ and are placed by God in His church and given the task of living as a missionary.

- **The Religious:** People who may share a common language, background, and set of ethical principles with those in the church. They tend to understand the language and thought patterns of believers and yet fail to grasp the gospel, hiding behind a thin veil of good works.

- **The Secular:** People who have little interest in the church and little to no understanding of the gospel.

- **The Marginalized:** People who may be religious or secular but often finds themselves increasingly removed from the church due to poverty or oppression.

- **The Antagonistic:** People who are angry and hostile to the gospel and the church due to conflicting worldviews or past woundedness. [1]

---

1. This illustration is adapted from Alan Hirsch, *The Forgotten Ways* (Grand Rapids: Brazos Press, 2006), 57.

You might picture it this way:

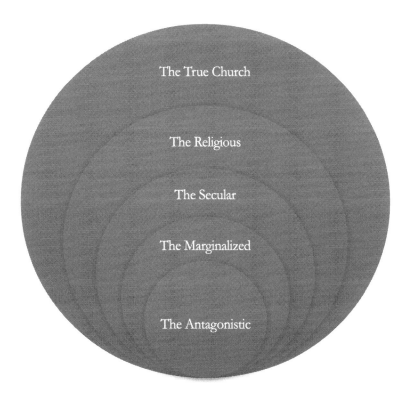

Consider your friendships with non-believers. Attempt to put two names in each of the above categories:

Religious	Secular	Marginalized	Antagonistic
1.	1.	1.	1.
2.	2.	2.	2.

What makes it uniquely challenging to share the gospel with people in each of these areas?

Religious: _____

Secular: _____

Marginalized: _____

Antagonistic: _____

Relationships with People of Peace

These developing relationships may draw your attention to people who have a disproportionate amount of influence in a relational network, workplace, town, or even city. Such people have been described as a person of peace because of their vast network of relationships with non-believers. This person, who may be a believer or non-believer, is:

- Connected to a large number of people through their relational capacity or their position in a city (i.e. a local coffee shop owner or city mayor);

- Respected by those people;

- Capable of providing you with relational credibility with others in that location.

This person may be a religious leader, or he may be a football coach, business owner, or artist. If this person is a Christian, he/she will often be a recent convert who still has a host of relationships with the lost (think about the original disciples or the Samaritan Woman at the well). Christians often have fewer and fewer deep relationships with the lost the longer they are Christian; therefore, it is vital to capitalize on these relationships as early as possible.

Whom have you observed that might match this definition of a person of peace?

_____

_____

How would you go about building a relationship with these people?

_____

_____

Relationships with Third Places

A final relationship, and one that we have already mentioned, is a relationship with the locations in which non-believers spend the vast amount of their time. These locations are often referred to as "third places." They are neither the place where a person lives nor the place they work, but the place where they spend most of their disposable time.

In these "third places," people build relationships and share stories making them prime locations for missionary encounters.

Missionary disciples should see it as a vital task to develop relationships with the owners of these locations and those who frequent them. This will mean that you should attempt to make yourself a regular in these third places. For example, rather than rotating between a number of different coffee shops for your morning coffee, you would be well served to consistently visit the same one. While there you should buy something, tip well, talk to the patrons and owner, and bring your friends there to do the same.

Where are the people with whom you are building relationships hanging out?

_____

_____

Investing in relationships with non-Christians, the marginalized, people of peace, and third places is a time consuming process. At first it may seem challenging, but over time these missionary principles will become second nature. Don't loose heart if they feel awkward at first. You don't grow as a missionary overnight—it takes time. But the rewards are incredible.

Notice Paul's words in Colossians 4:2–6:

> *Devote yourselves to prayer; stay alert in it with thanksgiving. At the same time, pray also for us that God may open a door to us for the message, to speak the mystery of the Messiah, for which I am in prison, so that I may reveal it as I am required to speak. Act wisely toward outsiders, making the most of the time. Your speech should always be gracious, seasoned with salt, so that you may know how you should answer each person.*

Here, Christians are commanded to make the best use of their time, particularly with those who are outsiders. Reclaimed worshippers will counter this trend by meaningful investment in missionary living.

Week 9: Declare

"Woe to me if I do not preach the gospel!"

—*1 Corinthians 9:16*

*"Mission may not always begin with evangelism. But mission that does
not ultimately include declaring the Word and the name of Christ, the call
to repentance, and faith and obedience as not completed its task."*[1]

—*Christopher Wright*

God created the gospel to reclaim worshippers for relationship.

Relationships are key to effective evangelism—and yet relationships alone are not enough. Jesus did not commission His first followers to go and make friends with people to the ends of the earth. Rather, He called them to make disciples of all nations, baptizing them in the name of the Father, Son, and Holy Spirit, and teaching them to observe all things that Jesus commanded (Mt 28:18–20). Such a task is certainly not less than investing in friendships with people, but it is vastly more.

Define evangelism:

_____

_____

We have spent the first five weeks examining the theological foundations for missions, and then three more weeks considering the locations to which we are called.

When did you begin evangelism in this process? Was it when you conducted your city survey, when you started praying for people by name, or when you built your first strategic relationship with a non-believer?

_____

_____

---

1. Wright, *Mission*, 319.

There are dueling temptations at play in the answer to this question. On the one hand, we may be tempted to think that we haven't really done evangelism until we have walked someone through some type of gospel presentation and asked them to place their faith in Christ. Such an assumption can untether the message of the gospel from the relationships that are often necessary in order for the gospel to make sense.

On the other hand, there are those who are tempted to assume that evangelism can happen even if you never speak to declare the message of the gospel through the person of Jesus. This can lead to genuine love for the lost or acts of social justice that provide temporary relief for the needs of humanity, while failing to address their eternal need of a relationship with God.

Christopher Wright was quoted at the outset of this session as saying "Mission may not always begin with evangelism. But mission that does not ultimately include declaring the Word and the name of Christ, the call to repentance, and faith, and obedience has not completed its task."[1]

Do you agree or disagree with this quote? Why?

_____

_____

To which temptation are you more likely to succumb? All friendship and no declaration of the gospel, or all declaration of the gospel with little or no friendship?

_____

_____

Relationships are vital, yet the blazing center of the gospel is the claim that God sent Jesus to be a substitute for sinners so that they could be reclaimed as worshippers. As a result, all of creation can be freed from the effects of Satan, sin, and death. This is the good news. Our lives must be marked by the verbal proclamation of the gospel message at some point in the relationship. At this point, you have taken massive steps towards living the life of a missionary—but you are not yet done.

---

1. Ibid., *Mission*, 319.

We are all under obligation to preach Christ (Rom 1:14). It is essential that a missionary disciple declare the message of the gospel. Throughout the book of Acts, the message of the good news of Jesus Christ served as the basis of public and private proclamation (Acts 4:31; 6:2; 8:14, 25, 40; 11:1; 13:5, 7, 44, 46, 48; 15:7, 35, 36; 16:10, 32; 17:13; 19:10; 20:24). It was of first importance for Paul (1 Cor 15:1–8), it motivated his mission ministry (1 Cor 9:23), and it was his only hope for successful ministry (1 Cor 9:16–17). The goal was "to be about the obedience of faith among all the nations, on behalf of His name (Rom 1:5)."

While the verbal proclamation of the gospel may not be the initial point of contact, any true mission must involve a clear testimony about the person of Christ, His substitutionary death, and a call to personal repentance and faith.

> ***Evangelism Defined***: A verbal witness to the good news that Jesus Christ died to save sinners with an invitation for people to place their faith in His work on their behalf.

What do you notice about this definition?

_____

_____

Is there anything that you would add or take away from this definition?

_____

_____

When?

One critical issue to discern is when to speak of the person of Christ in the context of a developing relationship. There are several points in a friendship that serve as on-ramps to the highway of evangelism.

- **Common Pain or Joy:** Emotional highs and lows are prime places of vulnerability and openness to new truths. Pain allows you the chance to speak to hope in the face of great suffering, and joy allows you to speak to the source of all good gifts.

- **Common Frustrations:** Christians are not living in some alternative universe. They face the same culture and pressures as do the lost and are confronted with many similar implications of fallenness. It may be rebellious children, an unhealthy marriage, fears about finances, or a host of other felt needs. Each of these provides a natural "tripwire" to take the conversation towards spiritual matters.

- **Common Life Events:** Be it a similar life history, type of suffering, or a strange occurrence, common life events provide an immediate connection between people. The disciple has a chance to testify to the way in which Jesus provided help for a common situation that the non-Christian may be facing. For example, two women may share the fact that they have had a miscarriage. The pain of this life event can serve as a catalyst to speak to the hope of Jesus in the face of deep suffering.

- **Conflicting Values:** The fact that you and your friend share wildly divergent worldviews means that you will consistently encounter topics about which you disagree. These may be topics concerning social ethics (abortion, homosexuality, etc) or daily choices such as how to spend money or what to do for fun. Rather than saying "I can't believe you think that," view these conflicts as opportunities to share the reasons behind your values and priorities.

Think through the ten non-believers that you listed in 3.7 of *Aspire*. What facets of their story provide an inroad for you to speak of Christ?

1. _____

2. _____

3. _____

4. _____

5. _____

6. _____

7. _____

8. _____

How?

Another critical issues is how to speak of the gospel faithfully. Consider for a moment what you would identify as the essential items that must be included in order for you to affirm that you have "shared the gospel with a friend."

Does the mention of Jesus count as sharing the gospel? How about the affirmation that you are a Christian? What about the fact that you believe in the Bible? What must be included in order for the gospel to have been shared?

_____

_____

Various models have been proposed to assist Christians in sharing the gospel. You may have learned one at some point. What is the value of such models?

_____

_____

Perhaps you noted that a model ensures that you know the gospel, ensures that the necessary truths of the gospel have been covered, and that it provides confidence for the one sharing.

What are the downsides of such models?

_____

_____

There is no one model for sharing the gospel that will fit all people at all times. The key is that you know the essential elements of the gospel that must be communicated, and that you have a natural and conversational way to declare those truths to those in your relational network. Below are four models for gospel declaration. Spend some time thinking through how you might use these methods of declaring the gospel and the various strengths and weaknesses of each.

Creation, Fall, Redemption, Restoration

This method allows you to present the gospel as an all-encompassing story, focusing on the four main movements of redemptive history: creation, fall, redemption, and restoration. See each of these segments as buckets, and your gospel presentation as an attempt to empty those buckets with the person to whom you are sharing the gospel. Each bucket should be loaded with gospel themes about God's work at that stage in history. This might include the following:

- **Creation:** by God, through His Word, for His glory, man as His image-bearers, created for worship, given meaningful work;

- **Fall:** result of sin, violation of God's law, idolatry, deserving of God's wrath as a result of His holiness;

- **Redemption:** through Christ, not by works, substitution, atonement, justification, and propitiation;

- **Restoration:** sanctification, meaningful work, new heavens and new earth, worship.

The challenge for most of us is discerning how best to begin a conversation that allows us to empty these buckets. Here, Tim Keller is quite helpful in providing a number of transitional questions that can be used:

- **Creation:** "Where did we come from?" Here, you could use this question when looking at a beautiful sunset, watching a bustling inner city during morning commute, or celebrating the joy of a kid's soccer game. This will allow you to learn what the person believes about the origin of creation and God's role in the world.

- **Fall:** "Why did things go so wrong?" This question is ideal when confronted with the evils of humanity—such as the suffering and tragedy that litters our TV, newspapers, and social media feeds daily. This will allow you to learn what the person believes about the origin of evil and sin. Also, this question may help to ascertain how the person understands their own sinfulness.

- **Redemption:** "What will put things right?" This question could be applied to the frustration that accompanies life in a fallen world. Your teenager is rebellious…Is there any hope? Your husband got fired from his job…Is there any hope? Here you have a prime opportunity to speak of Jesus as the only way that a broken and fallen world can be made right.

- **Restoration:** "How can you be put right?" Finally, this question allows you to speak personally to the heart of the other person and call them to repentance and faith in Christ.[1]

What did you find helpful about this method of gospel declaration? What are the challenges to this model?

_____

_____

Finally, each truth should be supported by the weight of God's Word. Therefore, you need to memorize a number of Scriptures that would serve to help you empty that bucket. What would be the top five Scriptures you would want to use to explain the following:

- Creation[2] _____

- Fall[3] _____

---

1. Keller, *Center*, 33
2. For example Gen 1–2; Col 1:15–17.
3. For example Is 53:6; Rom 1:20–25, 3:20–23, 5:12, 6:23; Heb 2:11.

- Redemption[1] _____

- Restoration[2] _____

Two Ways to Live

The tract produced by Mathias Media entitled *Two Ways to Live* contrasts life lived with God as King and life lived with a person as king. It forces those who listen to confront their idolatry and ask who is in charge of their lives. Idolatry provides a unique way of engaging Western culture with the story of the gospel. The things that we love, fear, trust, hate, and need reveal that all of humanity worships something.[3] Because idols deprive God of His glory, distort the message of the gospel, and always disappoint, they provide a prime inroad to gospel proclamation if they can be exposed. Their deceptive and subversive nature means that the only things capable of expelling them from the life of an individual is the liberating power of the gospel.

Mathias Media provides an app that walks through a simple diagram to illustrate the path of idolatry and worship similar to that which is outlined in *Aspire*. You can find various presentations online or by searching *Two Ways to Live* in the App Store online.[4] Take some time now to review the tract.

What did you find helpful about this method of gospel declaration?

_____

_____

What are challenges to this model?

_____

_____

---

1. For example Is 53; Jn 3:16; Rom 5:6–8, 10:9–10; 2 Cor 5:17; 1 Pet 3:18.
2. For example 1 Cor 15; Rev 21:1–5.
3. Wright, *Mission*, 169.
4. You can find "Two Ways to Live" online at http://www.matthiasmedia.com.au/2wtl/

Ephesians 2:1–10

The person and work of Christ stands at the very center of the gospel message.[1] The creation, fall, redemption, and restoration model presents the holistic metanarrative of Scripture. *Two Ways to Live* provides a contrast on worship and idolatry. However, at times it may be best to zoom in and focus specifically on the work of Christ in His death, burial, and resurrection. The text of Ephesians 2:1–10 allows for a clear gospel presentation based on the natural divisions of the text:

- **The Truth About You:** A proper zoomed-in version of gospel declaration begins with a right understanding of human sin. Paul establishes this reality in the first three verses of Ephesians chapter 2:

    And you were dead in your trespasses and sins in which you previously walked according to the ways of this world, according to the ruler who exercises authority over the lower heavens, the spirit now working in the disobedient. We too all previously lived among them in our fleshly desires, carrying out the inclinations of our flesh and thoughts, and we were by nature children under wrath as the others were also (Eph 2:1–3).

    Paul uses a laundry list of terms to make his point of the desperate plight of humanity apart from Christ. We see, primarily, that a person is dead in their trespasses and sins, incapable of anything to please God or alter their fate. This deadness is then seen in a life of depravity, defined by sin and directed by Satan himself. As a result, people apart from Christ are the just and rightful targets of God's wrath (See also Romans 3:23; 5:12). This truth could be illustrated like this:

---

1. This model was adapted from Dr. Mark Liederbach's teaching at Southeastern Baptist Theological Semianry.

- **The Grace Given to You:** As we have seen throughout *Aspire*, the beauty of God's grace is greater than the horror of human sin. Paul writes about this grace in verses 4–9 of that same passage:

> *But God, who is rich in mercy, because of His great love that He had for us, made us alive with the Messiah even though we were dead in trespasses. You are saved by grace! Together with Christ Jesus He also raised us up and seated us in the heavens, so that in the coming ages He might display the immeasurable riches of His grace through His kindness to us in Christ Jesus. For you are saved by grace through faith, and this is not from yourselves; it is God's gift—not from works, so that no one can boast (Eph 2:4–9).*

Here a proper gospel declaration would want to establish that God initiated a way for mankind to be made right with Him by sending his Son to live a perfect life and die a substitionary death for fallen humanity, who, by faith and repentance can be reconciled to God. This provides a second facet of the way in which God relates to humanity—both in truth and in grace.

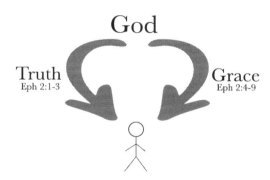

- **The Worship That Flows From You:** Finally, God saves a person for good works, not by good works. Paul writes:

> *For we are His creation, created in Christ Jesus for good works, which God prepared ahead of time so that we should walk in them (Eph 2:10).*

Those saved by grace through faith are given the privilege of fleeing sin and pursing Christ. This process of sanctification works it way out in a life of holiness from all of those who are truly God's children.

Finally, you would want to establish that while God did not save a person by good works, He does save them to do new works for His glory. They are to do this as they are increasingly transformed into the image of Jesus and led by His Spirit to proper worship.

What did you find helpful about this method of gospel declaration?

_____

_____

What are challenges to this model?

_____

_____

Testimony

A final method of gospel declaration is your personal grace story. This method is often the easiest way to speak of the gospel. It's potentially dangerous, however, due to the fact that most often the spotlight is on the person sharing the testimony and not placed clearly on the good news of Christ. Also, many testimonies devolve into a statement that "I once was bad, but now I'm good." This is not the gospel. The gospel is a declaration that you were once dead and God, through Christ, made you alive.

While the previous three methods focus on what God did for all people through Christ, this method focuses on what God did for you through Christ. Because it lacks universal validity, it is best to see your personal testimony as a path from one of the previous three methods of sharing the gospel.

In order to share your story well, it is best to describe your grace story by answering the following questions:

What did God save you from?

_____

_____

How did God save you?

_____

_____

What did God save you for?

_____

_____

Notice that God is the subject in each of these questions. He is the one doing the work. Your testimony is a way of putting Him on display. Try it out this week with a friend or your mentor. Tell your story of salvation in a God-honoring fashion. As you do, you will be surprised at how many opportunities you have to share the story with non-believers.

What did you find helpful about this method of gospel declaration?

_____

_____

What are challenges to this model?

_____

_____

Fear of failure may paralyze you from utilizing these tools. You must remember that God is at work to fulfill His sovereign purposes in the world and is gracious in using your missionary efforts. He can even redeem your frail, feeble, and even faulty declarations of the gospel to be a means of bringing the message of the gospel to many.

Week 10: Demonstrate

"For I didn't think it was a good idea to know anything among you except Jesus Christ and Him crucified. I came to you in weakness, in fear, and in much trembling. My speech and my proclamation were not with persuasive words of wisdom but with a powerful demonstration by the Spirit, so that your faith might not be based on men's wisdom but on God's power.

—*1 Corinthians 2:2–5*

"The Christian church in general and the Christian mission in particular are today confronted with issues they have never even dreamt of and which are crying out for responses that are both relevant to the times and in harmony with the essence of the Christian faith."[1]

—*David J. Bosch*

If the good words of the gospel are not accompanied by the good deeds of the gospel, a missionary disciple is presenting a truncated version of the gospel.

Conversion to Christianity is often the result of a lengthy process. We must learn to think in process and allow people time to embrace of the truths of the gospel. We have already seen that relationships and care is vital to the work of evangelism but it is insufficient in and of itself if it does not address the ultimate realities of human sin and the substitutionary work of Jesus.

This need not create an unnecessary dichotomy though. Gospel declaration must be matched by gospel demonstration in the life of a missionary disciple. We should engage because we believe that God is not only redeeming fallen humans, but also restoring all of the created order that is wrecked by the implications of sin.

This gospel demonstration should not only lead to Christians living exemplary lives of holiness, but also to them working to bring peace and wholeness to a world broken by sin. Such social action is a necessary and helpful corollary to the work of evangelism.

---

1. Bosch, *Tranforming*, 188.

Reclaimed worshippers fulfill their created design as they work to bring order, beauty, and wholeness in God's world and increasingly expose His glory to a watching world. For this to happen, we must target all areas of life that are broken by sin:

- Declining physical abilities as a result of aging or sickness;

- Poverty that results from economic oppression, joblessness, or poor life choices;

- Inability to read and write that hampers one's job opportunities;

- Addictive behaviors that cause people to hurt themselves and others;

- Isolation due to poor social skills, life stage, or family dynamics;

- Divorce that shatters families and deprives children of their parent's love and care.

How are missionary disciples to make a difference in these areas? The answer is found in three primary ways of demonstrating the gospel.

Living

People need a model for Christian living. Unfortunately, for most the model that they have of a Christian is not healthy. As a result, you have to live in such a way that your life challenges their stereotypes of Christians. As you live an authentically sanctified life around your non-Christian friends, they can increasingly say, "So, that's what life would look like if I were a Christian." Christopher Wright says, "The life of God's people is always turned outward to the watching nations, as priests are always turned toward their people as well as toward God."[1] Mission is propelled by faithful living. Mission is crippled by rebellion.

Paul provided such models for his converts and churches. As he leaves, he is able to consistently remind them that they can follow the pattern of life that he established while He lived among them. If they follow his model they will be following Christ (1 Thess 1:6–9; Phil 3:17; 1 Cor 11:1). He says, "Do what you have learned and received

---

1. Wright, *Mission*, 371.

and heard and seen in me, and the God of peace will be with you (Phil 4:9)." This only happens as Christian learn to share their lives with others (1 Thess 2:8).

In 1 Peter 2:11–12, Peter reminds Christians to "conduct yourselves honorably among the Gentiles, so that in a case where they speak against you as those who do what is evil, they will, by observing your good works, glorify God on the day of visitation." These good lives should be marked by gospel demonstration in the following areas:

- **Faith:** A person who trusts God to be and do what He says He will do;

- **Holiness:** A person who repents faithfully and flees from known sin;

- **Joy:** A person who lives as one who has found a treasure hidden in a field;

- **Simplicity:** A person who lives with contentment and rest in the faithful and generous provision of God;

- **Perseverance:** A person who has learned how to bear up under the weight of suffering by clinging to the gospel;

- **Love:** A person who demonstrates genuine love to his family and friends.

These should be seen as compelling alternatives to the brokenness of the world. For example, Christians can demonstrate a life of simplicity and generosity to non-believers who are both oppressed by cycles of poverty or who are running after idolatrous economic investment. Or, the Christian family may model a healthy, loving, and persevering marriage in the face of a culture in which divorce has run amuck. The Christian presents a counter-culture through their godly living.

In what ways are your lost friends learning what it means to follow Jesus by looking at your life?

_____

_____

This is also a vital catalyst towards your own personal transformation. Such transformation comes through mission and not before it. In this way, mission becomes a primary means of your own sanctification. Your sin, idolatry, and need for Christ is exposed and you are forced, once again, to cling to the gospel. Rather than waiting for your life to be a perfect representation of holiness, engage in mission, and allow God to bring about the needed transformation. For example, if you find yourself with an anemic prayer life, live on mission and see if God does not cause you to pray like you never have before.

How are you seeing your sin exposed as you seek to live on mission?

_____

_____

How does living on mission enhance your understanding of the gospel?

_____

_____

Serving

Gospel demonstration also takes the form of service. Servant evangelism in the context of relationships can be profound and lead to opportunities for gospel declaration. Jesus says that this is the path to leadership in the economy of the Kingdom of God—He who wants to be first, must become a servant to all (Mt 20:20–28).

Thankfully, our world presents a steady stream of opportunities to serve. Life in a fallen world will do that. Every day we are presented with ways to love and care for people—from a ride to the hospital, to the provision of a meal after childbirth, to help repairing a leaky facet. These provide an easy and effective means to continue to build relational credibility for the message that you are declaring.

There is no shortage of ideas for servant evangelism. Think about them in terms of the holistic needs of the people with whom you are seeking to build friendships. Their needs may come in a number of different areas, and you should be intentional in targeting your service to the area of need:

Physical Needs	Financial Needs	Social Needs	Emotional Needs
• Helping a disabled person with transportation • Providing childcare for a single mother • Working together on a minor home repair project • Providing a meal after a birth or death in the family • Preparing a homemade meal for someone living in poverty and inviting them to your home to share it together	• Paying for a neighbors power bill • Repairing or purchasing a broken appliance • Helping a buddy fix a car in order to save him money from buying parts • Creating a budget or helping with tax preparation • Blessing a friend with a struggling marriage with a gift card for a date night	• Hosting a game night for your neighbors to get to know one another • Planning a mother's play date to meet other mom's that live nearby • Sitting at the home or retirement center of an elderly person and listening to them attentively • Watching a football game with a man struggling with addiction who would typically only watch it at the local bar	• Listening to a couple talk about the pain of their recent cancer diagnosis • Sharing your story of grief and loss with a couple who has just experienced a miscarriage • Providing an outlet for a man with a "mid-life crisis" to avoid the pursuit of worldly pleasure • Providing an outlet for Biblical community and friendship for a man living in a local addiction recovery center • Talking with a teenager watching her parents walk through a nasty divorce

Which of these ideas could you use within the friendships that you are developing with the lost? What additional ideas come to mind?

_____

_____

_____

_____

Each of these ideas share something in common—they all come with a cost. They will cost you time. They will cost you money. And, they may even cause you pain and frustration. Love isn't love until it comes with a cost. You are never more like Christ than when you are giving of yourself in service to others (2 Cor 8:9).

Engaging

Missionary disciples must also find meaningful ways to engage in the critical issues of social justice at a systems level. Not only are individuals trapped in systems of oppressions, dysfunction, and pain, but there are also entire systems that bread these situations.

Missionaries can seek ways to bring macro-level change by engaging in an issue for which they are particularly broken. As Bosch says, "In our time, God's yes to the world reveals itself, to a large extent, in the church's missionary engagement in response of the realities of injustice, oppression, poverty, discrimination, and violence."[1]

This may come through initiatives undertaken by your local church. Pastors may see fit to lead their people to adopt certain city needs in order to make significant headway into bringing about change. This may come by funneling the people and the financial resources of the local church towards meeting a particular need. For example, the pastors of a local church may challenge their people to tutor children at a local elementary school in order to combat childhood illiteracy. You should attempt to find ways to partner with such projects as a missionary disciple and a meaningful member of your local church. Does your church have any particular projects that they have adopted?

The location of the church facility (if it has one) provides another way to think about city engagement. Leaders of the local church could figuratively draw a one mile circle around their churches facility and attempt to assess the social needs that are present in that defined geography. Such a project could allow the church to target needs, while having an easy means of integrating the people they serve into the life of the church. Take a minute to image the locations around your church's facility (if your church is meeting in a temporary facility use that location). Make a rough sketch of these neighborhoods on the chart below, noting anything you know about the needs present in these communities.

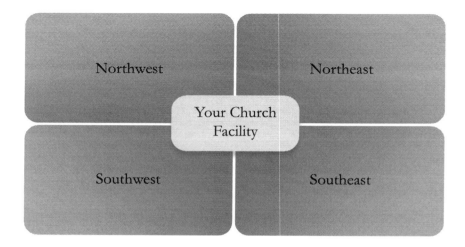

---

1. Bosch, *Transforming*, 10.

The location of your local church's facility could serve to define your church's circle of accountability. Consider the difference that could be made if each local church took responsibility for caring for the needs of those that lived near their location. This need not mean that each local church address every issue in a given city, but it does mean that each church could do something. And the cumulative effort of all churches doing something, or even doing some of the same things together, could result in significant changes to a city.

Such engagement need not come at the direction of the church. As the church seeks to equip the saints of the work of the ministry, it should see its people seeking to find ways to leverage their unique gifts, abilities, and financial resources to serve the needs of the world.

Circles of accountability could even be further divided into small cells of members of the local church who live near one another. Rather than commuting 20 minutes to the church facility, these families might determine that there was a need in their own community that needed to be addressed. Local church members could then find strategic ways to come together to address that need. For example, consider a local apartment complex with highly transient tenants. If the church has a small group that lives in or near that apartment complex, then those individuals could throw an apartment-wide cook out to allow people to get to know one another quickly. Such a project requires little effort on the part of an intentional missionary. They would simply seek permission from the apartment, plan the date, promote it via apartment flyers, newsletters, or social media and provide a little food and music.

Here the role of the church as an institution could be minimal. Perhaps, let your pastors know so that they could be praying for you. And, if you are going to advertise it as something that your church is doing, then you would certainly want to ask the pastor's permission. But, better yet, just do it for the sake of being a good neighbor. Making it a church event may add to the intimidation of those who attend and might add to the stress of your pastors, who may think that they have another event that they have to lead. Simple love for one's neighbor is a sufficient motive for engaging in these projects.

Trimester 3: Mission

What project like this could you implement in your immediate circle of accountability to meet a recognized need (for example, landscaping an area school, cleaning a local park, planning a flag football game for the teenagers of an apartment complex)?

_____

_____

Missional living is not rocket-science, but it does require intentionality. Take the ideas you have developed in this week's study and put them to work this week. Trust God to produce gospel fruit.

Week 11: Connect

"Consequently, you are no longer foreigners and aliens, but fellow citizens with God's people and members of God's household, built on the foundation of the apostles and prophets, with Christ Jesus himself as the chief cornerstone. In him the whole building is joined together and rises to become a holy temple in the Lord. And in him you too are being built together to become a dwelling in which God lives by his Spirit."

—Ephesians 2:19–22

"Just as we must insist that a church which has ceased to be a mission has lost the essential character of a church, so we must also say that a mission which is not at the same time truly a church is not a true expression of the divine apostle. An unchurchly mission is as much a monstrosity as an unmissionary church."[1]

—Lesslie Newbigin

The goal of the gospel is to connect people in relationship with Christ and His church.

Living as a missionary is not a linear process. You don't simply complete one portion of this process and then move on to the next step. The reality is that you will be praying, investing, declaring, and demonstrating all at the same time. The same is true for this week's topic: connecting. Connecting non-believers to Christ and to the church may happen very early in the process or after many years of relational investment. Either way, the missionary journey is not meant to end with you. Rather you are to build relationships with the lost in order to connect them to two other vital relationships that are in fact much more important: a relationship with Christ and a relationship with His church.

This process is much like being a parent. As a parent, my task is not simply to see to it that my children need me for the rest of their lives. In fact, for many of us, our children will outlive us by many years. The purpose of our parenting is to prepare them well so that they can know God, function meaningfully in the world, and build healthy relationships with other people, such as a spouse. Dependency is not the goal, neither is it the goal of the missionary's relationship with the non-Christian.

1. Lesslie Newbigin, *The Household of God: Lectures on the Nature of the Church* (Eugene, OR: Wipf & Stock, 2008), 169.

Connecting Them with Christ

The first, and most vital relationship, is obviously the focus of the entire process—to see the person enter into a relationship with Jesus. The gospel demands a response (Rom 10:9). It is not enough to simply declare and demonstrate the gospel, but you must also be bold enough to invite people to repent and believe this good news (Mk 1:15). For many, this is the most challenging step. The relationship is in place; they know you are a Christian; you have explained the gospel clearly through your words and your life. Now, the question is, are they ready to believe the gospel?

How do you typically invite someone to trust in Christ?

_____

_____

What is involved in trusting in Christ? What must they do to be saved?

_____

_____

The language of the Scriptures for salvation involves two key elements: repentance and faith.

Look back at the previous trimesters of *Aspire.* Define repentance and faith based on the material we have covered to this point.

_____

_____

_____

_____

Repentance and faith express worship.

- Repentance declares that I am not God.

- Faith declares that Jesus is.

Repentance is the act of acknowledging that one has disobeyed God, violated His holiness, and become the object of His wrath. Faith is the act of trusting in the finished

362

work of Jesus to pay the penalty one's sin deserves and to provide the righteousness that one could not earn.

Such an acknowledgment will take the form of a prayer to God, because sin is fundamentally against God. This does not need to be a formal prayer done in a church service. In fact, it may happen while the person is all alone. Certainly, there are no magic words that must be said. Salvation is made available to those who seek God's forgiveness through repentance and faith. Notice Paul's words in Romans 10:9, "If you confess with your mouth, 'Jesus is Lord,' and believe in your heart that God raised Him from the dead, you will be saved."

This confession does not save—God does. It does demonstrate, however, that God has done the work of bringing a person from death to life (Eph 2:1–10).

What might such a profession of repentance and faith look and sound like for the following people:

- A seven-year old child from a broken home;

  _____

  _____

- A 30-year old high school drop out working in an auto-mechanics shop;

  _____

  _____

- A 50-year old mother of four who has attended church her entire life;

  _____

  _____

- A Ukrainian businessman who has recently moved to the US for work;

  _____

  _____

In each case, the critical factor is their understanding of Jesus. He is the hinge on which salvation turns. In our rush to win converts, we may fall prey to the scene described by Graeme Goldsworthy:

> *There are evangelicals who are so earnest in calling for decisions for Jesus that they seem to forget to tell people why they should decide for Jesus. I remember listening to a speaker at an evangelistic meeting whose only mention of the death of Jesus was a passing reference in his closing prayer. I was acting as an advisor to follow up on the after-meeting counseling. I spoke to a young couple who had heard the talk, gone out to the front, been 'counseled' and then brought to me. They obviously had not heard any gospel in either the address or the counseling. They had no idea about being justified by faith in the doing and dying of Christ. It seems the decision can become everything. People are exhorted to turn to Christ, to receive Christ, to ask Jesus into their hearts, and the like, even when they have been given no substantial idea at all of who Jesus was and what He has done to save us.*[1]

What questions might you ask a potential disciple in order to discern if they truly understand who Jesus is and His role in salvation?

_____

_____

_____

_____

People may also hear the message of the grace and mercy that is offered through Christ, but not be given a clear exhortation to repent and turn from sin. They hear a message that says, "Come to Jesus just like you are because He loves you and died for you." What they hear is, "Come to Jesus and go to heaven when you die and yet continue to live just like you're currently living."

---

1. Graeme Goldsworthy, *Gospel-Centered Hermeneutics: Foundations and Principles of Evangelical Biblical Interpretation* (Downers Grove: IVP, 2006), 173–74.

What questions could you ask a potential disciple to ensure that they were repenting of their sins?

_____

_____

Paul provides a wonderful contrast of worldly sorrow vs. genuine repentance in 2 Corinthians 7:9–11

> *Now I rejoice, not because you were grieved, but because your grief led to repentance. For you were grieved as God willed, so that you didn't experience any loss from us. For godly grief produces a repentance not to be regretted and leading to salvation, but worldly grief produces death. For consider how much diligence this very thing—this grieving as God wills—has produced in you: what a desire to clear yourselves, what indignation, what fear, what deep longing, what zeal, what justice! In every way you showed yourselves to be pure in this matter.*

Worldly sorrow consistently masquerades as repentance. People naturally feel remorseful for their poor decisions, particularly those that cause them significant pain. Such people may seem repentant, yet they lack true, God-given heart change. According to Scripture, only time can tell whether or not someone is genuinely repentant. Time reveals whether a person produces fruit consistent with repentance (Mt 3:8).

What marks of a repentant life would you observe in light of the text above from 2 Corinthians 7?

_____

_____

Scripture also indicates that obedience to Christ will come with a cost for new Christians. Jesus indicated the life-encompassing nature of conversion in places such as Luke 14:26–27: "If anyone comes to Me and does not hate his own father and mother, wife and children, brothers and sisters—yes, and even his own life—he cannot be My disciple. Whoever does not bear his own cross and come after Me cannot be My disciple." The cost of discipleship will test the validity of a person's profession of faith in Christ. The person's love for Christ will be validated by His obedience to the commands of Christ (Jn 14:15).

How would you respond to the following would-be disciples:

- A young man unwilling to give up his adulterous relationship with a co-worker;

  _____

  _____

- A wealthy businessman known for shady business practices;

  _____

  _____

- A needy teenage girl bouncing from relationship to relationship.

  _____

  _____

Connecting Them to the Church

Baptism

Baptism is the first step of a new Christian according to the Scriptures (Acts 2:38, 41; 9:18; 10:48; Rom 6:2–4; Titus 3:4–7). This act provides a vivid picture of the transformative work of the gospel in burying the old life of sin and depravity and raising the person up to new life in Christ. Jesus commissioned his disciples, and thereby His church, to be about the task of "baptizing new disciples (Mt 28:18–20)." When the church was inaugurated at Pentecost, thousands of new believers publically professed their faith through the act of baptism (Acts 2:33–34). Baptism is meant to be public so that new believers can boldly declare their repentance and faith to the watching world. It also serves as a means of integrating them into church membership and the care of the body.

Baptism is meant to be public. It provides the means where by a new believer can boldly declare his or her repentance and faith to the watching world. Baptism does not save, but it does provide a public testimony to the work of God in salvation. It also serves as a means of integrating a new disciple into the church and the care of the body (Col 2:12; Rom 6:4).

Baptism is a far superior marker of faith and repentance than walking down an aisle or praying a prayer. These actions may be helpful, yet it is the public act of profession though baptism that is most needed. Generally, most churches have consistent times for baptism. If you are discipling someone who has expressed faith in Christ, you should connect him or her to your church's pastors in order to schedule a time for them to be baptized.

Baptism provides an easy segway into the life of the church family. For many, this connection may have started long before they actually place faith in Christ. A longing for community is a mark of God's common grace in our world. Most people long for relationships, as evidenced by the local club or bar, or the proliferation of social media. Here they can share stories, have fun, laugh, cry, mourn, and celebrate.

The local church can and should provide a more robust form of community for those with whom we are trying to build relationships. They need not run to the local bar, when they could come to a cook out at your house with those from your church's small group. Here the relations may meet their felt-needs for relationships, while providing a depth and permanence that other relationships may lack.

A healthy church is a tremendously powerful evangelistic tool in this regard. Think about the ways that you could introduce your non-believing friends to the community of the local church, even before they trust Christ. Keller argues that "most people in the West need to be welcomed into a community long enough for them to hear multiple expressions of the gospel."[1] This will require you to know people well and think strategically about the best entry point for them.

For some it may be by inviting them to a standing lunch appointment that you have with a member of your local church. Here, in a casual lunch setting, they can listen to you talk about life, marriage, parenting, God, and the church. For others, it may happen by inviting them to attend a gathering of your small group or Sunday school class. Here, they may sit in on a Bible study or discussion group or simply hang out with your group while you do something fun, such as watch the Super Bowl. This may help

---

1. Keller, *Center*, 281.

abate the stigma of weirdness that tends to shroud the local church and might make your friends more willing to attend a larger gathering of the church. Finally, some may enter through the weekly gathering of the church. Here, the anonymity may be helpful in orienting them to the life of the body without forcing them into awkward conversations with strangers. Those who have a background of church attendance may already be predisposed to such gatherings.

Think through the friends you are making with the non-believers. What setting might be the best for introducing them to the life of the church?

_____

_____

People may then be drawn to the gospel as they see groups of Christians:

- **Loving One Another:** The love of Christians for one another, and the unity they experience together, is a compelling motive for life transformation (Jn 13:34–35).

- **Serving One Another:** The care of the members of the church for another can be a compelling missionary tool.

- **Fighting Sin:** The confession of sin among Christians is one of the most genuine moments of brokenness that can be seen by a non-Christian. When a disciple explains his failures and his need for the gospel, it serves as a mirror for non-Christians to see their own sin and be drawn to repentance.

- **Living on Mission:** Churches should be marked by groups of people intentionally living on mission as a team. This group missionary concept is fueled by a desire for the church's cells (small groups, Sunday school, etc.) not simply to gather as introverted communities of believers but to live together on mission in the world.

How might the following practices be useful in drawing someone to faith in Christ:

Romans 12:5 _____

Romans 12:10 _____

Romans 12:16 _____

Romans 15:7 _____

Romans 15:14 _____

Galatians 5:13 _____

Galatians 6:2 _____

1 Thessalonians 5:11–15 _____

Ephesians 5:21 _____

Colossians 3:13 _____

James 5:1 _____

The local church is a vital means of grace, both before and after one's conversation. After conversion connection with the local church should be the natural byproduct of any personal who has been genuinely converted and baptized in the local church. People who know God as Father should long to be connected to His family, the church.

Imagine that you and your spouse legally adopt a child into your family. The kid, however, is unwilling to enter your home and become a participant in the shared life that you have together. You would be foolish to allow such a dichotomy to exist—for the child to be a adopted into your family, it is vital that the child actually becomes a part of your family. The same is true of the local church. New believers, adopted into God's family, will integrate into the life of the church. Such integration should take on a number of forms:

Consistent Attendance

New believers should make it a priority to gather with the church consistently, either in one-on-one discipleship relationships, small groups, Sunday school classes, or the gathered worship service. The author of Hebrews exhorts his readers to "hold on to the confession of our hope without wavering, for He who promised is faithful. And let us be concerned about one another in order to promote love and good works, not staying away from our worship meetings, as some habitually do, but encouraging each other, and all the more as you see the day drawing near (Heb 10:23–25). This challenge is not simply so that the church can pad its attendance numbers. *New believers need the church, and the church needs new believers.*

Why do new believers need the church?

_____

_____

Why does the church need new believers?

_____

_____

Genuine Partnership

The church and the new believer need more than simple attendance, however. They need to partner together in mission. Passive consumption is not the goal. Active mission is. New Christians seek to involve themselves in the mission of the church by using their gifts for the building up of the Body. This should, first of all, involve loving other believers and practicing the "one another" commands listed above. There is not a maturity threshold that someone must cross in order to love and care for people. Anyone, regardless of how long they have been a believer, can do this.

How might you encourage a person who has been a Christian for six weeks to begin to express love to other believers?

_____

_____

How might this change once someone has been a believer for five years?

_____

_____

New Christians should also be encouraged to serve the Body. This may be something as simple as holding the front door and greeting new guests on Sunday mornings. Or, it may be through serving to care for the children or through a host of other service roles that are needed in order for the church to function effectively. While there may be certain tasks that require age and maturity (such as teaching or pastoring), there are many ways that new Christians can begin to serve immediately.

How might you encourage a person who has been a Christian for six weeks to begin to serve other believers?

_____

_____

How might this change once someone has been a believer for five years?

_____

_____

Meaningful Membership

Finally, new Christians should pursue membership in the local church. Membership is a necessary corollary of meaningful involvement in the life of the church family. First, it provides a tangible commitment that protects against the consumerism that is pervasive in the evangelical church. Membership functions like an engagement ring, solidifying a commitment to a certain group of people.

Membership allows the pastors of a local church to know who is entrusted to their care. They are given the task of shepherding the sheep, and obviously they cannot effectively shepherd all of the Christians in any city. Rather they are to shepherd the sheep that God has given them, as evidenced by those who are members of their local church. It also helps the people know which leaders they are to follow. They are commanded to respect and follow their leaders (Heb. 13:7, 17). Obviously they cannot do this to every leader, so membership allows them to know to whom they are to submit.

Membership provides a context for the living out of the commands of Scripture. Here, in the context of commitment to a local church, believers can love one another, spur one another on to love and good deeds, and serve one another. You simply cannot do this by watching a church service online or randomly attending a series of churches. Only through long-term commitment of people to the church and church to the people can the church truly live out what it means to be the church (1 Cor 12).

Membership provides for the meaningful practice of church discipline. Paul, in places such as 1 Corinthians 5, prescribes church discipline as the way churches are to handle sin in the body. They are to lovingly, graciously, and humbly walk through a process of prayer and pleading in the hopes that a wayward member would turn from their sin and be restored to Christ and His church. This practice, while atypical for many churches, is a necessity in order to maintain the health and purity of the Body. And clearly, it requires some form of membership for such a process to have any effect. Can you imagine trying to practice church discipline on a random stranger or someone who attended the church for the first time? It would never work. Restorative discipline can only happen in the context of commitment. A new believer needs such accountability. They need to know that, while they may not like it, the church is going to love them enough to pursue them if they are wayward.

Consider the following case studies. How would you use God's Word to counsel professing Christians who say something like this:

- "I don't really need the church. My relationship with God is my business."

    _____

    _____

- "I hate organized religion. There is so much hypocrisy and politics. I'll just go at it alone."

    _____

    _____

- "When I was a kid I watched a church fire their pastor. It was ugly and I grew to hate the church. Any place that can cause that much pain is something I want to avoid."

  _____

  _____

- "Why go to church when I can listen to the best preachers in the world via podcast every week. Now I can even watch entire church services online now, music and all. I'm not missing anything."

  _____

  _____

- "If I go to church people will judge me. They all seem to have their act together, and I am such a mess. Let me clean up my life a bit and then I'll go."

  _____

  _____

- "There are so many good churches in my city. I can't settle for just one. I'll just pick the one that suits me each week and go there."

  _____

  _____

- "I've got such a busy life. Between work, soccer games, helping kids with homework, and taking care of the house, Sunday is my only day to rest. Surely God would rather me rest than do all the work necessary to gather with the church each week."

  _____

  _____

The necessity of the local church is no longer an accepted culture norm. Rather, people must be taught why it matters in their new relationship with God. This teaching is only the beginning of the work of discipleship that will be needed in the life of a new

Christian. And it is vital that you continue this work. To simply walk with someone to the point of his or her conversion and not continue to disciple them in their faith is sinfully negligent. It is your responsibility to see to it that you, or someone in your local church, walk with them on their discipleship journey by teaching them to obey all things that Jesus commanded (Mt 28:18–20).

Week 12: Disciple

"You, therefore, my son, be strong in the grace that is in Christ Jesus. And what you have heard from me in the presence of many witnesses, commit to faithful men who will be able to teach others also."

—2 Timothy 2:1–2

"Accordingly, the chief way in which we should disciple people…is through community. Growth in grace, wisdom, and character does not happen primarily in classes and instruction, through large worship gatherings, or even in solitude. Most often, growth happens through deep relationships and in communities where the implications of the gospel are worked out cognitively and worked in practically—in ways no other setting or venue can afford."[1]

—Tim Keller

Disciple-making is the primary purpose of the church.

It does not take long to determine what a church values. You may quickly spot formal statements of the church's values on their website, promotional material, or on the walls of their church facility. More often, you will discern their values more passively. It will seep out of the people of the church. People might say things like:

- This church is not at all like the church I grew up in;

- This church lets me come just like I am;

- This church is so loving;

- This church cares for the poor.

These statements help you get a sense of what the people really value. These values, those owned and affirmed by the people, are what really matters in the life of a church. A pastor can say that his people are about the work of missions, but unless they are actively sharing the gospel, then they do not really value missions.

---

1. Keller, *Center*, 311.

The same is true for the task of making disciples. You will rarely find a pastor that says "Oh, yeah… discipleship. We don't really care about that." Most will heartedly agree that the mission of the church is to make disciples that bring God glory in all the earth. And yet we must wonder if that is what the people who attend the church would say. Are the people of the church consistently growing in conformity to the image of Christ? Are they giving their lives away to invest in others so that they can grow in grace and knowledge of the Lord Jesus?

What do you think people would say about what your local church values? What would they think about what the church values by looking at your life?

_____

_____

Aspire is written in an effort to help Christians understand how the gospel transforms them, and how they can invest their lives in seeing this same transformation in others. Disciple-making, according to Köstenberger and O'Brien, "Entails the nurturing of converts into the full obedience of faith, not merely the proclamation of the gospel."[1] This is the task with which you have been entrusted.

Perhaps this responsibility seems daunting to you. If so, consider your growth over the last year. You may have begun this workbook as a new believer, a recent college graduate, a summer missionary, or a developing pastor. In each case, the same Spirit uses the same Word to apply the same gospel for transformation.

In the space below write some clear evidences of transformation that you have seen in your life over the past year:

_____

_____

_____

_____

---

1. Köstenberger and O'Brien, *Salvation*, 105.

You are living proof that transformation is possible.

You are at this point in your spiritual life through the grace of God and the investment of others. As you finish this year of study, consider the people who have invested in your life in order to make this possible:

•   Who was the individual most instrumental in your conversion?

    _____

•   Who in your family has been praying for your salvation?

    _____

•   What pastor or church leader do you most admire?

    _____

•   Who has invested in you in order to aid in your disciple-making journey?

    _____

Before you complete the last session, take time to write each of the people above a handwritten note. In it, thank them for their investment in your life and recount the work that God is doing in your life currently. Use it as a way of showing honor to those who have invested in your walk with Jesus.

The same gospel that is sufficient to transform your life can do the same for those that you have been building relationships with over this trimester. Hopefully, you have had the joy of seeing someone place his or her faith in Christ, be baptized, and join your local church. *If so, praise God.* Be reminded that "neither the one who plants nor the one who waters is anything, but only God who gives the growth (1 Cor 3:7)." Praise God for His work and the privilege you have had of being a part of His mission.

Perhaps you have toiled and labored with little fruit to show for your investment. *If so, praise God.* James reminds us that we are to "consider it a great joy, my brothers, whenever you experience various trials, knowing that the testing of your faith produces endurance. But endurance must do its complete work, so that you may be mature and complete, lacking nothing." (Js 1:3–5) Praise God for His work and the privilege you have had of being a part of His mission.

Welcome to the journey of disciple-making. You get the joy of spending the rest of your life investing in this great mission.

So, where do you go from here? *You multiply.*

Paul's words to his protégé Timothy provide a guide for the work that lies ahead for each of us. "You, therefore, my son, be strong in the grace that is in Christ Jesus. And what you have heard from me in the presence of many witnesses, commit to faithful men who will be able to teach others also (2 Tim 2:2)."

Discipleship happens when the life-changing truth of Scripture is infused into genuine relationships over an extended period of time.

His instructions start with Timothy himself. He reminds Timothy that he is not to move beyond the gospel, but rather to continue to grow strong in it. There should never be a time in a Christian's life when they feel like they have grown enough. They should consistently be striving to plump the depths of the gospel. And, thankfully, the gospel is so vast that you will never hit bottom. You will always be going further and further into the well of God's grace and mercy. It is not essential that you pursue vocational ministry in order to make disciples. You can do this work faithfully as a lawyer, school teacher, auto-mechanic, or salesman.

Thankfully, you have already grown comfortable with the tools for multiplying your disciple-making efforts.

A Discipleship Relationship

Start by encouraging those with whom you have been investing to multiply through their relational networks. The goal is that those who are disciplined through your efforts would then take the responsibility of making disciples themselves. Consider how the gospel spreads through multiplying relationships:

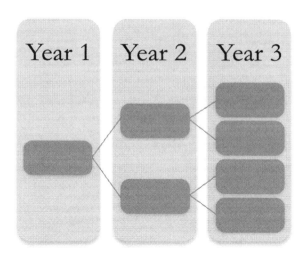

Imagine that you are the person illustrated above. You invest yourself in two relationships in the first year and commit to making a healthy disciple. These individuals are then given the task of doing them same in the lives of two other people in the following year and so on year after year. Missionary disciples pray for a vast family tree. The results would be astounding:

Year 1 = 2 Disciples

Year 2 = 6 Disciples

Year 3 = 14 Disciples

Year 4 = 30 Disciples

Year 5 = 62 Disciples

Year 6 = 126 Disciples

Year 7 = 378 Disciples

In seven years, you could have played a significant role in the spiritual formation of almost 400 people. And that is simply one of your family trees. In Year 2, you could invest in two new disciples and see the process reproduced in their lives also, starting a new branch on your family tree.

Try your hand at it. Ask a couple of young believers who you have been investing in to share the names of two of their friends who they could begin to meet with as well and write their names below

Person 1 _____

    Friend 1 _____

    Friend 2 _____

Person 2 _____

    Friend 1 _____

    Friend 2 _____

Now take this same multiplication and infuse it into the life of the church. Now, you do not simply have one person multiplying their influence, but you have dozens, perhaps hundreds of people doing the same. This type of disciple multiplication would have a radical and far-reaching impact on our cities and our churches.

A Discipleship Resource

God has supplied His church with all things necessary for life and godliness through His Spirit and His Word. The Scriptures are "living and effective and sharper than any double-edged sword, penetrating as far as the separation of the soul and spirit, joints and marrow (Heb 4:12)." The Bible is a sufficient tool for the task of disciple-making. The tools you have learned this year should equip you with a simple and reproducible way to read the Bible with someone for the purpose of disciple-making (refer back to session 2.5 for the introduction of the seven arrow hermeneutic that we have used throughout the text).

God has also provided tools like *Aspire* that are useful in the task of disciple-making. My prayer is that God has used this journey to help you understand His mission, His church, and your mission in a fresh way. In fact, this workbook was written out of a desire to provide the church with a simple tool for creating a disciple-making culture in the church.

You could give another copy of the *Aspire* workbook to the people with whom you are investing and ask them to journey with you through these first three trimesters. Teaching something to others is a valuable way of burning these truths into your heart and mind. Additionally, it may serve as a catalyst for life change for others to hear you talk about how God used these truths to bring transformation in your life.

Who are two young believers in your local church that you could commit to taking through *Aspire* next year?

1. _____

2. _____

A Disciple-Making Church

Hopefully you have this already. You may be positioned, by God's grace, in a church that is aggressively working to build an ethos of disciple-making into its DNA. If so, do you plan to give your life to the mission of the church and make disciples aggressively and often. If not, there are two primary options:

- Start where God has you. You may not be a pastor of a local church and in the position to create an overall disciple-making culture. This need not mean that you are helpless. You can begin with the people with whom you have influence. Certainly this will involve those you have invested in over the course of this year. It can also involve your friends within the local church who share your level of spiritual maturity but are not invested in making disciples. You can, and should, encourage them to get in the game as well.

    Who are the names of some people in your church family that have been walking with Jesus for some time who may not be involved in the work of disciple-making?

Write their names below, and be intentional about finding a way to challenge them to begin this journey themselves.

_____

_____

You may also have a level of influence over a small group of people in the church; such as a community group, youth ministry, or Sunday school class. This would provide a prime context for you to encourage others to make disciples. For example, you may begin this process with the high school students in your youth group by pairing them all with a college mentor who can walk them through *Aspire*. Imagine the fruit that could come if you helped to create a culture of active disciple-making that started in middle and high school. These young, future leaders would then have decades in which to multiply their influence. Not only that, but many of the future missionaries, church planters, deacons, and pastors for God's church are currently sitting in the youth ministries of our churches. The same could also be true of your small group or Sunday school class. Why not challenge the mature Christians in that group to walk through an intentional discipleship process using this text.

What positions of influence has God given you in the church? What steps could you take to create a discipleship culture among that group?

_____

_____

- Consider vocational ministry or church planting. Church planting and pastoral ministry is the fruit of effective disciple-making. Some of you may be sensing a prompting from the Lord to serve Him vocationally though pastoral ministry in the local church. Paul's says that "if anyone aspires to be an overseer, he desires a noble work (1 Tim 3:1)." The noble work of gospel ministry is a glorious gift from the Lord. It is not easy, however. As a result, the second volume of *Aspire* is written to train those who wish to pursue such a role. Like volume one, you will find three trimesters, comprised of twelve, weekly sessions. The trimesters will focus on three vital functions for pastors: teaching, building, and leading. Some of you may feel led to continue this journey towards vocational ministry.

What is your one-sentence personal mission statement. Write it in the space below, and share it with your mentor during your final session of the trimester.

_____

_____

Your task is the same though your role may differ. You will give your life to the great and glorious task of filling the earth with worshippers of Jesus until the day when the knowledge of the glory of God covers the earth as the waters cover the sea (Hab 2:14). Praise God this mission is big enough to encompass the rest of our lives. So let's get to work!

Trimester 3—Top Ten List

What are the top ten take-aways that you have from this trimester of *Aspire*? In each area, note how God is bringing transformation in your life.

1. _____

2. _____

3. _____

4. _____

5. _____

6. _____

7. _____

8. _____

9. _____

10. _____

Suggested Reading List

Allen, Roland. *Missionary Methods: St Paul's or Ours?* Grand Rapids: Eerdmans, 1962.

Ashford, Bruce ed. *Theology and the Practice of Mission: God, the Church, and the Nations.* Nashville: Broadman & Holman, 2011.

Beale, G.K. *The Temple and the Church's Mission.* Downers Grove: IVP, 2004.

Bosch, David J. *Transforming Mission: Paradigm Shifts in Theology of Mission.* Maryknoll, NY: Orbis Books, 2005.

Colman, Robert. *The Master Plan of Evangelism and Discipleship.* 2nd ed. Grand Rapids: Baker, 2010.

Dever, Mark. *The Gospel and Personal Evangelism.* Wheaton: Crossway, 2007. Frost, Michael and Alan Hirsch, *The Shaping of things to Come.* Peabody, MA: Hendrickson, 2003.

Goheen, Michael W. *A Light to the Nations: The Missional Church and the Biblical Story.* Grand Rapids: Baker, 2011.

Goheen, Michael W. and Craig Bartholomew. *Living at the Crossroads: An Introduction to Christian Worldview.* Grand Rapids: Baker, 2008.

Guder, Darrell L., ed. *Missional Church: A Vision for the Sending of the Church in North America.* Grand Rapids: Eerdmans, 1998.

Hirsch, Alan. *The Forgotten Ways.* Grand Rapids: Brazos Press, 2006.

Hunter, George G. III. *The Celtic Way of Evangelism: How Christianity Can Reach the West…Again.* Nashville: Abingdon Press, 2000.

Hunter, James Davidson. *To Change the World: The Irony, Tragedy, and Possibility of Christianity in the Late Modern World.* Oxford: Oxford University Press, 2010.

Keller, Timothy. *The Prodigal God: Recovering the Heart of the Christian Faith.* New York: Riverhead, 2008.

Keller, Timothy. *Center Church: Doing Balanced, Gospel Centered Ministry in Your City.* Grand Rapids: Zondervan, 2012.

Keller. Timothy. *Ministries of Mercy: The Call of the Jericho Road.* 2nd ed. Phillipsburg: P&R, 1997.

Köstenberger, Andreas J. and Peter T. O'Brien. *Salvation to the Ends of the Earth: A Biblical Theology of Mission.* NSBT; Downers Grove: IVP, 2001.

Metzger, Will. *Tell the Truth: The Whole Gospel Wholly by Grace Communicated Truthfully and Lovingly.* 4th ed. Downers Grove: IVP, 2012.

Neibuhr. Reinhold. *Christ and Culture*. New York: Harper, 1951.

Neill, Stephen. *A History of Christian Missions*, rev. London: Penguin, 1990.

Newbigin, Lesslie. *The Gospel in a Pluralistic Society*. Grand Rapids: Eerdmans, 1989.

Newbigin, Lesslie. *Open Secret: Sketches for a Missionary theology*. Grand Rapids: Eerdmans, 1978.

Packer, J.I. *Evangelism and the Sovereignty of God*. Downers Grove: IVP, 1991.

Piper, John. *Let the Nations Be Glad! The Supremacy of God in Mission, 3rd ed*. Grand Rapids: Baker, 2010.

Piper, John and Justin Taylor. *The Supremacy of Christ in a Postmodern World*. Wheaton: Crossway, 2007.

Schnabel, Eckhard J. *Paul the Missionary: Realities, Strategies, and Methods*. Downers Grove: IVP, 2008.

Stark, Rodney. *The Rise of Christianity*. San Francisco: HarperCollins, 1997.

Stiles, J. Mack. *Marks of the Messenger*. Downers Grove: IVP, 2010.

Stott, John. *Christian Mission in the Modern World*. Downers Grove: IVP, 1975.

Veith, Gene Edward, Jr. *God at Work: Your Christian Vocation in All of Life*. Wheaton: Crossway, 2002.

Willis, Dustin and Aaron Coe. *Life on Mission*. Chicago: Moody, 2014.

Wright, Christopher J.H. *The Mission of God: Unlocking the Bible's Grand Narrative*. Downers Grove: IVP, 2006.

Wright, Christopher J.H. *The Mission of God's People: A Biblical Theology of the Church's Mission*. Grand Rapids: Zondervan, 2010.

Appendix 1: Overview

"You then, my son, be strong in the grace that is in Christ Jesus. And the things you have heard me say in the presence of many witnesses entrust to reliable men who will also be qualified to teach others."

2 Timothy 2:1–2

Aspire is written as a two-year disciple-making journey. Year 1 is designed to provide a strategy for developing any disciple through the local church. This could be anyone—from a recent college student who professed faith in Christ, to a lawyer who leads a small group, to a future church planter or pastor.

This year is broken down into three twelve-week trimesters, each with an essential area of focus:

- Year 1 Trimester 1: **GOSPEL**

  Disciples will understand the grand announcement of the good news of the gospel in the hopes that they will know, love, and serve out of awed gratitude for the stunning and overwhelming grace they have been shown in Christ Jesus.

- Year 1 Trimester 2: **MINISTRY**

  Disciples will learn to apply the gospel to their lives in order to discover how it is a catalyst for personal life transformation and, in turn, allows for fruitful ministry to others in the church.

- Year 1 Trimester 3: **MISSION**

  Disciples will be mobilized to live on mission as they declare and display the gospel message to those who have yet to trust in Christ for salvation.

Suggested Year At-A-Glance

Trimester 1	Break	Trimester 2	Break	Trimester 3	Break
September–November (12 weeks)	December	January–March (12 Weeks)	April	May–July (12 weeks)	August
GOSPEL		MINISTRY		MISSION	

Men desiring to pursue vocational ministry will then move on to Year 2 (Pastor). Though the content for the second year of *Aspire* will be provided in a subsequent book, the model will be as follows:

- Year 2 Trimester 1: **PROCLAIM**

  Leaders will learn to apply the Scriptures to the lives of those they lead through pastoral counseling, preaching, and teaching.

- Year 2 Trimester 2: **BUILD**

  Leaders will confront the complexities of creating intentional structures and systems in and through their local church contexts that facilitate disciple-making.

- Year 2 Trimester 3: **LEAD**

  Leaders will develop the essential leadership skills necessary to lead God's people on mission to make disciples of the nations through God's church.

Suggested Year At-A-Glance

Trimester 1	Break	Trimester 2	Break	Trimester 3	Break
September–November (12 weeks)	December	January–March (12 Weeks)	April	May–July (12 weeks)	August
PROCLAIM		BUILD		LEAD	

Year 1 Sessions

Year 1	Trimester 1: GOSPEL	Trimester 2: MINISTRY	Trimester 3: MISSION
Week 1	Creation	Worship	Mission of God
Week 2	Rebellion	Transformation	Mission of Church
Week 3	Covenant	Idolatry	Mission of Disciple
Week 4	Israel	Character	The Nations
Week 5	Law	Holy Spirit	Your Culture
Week 6	Judgment	Discipleship	Your Context
Week 7	Incarnation	Gifting	Pray
Week 8	Ministry	Calling	Invest
Week 9	Cross	Marriage	Declare
Week 10	Resurrection	Family	Demonstrate
Week 11	Church	Time	Connect
Week 12	Consummation	Rest	Disciple
Desired Outcomes	A disciple of Jesus • will have a clear understanding of the metanarrative of Scripture. • will be able to understand how the "micro-stories" of Scripture fit into the "macro-story" of God's redemptive plan. • will be able to articulate a holistic gospel. • will grow in love and appreciation for the gospel.	A disciple of Jesus • will grow in applying the gospel to his/her daily life. • will develop the tools necessary for making disciples. • will understand how the gospel informs his or her sense of calling and giftedness. • will develop daily disciplines in life, marriage, and parenting that support gospel transformation.	A disciple of Jesus • will understand God's mission in the world and the role of the church in that mission. • will develop a missional vision for the local church. • will personally live on mission and be able to disciple others to do the same.

Appendix 2: How does *Aspire* address the four critical areas of growth?

Churches and disciple-makers can utilize *Aspire* to address each of the four key areas of development for a disciple.

Know

- **Weekly Sessions:** *Aspire* provides the church and its developing disciples with a weekly "field guide." It is designed to provide a systematic method for growth in understanding and application of the gospel. The guide provides content as well as application questions that allow for fruitful mentorship.

- **Scripture Immersion:** *Aspire* will point a reader to God's sure and authoritative Word as a guide for life transformation. A key Scripture verse will also be provided at the outset of each week's guide. This verse can be memorized in order to store God's Word in the heart of the disciple. Finally, some readers may choose to use a Bible reading plan throughout their first year of *Aspire* which will allow them to read through the Bible in its entirety.

- **Supplemental Reading:** Throughout *Aspire* you will see suggestions of a number of helpful books and resources that aid in the understanding of the concepts under consideration. However, pastors and churches should feel free to add or subtract as they see fit based on the needs of their developing disciples and their own passions.

- **Classroom Instruction:** Some churches, particularly those with an abundance of disciples, may see fit to gather all of those going through *Aspire* for a weekly time of training. This would allow for people to form relationships with one another and for gifted leaders to speak into the lives of the maturing disciples in a formal training environment.

- **Seminary Credit:** Pastors and churches should seek out partnerships with evangelical seminaries in order to secure seminary credit for developing disciples who desire such credentials.[1]

Be

- **Mentorship:** Disciples should meet with a pastoral mentor or known disciple-maker within the church for at least one hour each week in order to discuss their journey through the *Aspire* material.

- **Accountability:** This mentoring relationship can provide a context in which the leader can be held accountable for pursuing a life of holiness and fighting known sin.

- **Discipline:** This mentoring relationship provides a context where the leader can grow in his or her practice of the spiritual disciplines.

- **Assessment:** The mentor is in the best position to assess the calling and character of the developing disciple and affirm his or her role and responsibility as a leader among God's people.

- **Encouragement:** Finally, mentorship serves as a context for encouraging the leader as he or she faces the growing pains that come to all developing disciples.

Do

- **Personal Discipleship:** Disciples should be encouraged to replicate their disciple-making journey through their own network of friends. Ideally, a growing disciple would take a newer believer through *Aspire* after completing year 1.

- **Missionary Living:** Disciples should have a web of relationships with the lost and seek to foster new relationships in which they can declare and demonstrate the gospel.

---

1. For example, many Southern Baptist seminaries have distance learning programs which will partner with local churches for formal, theological education.

- **Ministry Service:** Disciples should be placed in roles in the church where they gain experience at vital tasks such as teaching, administration, or counseling, and they should be evaluated based on their performance and growth.

Love

- **Genuine Relationships:** Disciples should have a number of genuine and deep friendships that are growing through the discipleship process, which serve to provide informal support, encouragement, and accountability.

- **Prioritized Marriages and Families:** Those disciples who are married are encouraged to love their spouses in a way that honors Christ. During year 2 of *Aspire*, churches are encouraged to connect the fiancés or spouses of developing disciples with the spouses of their mentor, who can then guide them through *Aspire* as well.

Appendix 3:
Frequently Asked Questions

Who is *Aspire* designed for?

Ideally, any disciple-maker and disciple in the local church can use the first year of *Aspire*. One need not be a seminary trained leader to benefit from this model, nor does the church utilizing *Aspire* need to be a mega-church equipped with a vast array of resources and manpower. All that is needed is willingness. Year 1 is specifically designed for all disciples, men and women, who desire to walk through an intentional process of development. As *Aspire* moves into year 2, the material is designed to be utilized by men who are aspiring to vocational ministry in the local church.

Why is *Aspire* so long?

It is better to train disciples *well* than to train them *quickly*. There is simply no way to assess, equip, and place someone into leadership quickly. Discipleship will take time, a host of mistakes, and strategic discernment on the part of everyone involved. Many will grow as a disciple of Jesus and spend their lives replicating this process in the lives of others. For some, formal leadership roles may be further in the future than they desired. For others, they may never enter vocational ministry. For a few, they will disqualify themselves due to unrepentant sin. For all, they will need time to develop and deploy in a successful fashion.

Where should we take breaks?

The breaks in *Aspire* are not simply designed to coincide with busy seasons in the calendar (Christmas, Easter, and summer). They are also placed at intentional points to allow the disciple-maker time to have strategic conversations with the developing disciple about areas of weakness or needed growth. By year 2, these conversations can be used to help position the disciple to launch into ministry leadership by pointing them in a direction that best fits their maturity and giftedness. Also, this time allows for formal assessment or strategic training through supplemental meetings that may be difficult to squeeze in during the trimesters themselves.

Where do we start?

There are two strategic places for local church leaders to start. First, they need to find those in need of discipleship. Regardless of the number, every church has disciples in need of investment. Start by considering those who have trusted Christ recently in the life of the church. They are often ready and willing to invest in a development plan. Another place to look is within the ranks of a local church's student or college ministry, or among those already holding some type of leadership position (for example, all of a church's current small group leaders). These aspiring leaders should be invited into the *Aspire* process. Disciple-makers may be harder to come by. Look for people who have either been discipled themselves (thus, understand the value of such a process) or those who are hungry to invest their lives in others and would be quick to learn. The key is to start somewhere, even if it is just with a few people in the church. The rest of the church may catch on as God provides fruit through the process.

At the outset, there need not be a formal application process, in which interested candidates apply to the program. Local church pastors can simply invite an aspiring disciple into the process. Expanding capacity may necessitate that local churches create more formal pathways for leadership candidates. *Aspire* encourages churches to create a formal application process as well as well as purchase additional resources for disciples going through this process.

When should we meet?

If the church chooses to gather groups of disciples, it is best to do so at times which do not preclude those with jobs from being able to participate. Early morning hours (6–8AM) provide a suitable time that does not conflict with most work schedules and that does not encroach on family time in the evenings. The labs included in *Aspire*, however, do not require a weekly class component in order to be successful. They can be given to a developing disciple who completes the work on their own and then sets up a time to meet with a mentor. This can happen at any time. Ideally, this time will be consistent each week, and the location will allow for genuine and heartfelt conversation. If the church chooses to gather them into groups, it is vital that *Aspire* not become simply another class. One-on-one mentoring is far superior to classroom instruction for disciple-making. The weekly labs may be helpful in creating momentum or in supplementing the mentorship process, but it should not be seen as a substitute.

Where should the developing disciples serve?

Hands-on training is a vital component to the *Aspire* model. However, it is essential that growing disciples are serving, not that they are serving in the ideal role from the beginning. A bit of trial and error is required. A new convert may have no clue where he or she is gifted to serve the church. Some growing disciples are predisposed to one of three areas of gifting: (1) those gifted in proclaiming God's word; (2) those gifted in personal care for God's people; (3) those gifted in administrating God's church. In most cases, however, the disciple's primary gifting is not readily apparent. Local church leaders must work in tandem with individuals to aid them in discerning the roles in which they excel, the roles in which they can develop, and the roles that do not fit their gifting. For this to happen, it may be wise to place the person in different types of service roles within the church each trimester. For one trimester, the disciple may spend time working with the youth (teaching), for another he or she may help coordinate a church-wide ministry program (administration), and for another he or she may assist in pastoral counseling (caring).

How much time will we need to allocate for mentorship through *Aspire*?

Both existing pastors and aspiring disciples will get out of *Aspire* what they put into it. For this reason, *Aspire* will necessitate a time commitment from both parties.

Disciple-makers will need to devote time to reading the material and preparing to ask good questions each week. The beauty of the *Aspire* model, however, is that much of this work is already done in advance. A disciple-maker can simply ask the person with whom they are meeting to discuss his/her answer to a certain question each week. Also, as the disciple-maker utilizes the model with more and more people, he/she will become increasingly familiar and fluid with leading a spiritual conversation. The expectation would be that disciples and their mentors meet for at least one hour per week to discuss the person's journey through *Aspire*. The hope is that this does not add another task to the leader's plate, but streamlines a task to which they are already committed.

Who mentors each disciple?

Any disciple of Jesus who demonstrates a consistent walk with Jesus is capable of making a disciple. However, churches may see fit to pair developing disciples with existing mentors who match the young leader's personality or sense of giftedness. For example, if a young disciple aspires to church planting, it may be best for him to be mentored by the lead pastor. If another young female aspires to work with widows and orphans, it may be best to pair her with a female who has experience in this vital ministry role.

Can churches collaborate?

Yes. There are multiple avenues for church collaboration through *Aspire*. The weekly sessions may provide a time where pastors gifted in a particular topic can serve to facilitate the discussion for the week. A young, newly married pastor may not be the best person to lead a workshop on marriage. It may be best to ask an elderly pastor from the city to address that topic. A church planter may be best suited for leading the discussion on contextual strategy, and so on. Also, collaborating around the weekly labs gives individuals from churches with few young disciples a chance to place those people in a context for building relationships with other like-minded, aspiring disciples.

City collaboration also provides a context for God to form church planting teams. Perhaps a church does not have a fully formed team for planting a church in an urban context, but through partnership with other churches, people committed to church planting may be exposed to one another, and their hearts may be knit together. Multiple churches can also strategically select various church planting contexts and partner together for the sake of maximum impact. For example, the churches in a city may choose to funnel disciples to a couple of strategic city centers, such as Washington, DC or Salt Lake City, Utah. Church pastors can also partner together to provide the vital financial and marital support essential for sending disciples. The relationships forged during *Aspire* groups can provide the fuel for such healthy, supportive relationships.

What about seminary?

Aspire is not designed to be an alternative pathway for seminary training, but may be a means by which participants can receive seminary training in the context of the local church. Walking through a process such as *Aspire* can bolster the theological training one will receive through our partnership with evangelical seminaries such as Southeastern Baptist Theological Seminary (SEBTS). Churches should consult with like-minded seminaries to discern how they may partner with churches that are utilizing intentional discipleship tools such as *Aspire*.

How is *Aspire* funded?

It doesn't have to be funded. Training disciples does not require funding, only intentionality. Disciples can pursue *Aspire* training while holding a full-time vocational job. Those aspiring to pastoral ministry during the second year of training may see fit to raise funding for an internship with the local church in order to allocate more time to the process. Leaders could raise a minimal amount of support from their relational networks to offer a strategic internship in the church. For example, a future church planter may serve as an intern or apprentice with the North American Mission Board and utilize a tool such as *Aspire* prior to going to plant a church in a strategic city. Churches may also determine to allocate money to the process when a leader is clearly positioned to hold a higher mantle of leadership responsibility in the church.

What will it cost the church?

In one sense, developing disciples is free. But, on another and more important level, developing and deploying disciples and leaders comes with a great cost. *It will cost time.* Existing pastors must allocate time for implementing the *Aspire* model and for the necessary relational discipleship that it requires. *It will also cost money.* Churches who develop leaders will want to find every possible way to finance their developing ministries. Thus, increasing percentages of a church's budget will be spent leveraging the calling of aspiring leaders. Lastly, *it will cost love.* Pastors who care about multiplying disciples will find themselves personally invested in the lives of those they mentor. They will both rejoice and weep as they watch these young disciples undergo the travails of spiritual formation and leadership.

For additional information, contact Seed Publishing Group or Matt Rogers for more information on how the *Aspire* model is utilized in different church contexts in order to produce disciples and leaders in God's church. Personal consultations about implementing a strategy for disciple-making and leadership development can be requested by contacting the author.

Made in the USA
Charleston, SC
02 July 2015